Physical Theatres

ed on c

Physical Theatres: A Critical Introduction is the first account to provide a comprehensive overview of non-text-based theatre, from experimental dance to traditional mi e. This book synthesises the history, theory and practice of physical theatre for stur its and performers, in what is both a core area of study and a dynamic and innovative aspect of theatrical practice.

Insisting that there are many physical theatres and arguing for the essential physicality of all theatrical forms, this book not only examines the acknowledged luminaries of physical theatre, but forges a new lens through which the physical and visual practices of the twentieth century's most exciting dramatists and theatre makers can be viewed.

This comprehensive book:

- traces the roots of physical performance in classical and popular theatrical traditions
- looks at the Dance Theatre of *DV8*, Pina Bausch, Liz Aggiss and Jérôme Bel
- examines the contemporary practice of companies and artists such as Théâtre du Soleil, Complicité, Goat Island and Dario Fo
- focuses on principles and practices in actor training, with reference to figures such as Jacques Lecoq, Lev Dodin, Philippe Gaulier, Monika Pagneux, Etienne Decroux, Anne Bogart and Joan Littlewood.

This book can be used as a stand-alone text, or together with its companion volume, *Physical Theatres: A Critical Reader*, to provide an invaluable introduction to the physical in theatre and performance.

Simon Murray is a performer, director and academic. He is currently Director of Theatre at Dartington College of Arts, and author of *Jacques Lecoq* (2003).

John Keefe is a senior lecturer at the London Metropolitan University Undergraduate Centre, and a lecturer and visiting fellow at Queen's University International Study Centre (Canada), specialising in perf   ance director and performance dramaturc

cirencester
college
a beacon college

Physical Theatres

A Critical Introduction

Simon Murray
and John Keefe

Routledge
Taylor & Francis Group

LONDON AND NEW YORK

First published 2007
by Routledge
2 Park Square, Milton Park, Abingdon, Oxon OX14 4RN

Simultaneously published in the USA and Canada
by Routledge
270 Madison Ave, New York, NY 10016

Routledge is an imprint of the Taylor & Francis Group, an informa business

© 2007 Simon Murray and John Keefe

Typeset in Helvetica and Avant Garde by
Florence Production Ltd, Stoodleigh, Devon
Printed and bound in Great Britain by
Antony Rowe Ltd, Chippenham, Wiltshire

British Library Cataloguing in Publication Data
A catalogue record for this book is available from the British Library

Library of Congress Cataloging in Publication Data
Murray, Simon David, 1948–
    Physical theatres: a critical introduction/Simon Murray and John Keefe.
        p. cm.
    Includes bibliographical references and index.
    1. Movement (Acting)   2. Mime.   3. Dance.   I. Keefe, John, 1950–   II. Title.
    PN2071.M6M87 2007
    792.02′8 – dc22   2007016261

ISBN10: 0–415–36249–0 (hbk)
ISBN10: 0–415–36250–4 (pbk)
ISBN10: 0–203–01282–8 (ebk)

ISBN13: 978–0–415–36249–8 (hbk)
ISBN13: 978–0–415–36250–4 (pbk)
ISBN13: 978–0–203–01282–6 (ebk)

For Wendy and Isla

For Ivy, David (Manjusvara) and Will

In memory of Bill

Contents

List of illustrations   xi

Acknowledgements   xiii

Introduction   1

So why pluralities?   3

This book   8

Omissions and absences   10

In three senses   11

Ownership   11

1   Genesis, Contexts, Namings   12

Contemporary Contexts   12

   Namings   14

   Physical theatres and devising   17

   A word on mime   18

   Acting and performing in physical theatres   20

Physical theatres: cultural and philosophical contexts   22

   Reading gestures: the significant action   23

   Subjectivity and feeling: the phenomenologist's case   25

   Cultural materialism: framing the bigger picture   27

   Feminism, sexuality and gendered bodies   29

   Perceiving theatre: the contribution of reception theory   31

Afterthoughts on contexts   33

2   Roots: Routes   34

Deep traditions: classical and popular   35

   Words, signs and actions   35

   A path backwards   36

Mimesis and empathy 38
The cognitive and neurological roots of mimesis-empathy-play 44
Popular playing 46
Drama versus the dramatic 47
The Trickster's play 49
Official and everyday bodies: conflicts in culture 52
Hybrid pathways 53
Miming bodies 53
Expressive bodies 54
Masked bodies 56
Illusionary bodies 57
Dancing bodies 59
Avant-garde bodies 64
Visceral theatre 68
Into the millennium 71
Afterwords 72

3   Contemporary Practices   73
Some warnings on writing theatre 73
Theatre in dance theatre, dance in physical theatres 75
Pina Bausch and the Wuppertal Dance Theatre 77
Lloyd Newson and DV8 81
Liz Aggiss and Divas Dance Theatre 84
Jérôme Bel and performance dance 87
Physicalising narrative 92
Théâtre du Soleil and Ariane Mnouchkine, 1789 93
Complicité: The Street of Crocodiles 96
Goat Island Performance Group: The Sea and the Poison 107
Dario Fo: Mistero Buffo 112
Afterwords 116

4   Preparation and Training   117
Pedagogy as a creative act 117
Physical preparation for theatre: histories and contexts 119
Training as cultural production: models of provision 121
The director and actor as professional trainer 121
Professional theatre schools and the modern university 123
The rise and rise of the workshop as training opportunity 129
Contemporary training: principles and practices 135
Lev Dodin and the Maly Theatre of St Petersburg 137
Eugenio Barba and the Odin Teatret 139
Anne Bogart: viewpoints and composition 142
Jacques Lecoq 144
Monika Pagneux 147
Philippe Gaulier 149
Joan Littlewood and the Theatre Workshop 152
Etienne Decroux 155
Afterwords 158

5   Physicality and the Word   159
Against a hierarchy of theatre languages 161
Agamemnon: the morning watch 162

Realism and the *realistic*   165
Space as 'silent character'   167
Articulate stillness   170
The silent cry   172
(Physical) text as transformation and imagination   174
Reaching for comedy and pathos   175
Improvising or fixing the text?   179
Fantasia, furbizio, tecnica   181
Playing the audience   181
Afterwords   184

6 Bodies and Cultures   185
Flattening differences   186
Borrowings, takings and muddled thinking   187
Bodies from other cultures   189
Meyerhold, Artaud and intercultural theatre   192
Contemporary case studies   196
     The Mudrooroo/Müller Project   197
     Dry Lips Oughta Move to Kapuskasing   198
Universal bodies   199
Rhetoric, optimism and utopias   201

7 Conclusion by way of Lexicon   204
Lexicon   204

Glossary   209
Bibliography   213
Index   223

Illustrations

2.1   *I Miss You* (2002) Franco B, Malmo, Sweden. Photo: Manuel Vason.   40

2.2   *Street of Crocodiles* in rehearsal (1992) Complicité. Photo:
       Pascal Couillard.   41

2.3   *King Ubu* (1964) (Alfred Jarry), Theatre on the Balustrade, Prague,
       Czechoslovakia. Copyright: Josef Koudelka/Magnum Photos.   41

2.4   *Waiting for Godot* (1964) (Samuel Beckett), Theatre on the Balustrade,
       Prague, Czechoslovakia. Copyright: JK/Magnum Photos.   42

2.5   *Haunted, Daunted and Flaunted* (1997) Wendy Houstoun.
       Photo: Chris Nash.   43

3.1   *The Summit* (2006) Ralf Ralf, Jonathan and Barnaby Stone, Cairo
       Festival of Experimental Theatre. Photo: unknown.   97

3.2   *The Harry Stork Cabaret* (2006) 'Dog', Théâtre Décalé, Alan Fairbairn
       and Eline van der Voort. Photo: Caroline Buyst.   98

3.3   *Bartleby* (1993) Kevin Alderson and Adrian Preater, Wall Street
       Productions. Director: Simon Murray. Photo: Keith Pattison.   99

3.4   *A Minute Too Late* (2005, revival) Complicité. Photo: Sarah Ainslie.   100

3.5   *The Government Inspector* (2003) Théatre de l'Ange Fou. Steven
       Wasson/Corinne Soum. Photo: Geraint Lewis.   100

3.6   *In Close Relation* (1998) Louder than Words, directed by Ruth
       Ben-Tovim and Peader Kirk, Young Vic Studio commission, London.
       Photo: Liane Harris.   101

3.7   *The Hansel Gretel Machine* (1997/8) T.C. Howard, David Glass
       Ensemble. Director: David Glass. Photo: Keith Pattison.   102

3.8   *Time Flying* (1997) Bouge-de-la. Photo: Richard Heaps.   103

3.9   *DiveUrgence* (1999) Dark Horse. Director: Bim Mason. Photo: Pau Ros.   104

4.1   Kenneth Davidson (1994) *Moving into Performance* Workshop-
        Symposium, Manchester, England. Photo: Simon Murray.   126

4.2   Dugald Ferguson (2005) Theatre student, Dartington College of Arts,
        Devon, England. Photo: Kate Mount.   127

4.3   Theatre movement class at Dartington (1995) Dartington College of Arts,
        Devon, England. Photo: Kate Mount.   127

4.4   *Tea Without Mother* (2005) Lynette Oakey and Mark Stephens, National
        Student Drama Festival, Scarborough, England. Photo: Allan Titmuss.   128

5.1–5.6 *Footfalls* (1976) Billie Whitelaw. Royal Court Theatre, London.
        Writer/director: Samuel Beckett. Designer: Jocelyn Herbert.
        Photos: John Haynes.   166–67

5.7   *Mother Courage* (1949, Berlin) (Bertold Brecht) 'Mother Courage
        prepares to pull her wagon alone', Helene Weigel. Copyright:
        Ruth Berlau Estate/Hilda Hoffmann. Photo: Heiner Hill.   168

Acknowledgements

Our thanks go to Talia Rodgers and Minh Ha Duong for commissioning this project, and for their generous support, advice and encouragement as the volumes have progressed.

Assembling the images for this book has been a largely pleasurable and rewarding task, but only made possible through the help of certain key people. In this respect our thanks go to Joel Anderson for advice and practical help in selecting images, and particularly over securing the Magnum photographs. Thanks also to Dartington colleagues Emilyn Claid, Graham Green, Joe Honywill, Jane Nevin and Simon Bertram for various help in assembling photographs and images. Our thanks, too, to Felicity Hall of Total Theatre Network for her help in sourcing many of the images used.

Although they do not figure directly in this book, our thanks must also go to the six 'essayists' – Dick McCaw, Jonathan Pitches, Franc Chamberlain, Lorna Marshall, Phelim McDermott and David Williams – for accepting our invitation to contribute original material to our companion volume, *Physical Theatres: A Critical Reader*. The conversations we have had with them about their essays have informed our thoughts, the choice of lenses through which we see physical theatres, and have provided a stimulating range of responses to our choices and ideas. We thank them for their energetic engagement in this project.

American colleagues, Tom Leabhart (Pomona College, California) and Michael Costello (Texas State University), offered useful advice and information on physical theatre training opportunities in the USA, and our thanks must go to them too. We also both owe an acknowledgement to all those students, practitioners and colleagues who have been part of our learning journeys over many years: journeys which continue to delve into the 'messy' nature of theatres.

Simon Murray

Dartington College of Arts provided me with four months' research leave at a very busy time in 2006 to start preparing for these books, and therefore particular thanks go to Antonia Payne, our Dean of Research, for helping to make this happen. My colleague, David Williams, has contributed to these books in all manner of ways through conversations, more or less formal, and thanks to him for providing detailed feedback on Chapter 3, 'Contemporary Practices', and for refining the football dimension to physical theatres.

My special thanks go to the theatre team at Dartington of Joe Richards, Catriona Scott, Misha Myers, Misri Dey, Paul Clarke, Simon Persighetti, David Williams and Sue Palmer for supporting my various absences to write and construct these books. These Dartington colleagues are among the most generous people I have ever worked with, and have consistently generated a culture of thoughtful questioning and stimulating dialogue around contemporary theatre practices, which in turn has sharpened my own thinking about the perplexing nature of physical theatres. Thanks also to Joy Owen and Chantal Vosloo for administrative help, and to the Dartington College library team for endlessly efficient and friendly detective work.

In these, and many other respects, thanks go to Alan Fairbairn for numerous productive conversations around contemporary mime and physical theatres. And thanks to my co-writer and editor, John Keefe, for embarking on this journey with me, for challenging my received wisdoms and for sharing a perspective which has led to these publications.

Finally, unquantifiable thanks go to Wendy Kirkup for her unflagging support and *domestic labour* in helping to make these projects happen, and to my daughter Isla for reminding me that there is much more to life than writing books about physical theatres.

John Keefe

My thanks go to all my colleagues at London Metropolitan University Sir John Cass Department of Art, Music and Design, and Queen's University International Study Centre (Canada) for their understanding and stimulation as this project has wended its way forward.

David Bevan at the International Study Centre, and Brian Falconbridge and Lewis Jones at London Metropolitan University gave their support, advice and encouragement in matters of research and writing which has been greatly appreciated.

Without Eugene Svoboda, the marvellous librarian at the International Study Centre, the research for these volumes would not have been possible; I am indebted to him for his help in obtaining the books and journals needed.

I must also thank Julia Ferguson, Robin McLean and Brian Jones, also of the ISC, for their patience and assistance with scanning and technical advice. My thanks go to Peter Carrier and Bettina Nethercott for help in translations, and to Eric Litwack for help with Wittgenstein; to Steffi Sachsenmaier for many lively discussions. My thanks go to Karen Aram for her patience.

Thanks go to my son Will for his bemused tolerance of my preoccupations while nevertheless having his own sense of play. Finally, thanks to Simon Murray for being a fellow traveller over many years in physical and total theatres, travelling which has led to these books.

Introduction

This is a book about intersections, cross-overs and spillages. It is a book which is trying to understand some key features of contemporary Western theatre practice, but at the same time striving to unearth and [re]articulate modes of theatre history which often seem to have been hidden from view or subject to a strange amnesia.

The impulse for the project – two connected books on physical theatres – may be identified partly through the personal (theatre) biographies of the two authors, but also in a wish to unravel and map out that complex network of propositions, actions, events and dispositions which arguably constitute – and have constituted – the landscape of *physical theatres* and the *physical in theatre*. As a starting point our account embraces – tentatively – the term physical theatres, but then proceeds to subject it to critical scrutiny as the book develops and reveals itself.

There are an increasing number of books of all shapes and sizes that explore, set out, methodologise, and give history and outline to our understanding of theatre. What is noteworthy here is the increasing prevalence of the plural in such articulation of theory(ies), history(ies), practice(s). The impulse to acknowledge and indeed celebrate complexity is not a perverse desire to complicate for the sake of complication, far rather a recognition that histories, influences and theatre makings are rarely ever simple and linear. To pretend that they are is alluring, but does little to take us towards an understanding of how theatre works in all its creative and often frustrating 'messiness'. We dig deeper into these issues shortly.

But when we first began forming the ideas and perspectives which lie behind these two volumes, pluralities were also a means of articulating theories, histories and practices that we had been following for some years in our own teaching, practice and understanding of what theatre was and is. Our individual and collaborative contributions towards the shaping and execution of the international 'Moving into Performance' workshop symposium in 1994 in Manchester speak of and reinforce the productiveness of such a perspective. Perhaps these ideas and approaches to theatres derive much from our particular political and social backgrounds; perhaps from our own education and professional paths; perhaps thus from ways of looking at and being in the post-war world, a world in flux.

We both began our theatre careers at a point when the languages of physical theatre were being enthusiastically articulated, promulgated and – from some quarters – denigrated within the landscape of non-literary and experimental theatre. Twenty-six years on there is – arguably – a considerable amount of physical theatre still being generated and seen across the Western world, but whether the term can continue to describe and encapsulate renewal and innovation in theatre and performance is open to question. To a certain extent, the locus of innovation, risk and challenge has moved elsewhere in the cosmology of theatre and performance making.

Perhaps the moment of physical theatre has passed and consequently this book may have an elegiac quality, wistfully remembering a period and a particular cultural context, highly significant in its time, but no longer possessing the same charge for contemporary makers and thinkers of theatre. If physical theatre in 2007 fails to enjoy the same cultural and theatrical resonance it had in the 1980s this tells us something important about the times – then and now – and throughout this book we engage with ideas which try to offer a social, philosophical and ideological context for the work we are examining.

Paradoxically, however, physical theatre has become embedded in the language of educationalists, actor trainers and their students. Modules, courses and perspectives on 'physical theatre' proliferate within training-education programmes across Europe, North America and Australia. Within the landscape of professional theatre, too, the vocabulary, aspiration and rhetoric of physicality, and of an actor's movement qualities, have become widely articulated and claimed. The extent to which these remain at the level of rhetoric, or represent a substantial shift in the business of acting and theatre making, is one of the purposes of this book to explore.

So, regardless of whether the cultural moment of physical theatre has passed, its presence both in the language of performance, and in a variety of diverse contemporary theatre practices, remains present and – at times – clamorous. What the 'it' of physical theatre is, and whether the 'it' has substance beyond shadow and phantom, disguising (by renaming) otherwise unremarkable performance events, we will investigate in the pages that follow.

So why pluralities?

There may be a dominant or **hegemonic** set of theatre conventions in any one era, perhaps of style or language. But such 'establishment' work will also be found to draw on the ideas or energies of the unofficial, the submerged, the subversive and the popular, all of which exist underneath or alongside the *official*. These influences and impulses then provide an impetus for change, while often becoming incorporated into the 'new' official theatre, or simply carry on in their own various manifestations, ignoring and being ignored by the works of official art.

Thus there have always been 'many theatres', but only 'One Theatre' that has dominated by virtue of its culturally and politically awarded-ascribed status, its presence in published or preserved manuscripts and other texts taking on a powerful authority and influence. It is in this spirit that we ground our insistence on talking about 'physical theatres/the physical in theatres' rather than a single form or practice. This has led to debates with fellow practitioners and academics over many years about whether the plays of Beckett or Chekhov are 'physical theatre', the work of Littlewood or Brecht is 'physical theatre', the stage practices of Shakespeare or Aeschylus are 'physical theatre'.

In a word, yes – they are, it is.

Our aim is to set out this plurality of theatre practice-theory-history as rooted in certain through-lines of principles of theatre itself; of embodied ideas that are in a **dialectical** relationship to the spoken word. Too often this physicality is relegated to a mere supporting role to the word, is regarded as vulgar or simply a means to an end – at its worst being the vehicle by which the words are delivered or moved around the stage; or reduced to the routine gestures and mannerisms sufficient to convey the stock character inhabiting and making familiar the world of the play.

It is such practices that give rise to the truism that all theatre is physical. Writer, director and actor Simon Callow expresses it thus:

> All sorts of other theatre experiences become more interesting than those which focus on acting: the musical theatre . . . or what is called physical theatre – as if theatre, in which the word is made flesh, could be anything other than physical!

(Chekhov 2002: xi)

Thus, torn between a perspective that states – with alluring simplicity – 'there is simply theatre', on the one hand, and positions that make confident claims about new and definable forms of body-based or physical theatre on the other, these books have had to negotiate a path which avoids both the closure of the first position and the over-excited polemic of the second.

The case for there being 'simply theatre' has all the attraction that a comfortable and safe position provides, but the arguments are worth restating none the less. Here, the 'physical' in physical theatre is redundant excess since all theatrical performance is an embodied activity. We witness live bodies on stage, and as spectators we invest every performer's action, gesture and spoken word – whether intentional or uncontrolled – with significance and meaning. That, as the semiotics of performance has taught us, is the nature of the transaction between actor and audience. Here, the turn of a head, the tone of voice or the scratching of a buttock are as much the gestural vocabulary of theatre – which has no choice but to be physical – as are the muscular and choreographed actions of the performer trained athletically in mime, dance or circus skills. This position tells us everything and nothing, for it is unable to offer any further analysis or explanation of what has been shown and received. Its virtue, paradoxically, is to invite the same degree of visual and kinaesthetic scrutiny to text-based theatre as we would wish to apply to all those theatre forms where visual and gestural languages are paramount.

The perspective that makes ambitious claims for innovative – physical – theatre forms and genres discovered and practised in the last few decades of the twentieth century is a seductive one. It offers the lure and 'shock of the new' (Hughes 1991), while inviting a sense of confidence and excitement about theatre's ability to re-invent itself in a mediatised age. The difficulties with this position are that it is unable to differentiate between significantly diverse physical languages and strategies within the 'physical theatre' mode. In its enthusiasm for proclaiming newness and innovation it fails to acknowledge theatre histories, and in so doing becomes fixated upon the contemporary.

Our book is predicated upon the basis that both these propositions possess their own truths. Consequently, we believe that it is a potentially productive quest to investigate the contours and possibilities of the physical *in* theatres, while testing and illuminating the claims that seem implicit in assertions made for new and discrete theatre genres which are indeed peculiarly physical and gestural. From the outset of this project we felt that if we were to risk constructing two books which signalled a conditional acceptance of the validity of the physical theatre label – both through their titles and in their structure – then we would employ only the plural usage. Hence, we have been ruthlessly insistent on *physical theatres* with all its consequent implications for suggesting a diversity of forms built from different roots and technical traditions. The physical or dance theatre of Pina Bausch looks very different from work anchored in the French mime tradition. The practices of Eugenio Barba's Odin Teatret apparently share little with those of Forced Entertainment or Goat Island. We return to these matters in Chapter 3, 'Contemporary Practices'.

To this end *Physical Theatres: A Critical Introduction* (hereafter *PT:I*) and *Physical Theatres: A Critical Reader* (hereafter *PT:R*) are being published as companion volumes, allowing a movement across and between the (paradoxical) network of issues and ideas **denoted** and **connoted** by the term 'physical theatres'.

We intend these books to be 'portals', pointing readers to many other sources of information which arise from these critical introductions to physical theatres/the physical in theatres; to avoid a *territorial* approach to ideas on our part, rather to open up territory and to signal connected inspirations and initiatives. To cite Schechner, it 'is an introduction ... there will be others and that suits me just fine' (2002/2006: 1). While it suits us 'just fine' that these will be two books among many that address the issues we look at here, they do form a particular set of engagements with a field that is characterised by a diversity of approaches and differences in emphasis. In this spirit we also hope the books demonstrate a principle of openness that is a reflection of the always messy, hybrid nature of theatres, an approach which always resists attempts to clean these up, to 'purify'.

We have tried to avoid creating a mere roll-call of practitioners and ideas, or a collection of esoteric theorising, or a 'how-to' manual. Rather we are attempting an investigation and interrogation of the principles, **tropes** and practices that make up physical theatres/the physical in theatres. Thus a necessary minimum of division and categorisation of ideas and themes is needed for reasons of coherence in structuring these books. But it must be emphasised that our organising framework is one that allows the principles of theatre to flow to and from one practitioner or style to another; thus encouraging the virtues of a clash of contrapuntal voices as these appear and reappear in different places and guises.

To this end, we have included a number of 'choric quotes' placed in boxes: to help readers through this flow of principles and materials by acting as signposts to that material; as provocations and commentaries on the ideas being presented and discussed. It is in this spirit that both volumes are intentionally heterogeneous with paradoxes, seeming contradictions and oppositions left in place – to allow the subject to be seen in its often unruly complexity.

To literature and drama undergraduates long ago, it was taught that 'tragedy is for those who think, comedy is for those who feel' – a formulation that never made sense at the time and does not to us today. As stated, theatre in all its guises is an embodied art form, and therefore demands embodied responses. If we are considering physical theatres/the physical in theatres then, as with all theatres, our response as spectator and audience will be physical, visceral, psychological and emotional. We feel ideas, we think about feelings. We understand, sometimes, on a level of grasping meaning almost without being able to articulate it to ourselves but simply *knowing* through our senses as we see and hear the physical in theatre. We explore a number of different theoretical positions on locating and understanding theatre in the first chapter, 'Genesis, Contexts, Namings'.

In this sense theatre is practical – of practice – and it is experienced and experiential. Whatever (re)framing, (re)conceptualising or (re)fashioning of ideas and practices occur, theatre remains an empirical, utterly human phenomenon which we come to from the equally sentient experience of play. In this way it is **syncretic** in more than its craft elements – the act of theatre also embraces the experience itself of presenting and receiving that act.

Such (re)working of the ideas and practices of theatre merely help us (at best) to enhance and articulate our understanding of that fundamental experience of being in the world. We see theatre as a distinct category of human behaviour, having at its centre the human body working with certain intentions outside the tasks of maintaining everyday life, in 'front' of a particular group – the audience.

(Re)considering considering

I use '(re)consider' to mark clearly the implicitly processual nature of 'considering'. This view invites us not only to see performance as processual, but also to see that 'both society and human beings are performative, always already processually under construction'.

(Philippe B. Zarrilli (2002:1), *Acting (Re)considered*, Routledge)

We consider our key terms – 'physical theatre', 'total theatre', etc. – as frames or lenses by and through which particular practices and ideas can be understood; as perspectives that help a dialectical engagement with fields of work, rather than closing these off from each other. To this end, we have used a minimal number of key technical or formal terms ('performance text' or 'production text') as part of the modern vocabulary of theatre discussion and discourse. These are not intended to be esoteric or exclusive but to offer a vocabulary by which such theatres can be discussed and understood across practices and investigations. As such, these will be explained within the body of the text, or will be shown in **bold** when first used to indicate their appearance in a glossary at the end of the book.

Thus, as part of our aim of providing 'portals' or points-of-entry to the subject, and perhaps reflecting our own pedagogical and political preferences (prejudices?), we seek to raise questions, to provoke investigations, rather than present a simple 'primer'. Our own points-of-entry embrace what might be called a 'multi-frame' approach. The aim is to give optimal understanding from the necessary range of viewpoints that reflects the messy reality of what theatre is: an unavoidable hybrid of inherited, borrowed, stolen and invented practices and ideas.

From these considerations and perspectives comes our grounding premise: that 'physical theatre' as a term, idea or concept captures the aims of certain movements in the nineteenth and twentieth centuries to confront the continuing hegemony of a theatre defined by its literary and verbal dimensions. But we also propose that such theatre must be contextualised within the historical and ongoing practices we call the 'physical in theatres' which are found in all theatres as centred on the (moving-speaking) body. These practices are **mimetic** in manifestation, playing to the empathetic and cognitive receptivity of the spectator gathered as audience; what Susan Bennett calls 'interpretive communities' (1990: 44).

Labyrinthine paths

Language is a labyrinth of paths. You approach from one side and you know your way about; you approach the same place from another side and you no longer know your way about.

(Ludwig Wittgenstein (1972: 83e), *Philosophical Investigations*, Blackwell)

'Physical theatre' then traces its origins in our contemporary sense to those ideologies and manifestos which sought to reverse a dualism and hierarchy of word over body. As such, 'physical theatre' is a construction of forms, beliefs and dispositions which takes its place alongside other and continuing suspicions of the word as the embodiment of Enlightenment reason, preferring what at its most extreme is an atavistic reifying of a mystifying instinct and a romanticised natural.

But we must also be careful of simply creating an inverted dualism here: be aware of the danger that preoccupations with body-based theatres reverse the mind–body dualism by privileging the body as an entity independent from mind, thought and feeling. In an understandable and overdue attempt to redress the balance from heavily psychological approaches to acting and theatre making, physical theatres have been guilty of not only romanticising the body, but fundamentally misunderstanding it. (See Zarrilli (2002) for a very useful summary of issues and arguments on this matter.)

Like all such constructions, 'physical theatre' is value-laden, and our discussion – any discussion – must in itself reflect our own values; thus the perspectives and prejudices we own up to. Such alternative modes of inquiry may be seen as of value in themselves; discussed by Richard Rorty as issues not to be settled, but differences to be lived with and used, and by Thomas Kuhn as the impossibility of there being value-free ways of looking at and advancing understanding. (See also Arthur Bochner (2000).)

Thus the different lenses for understanding these physical theatres are, *pace* Callery (2001), 'codifiable' and 'definable'. The terms 'physical theatres/physical in theatres' help us to escape from the counter-productive dualisms which constantly bedevil theatre understanding and analysis. Instead, we propose a three-point relationship between the physical-visual/scenographic/vocal-aural sign systems that make up the ***mise-en-scène*** of theatre.

Calcio (Football) Three qualities required for success:
Fantasia – surprise, unpredictability, imagination, flair
Furbizio – cunning, slyness, bending the rules, trickery, gamesmanship
Tecnica – technique, highly developed core skills

(Translation: David Williams 2007)

This book

The broad agenda outlined in the introductory and contextual statement above will be realised and amplified through six chapters.

Chapter 1, '**Genesis, Contexts, Namings**', establishes the landscape of the whole project and begins to map out the range of concerns and issues tackled in greater detail through the other five chapters. We indicate a number of axes around which the analysis and content of the book may be located:

- the fluidity and mutability of language and terminology
- contemporary practices and historical contexts
- the acting–performing/performance–theatre continuum
- the body in its philosophical and cultural contexts
- negotiations between East and West and the problem of 'Eurocentricity'
- training or preparation?
- celebrating the hybridity and multiplicity of theatre.

Chapter 2, '**Roots: Routes**', takes as its starting point a linguistic framework – roots or routes – enjoyed by Jatinda Verma, Director of the UK-based company Tara Arts. In deliberately offering a dual conceptual understanding of how we might trace influence and legacy, Verma refuses the singular and exclusive notion of a route, insisting instead that it is more useful to acknowledge a plurality of foundations – roots and routes – when trying to grasp the origins of particular theatre forms and practices. This chapter sets out our overall engagement with physical theatres in this project, namely inflecting our focus on contemporary practices with a strong sense of historical and physiological legacy and context. It is acknowledgement of the plurality of body-based practices that cross contemporary theatre performance and 2000 years of Western theatre history.

Schematically, we articulate two routes of practices which feed contemporary physical theatres, and the *deeper* roots that these rest on. Clearly, the relationship between current forms and these antecedents is rarely linear, straightforward and self-contained, and the account which follows attempts to articulate some of these complexities: multiple *routes* from multiple *roots*. The chapter is divided into two subsections as follows:

- *Deep traditions: classical and popular* – a recognition of the importance of the physical in theatres traced through 'classical' drama, medieval drama, the street, circus, music-hall/vaudeville, clown and agitprop, etc. But here we also outline and articulate the deeper cognitive and neurological foundations of mimesis, empathy and play which we believe underlie the physicality of all theatres.
- *Hybrid pathways* – a recognition of nineteenth- and twentieth-century intertwinings of dance-mime-perfomance-theatrical avant garde which immediately prefigure the practices of contemporary physical theatres. Again, we trace ideas on associated issues such as gazing-looking and perspectives on the body.

We deliberately explore a wide range of material through case studies and 'byways' into these associated issues as a means of creating arcs and linkages across the foundations we propose. These foundations again emphasise certain principles (hybridity, audience collusion) which run as theatrical tropes throughout the book.

Chapter 3, '**Contemporary Practices**', identifies and begins to explain some of the key tropes of Western physical theatres. Through a focus on dance-based physical theatres, and a perspective we identify as 'physicalising narrative', we provide case studies of particular productions and company/artist profiles. This section examines in detail the various compositional and dramaturgical strategies of practitioners who may or may not have embraced the language and labels of physical theatre, but whose practices explicitly and unapologetically foreground the visual and physical dimensions of theatre making and performing. Here, a multiplicity of aesthetics and compositional forms will reveal themselves as tendencies or dispositions towards particular ways of generating material, devising and constructing meaning. In focusing on the practices of different artists and companies we will of necessity consider the relationship of their work to other signifying systems of theatre – the spoken word, objects and props, scenography and the use of technology, light and music. This section also particularly cross-references the historical roots and technical traditions from which contemporary practices have their provenance.

Chapter 4, '**Preparation and Training**', examines the relationship between those forms of training and preparation which particularly engage with movement and the performer's physicality, and the dramaturgical strategies for theatre making which are shaped by these approaches. Any examination of the pedagogies of twentieth-century innovators in actor training immediately confronts us with the impossibility of that mind–body/voice–movement dualism we disavowed earlier in this introduction. Even those practitioners most associated with the physical training of the actor – Meyerhold, Lecoq, Barba or Pagneux, for example – never practised a narrow and reductive corporeal training, and all insisted, or continue to insist, on conceptualising their training methods as a rejection of this simplistic and regressive dualism.

One of the significant features of the ecology of late twentieth-century Western theatre has been an increase in, and professionalisation of, training opportunities for actors. This is marked not only by an expansion of courses offered by professional drama schools and universities, but also in a remarkable upsurge in the range and number of short workshops available for young or experienced performers and theatre makers throughout Europe, Australasia and North America. Through a series of short case studies this section explores the assumptions and conceptual paradigms which lie behind selected training strategies; considers how these different regimes deal with the body and physical expression in the creation and representation of character; and reflects on nuances and tensions between notions of 'preparation' and 'technical training'.

Chapter 5, '**Physicality and the Word**', considers how, in productions constructed from texts where the word is dominant, other theatrical languages – corporeality, movement and scenographies, for example – work with the spoken word. Here we are examining the dramaturgical relationships between words and bodies in order to harness and enrich the visual and physical qualities of both staging and acting.

We look at the physicality of the voice, and through a number of case studies (Aeschylus, Ibsen, Chekhov, Brecht, Cleese, Berkoff and others) examine how the physical and the word are used across a range of drama styles. Beckett's work, for example, through the meticulous details of his staging instructions, operates almost as movement theatre with actions and gestures timed and measured with the same precision that a choreographer might use for making dance.

These 'close readings' allow us to examine issues such as transformation, the comic, the poignant and improvisation which in turn lead us to the 'active' role of the audience across the range of theatres and when this is often dismissed.

Chapter 6, '**Bodies and Cultures**', completes the book with an acknowledgement – implicit in everything that has gone before – that this account is inevitably a partial one in that its centre of attention is on Western practices and histories. Given the highly codified and corporeal nature of many forms of Eastern dance dramas this is partiality indeed. None the less, we felt it better to be explicit and – in a sense – unapologetic about the North American and Eurocentric nature of our project than to dabble in, and hence perhaps tokenise, the rich complexities of Asian, African or South American theatre forms which might otherwise fit into our frame of reference.

However, what this chapter does offer is an overview of the relationships between twentieth-century Western physical theatre forms and those Eastern (and other) perform-ance traditions which have fed and influenced many European avant garde experiments. Here we reference the debate – sometimes passionate and angry – about cultures and their relationships and engagements. We consider the tension between a cultural exchange that is generous, equitable and mutual, and one that has often been accused of exoticism and cultural colonialism, and speculate on how the ethics of these intercultural encounters are inevitably framed by the politics of contemporary global capitalism.

[E]very cultural document contains within it a history of a contest of rulers and ruled, of leaders and led.

(Edward Said (2003: 59), *Orientalism*, Penguin)

Omissions and absences

What follows from this is a sharp awareness of the many omissions that any book which is not encyclopaedic has to come to terms with. Hence, in our aspiration not to write a superficial and generalist primer we have given virtually no attention to mask, puppets, site-specific theatres and voice as physical elements within theatre practice, although these are brought into discussion as necessary. We might also have written a book that examined physical theatres through the vehicle of specific theatrical genre and hence examined, for example, melodrama, clowning, musical theatre, Restoration drama, farce or Greek tragedy. 'Physicality and the Word' clearly enters this territory, but not explicitly through genre. Moreover, although not a book about scenography, we are fully aware of the importance of scenography when it becomes part of the totality of a production, and not merely a visual container for the words and characters. When properly used, and allowing for the verisimilitude or representation required, scenography becomes a 'character' in its own right – a composite signifier saying something about the substance and ideas of the play or drama text, and not merely locating action or period (see Chapter 5).

In three senses

It is in this sense that we understand the meaning of the performance or production text; the intertextual manifestation on stage of the totality of the constituent parts or signifying systems as identified by Tadeusz Kowzan (1968) in his seminal work on the semiotics of theatre.

It is in this sense that we would wish to play with Clifford Geertz's (1983) notion of 'blurred genres' or categories. By their very nature, theatres are blurred: at the centre, at the edges and in their processes.

It is in this sense that we would consider theatre to have always been 'total' as well as 'blurred'.

Ownership

In the writing and production of both books we have divided up the writing of chapters and undertaken different tasks, but they are finally our joint and shared responsibility as a collaboration of dialogue and constructive argument.

To understand theatre

Theatre is nothing if it is not understood. To understand is not a dry theoretical capacity, but a practice which combines the physical and the mental in equal measure, and denies that a solely intellectual response to experience is ever possible.

(Alan Read (1993: 62), *Theatre and Everyday Life*, Routledge)

CHAPTER 1

Genesis, Contexts, Namings

Letter to a young practitioner
Value the work of your hands and body

This physical body is the meeting place of worlds. Spiritual, social, political, emotional, intellectual worlds are all interpreted through this physical body. When we work with our hands and body to create art, or simply to project an idea from within, we imprint the product with a sweat signature, the glisten and odour which only the physical body can produce. These are the by-products of the meeting of worlds through the physical body. It is visible evidence of work to move from conception to production. Our bodies are both art elements and tools that communicate intuitively.

**Goat Island: C.J. Mitchell, Bryan Saner, Karen Christopher, Mark Jeffery,
Matthew Goulish and Lin Hixson.**

(From Maria Delgado and Caridad Svich (eds) (2002: 241), *Theatre in Crisis?*, Manchester University Press)

Contemporary contexts

The singular 'physical theatre' has had a popular currency among theatre publicists, critics and commentators in the UK, North America and Australia over the past twenty-five years. It is a term which many young theatre companies and artists have been prepared to use as part of a rhetoric that aspires both to encapsulate their practice and to sound fashionable, 'modern' and exciting to potential audiences. Regardless of whether the phrase actually describes, reveals and delineates theatre practices in any productive way, that certain practitioners, arts promoters and publicists should choose to use and propagate this term – or variations on it – tells us something significant about the times we live in. To be 'physical' in theatre is apparently to be progressive, fresh, cutting edge and risky, while at the same time it is a distancing strategy from a range of theatre practices that are perceived in Peter Brook's phrase to be 'deadly' (Brook 1965: 11), outmoded and laboriously word based. To be *physical* is to be sexy and to resist the dead hand of an overly intellectual or cerebral approach to theatre making. To be *physical* in performance connects you to territories not regularly associated with theatre – with, for example, sport (see *PT:R*), dance and club culture and (more theoretically) with contemporary discourses that articulate and rehearse the nature of embodiment in a wide range of public, personal and intellectual spheres.

We are aware, too, that the field of enquiry represented by this book connects closely to – and overlaps with – a number of other published accounts of the past decade that have sought to map changes and developments in Western theatre practice from the 1960s into the twenty-first century, and to identify the characteristics of new theatre forms and aesthetics. The writings of, for example, Hans-Thies Lehmann (2006), Philip Auslander (1997, 1999), Tim Etchells (1999), Matthew Goulish (2000) and Elenor Fuchs (1996) have all in their different ways traced shifts in modes of performance or acting, relations with dramatic texts and dramaturgical and compositional strategies. A publication entitled *A Performance Cosmology* (2006) marking 30 years of the Centre for Performance Research (CPR) (see Chapter 4) is an eloquent and emblematic statement that captures many of the preoccupations and focal points of theatre and performance writing over this period. It particularly characterises contemporary concerns felt by a number of commentators that *how* one writes about theatre and performance is as important – and problematic – as *what* one writes.

Connections and differences with some of these analyses will emerge as our own narrative unfolds, but at this point it is worth remarking that all these accounts note an increase in the role of the visual languages of theatre and a loosening of the relationship between dramatic text and performance composition. This sense of a slackening of the grip of historically dominant models of theatre formation does not in itself demonstrate the emergence of a new overarching paradigm, although Hans-Thies Lehmann's proposition of 'postdramatic theatre' comes close to this. Indeed, as Lehmann himself argues:

> At the same time, the heterogeneous diversity of forms unhinges all those methodological certainties that have previously made it possible to assert large-scale causal developments in the arts. It is essential to accept the co-existence of divergent theatre forms and concepts in which no paradigm is dominant.   (Lehmann 2006: 20)

Within these broader changes we are attempting to locate the changing role of the actor's body and the extent to which contemporary theatre has foregrounded physical expressivity and gestural composition as the main signifying drives for the work in question.

Chapter 2, 'Roots: Routes', traces the complex historical lineage of our inclusive models of physical theatre and the physical *in* theatre. While here we have argued for a deep historical framing and recognition of corporeal performance practices, conventional wisdom often suggests that physical theatre was a startling new departure in forms of theatre dating only as far back as the 1970s and 1980s.

Namings

In Britain, the term 'physical theatre' first came to public attention through the emergence of *DV8 Physical Theatre* in 1986 (but note our extended historical timeline explored in Chapter 2). Slightly earlier, in 1984, the London-based Mime Action Group (MAG) was founded, and in its first newsletter (autumn 1984) Nigel Jamison refers to 'physical based theatre' in response to the Arts Council's recently published report 'The Glory of the Garden'. By its third newsletter (Spring 1985) a MAG editorial refers to 'mimes or physical theatre people'. We return to the role and development of MAG later in this chapter. However, the genealogy is more complex and convoluted than this, as the term 'physical theatre' seems to appear in various places throughout the 1970s and, Baz Kershaw suggests, was possibly part of the rhetoric used by Steven Berkoff and Will Spoor in the London-based Arts Lab of 1968 (Standing Conference of University Drama Departments (SCUDD) email exchange, April 2006). Certainly, the term is invoked as a shorthand to identify a range of practices associated with Grotowski's laboratory, and *DV8*'s Lloyd Newson acknowledges this legacy in an (unpublished) interview with Mary Luckhurst in 1987 (www.*DV8*.co.uk). The term can also be traced in Peter Ansorge's book, *Disrupting the Spectacle*, where there is a suggestion of an American derivation:

(Ansorge 1975: 23)

> Nancy Meckler, as the American creator and director of Freehold, has been generally recognised as the most successful exponent in this country of the US-inspired style 'physical theatre' which was perhaps illustrated most succinctly by her adaptation for Freehold of Sophocles' *Antigone*.

While explicit usage of the term does not seem to pre-date 1968 at the earliest, it is a central contention of this book that there are theatre practices down 2000 years of theatre history that might conceivably have claimed, or been ascribed, the physical theatre appellation had the terminology been culturally available. As we argue throughout this book, the work of such diverse twentieth-century Western theatre practitioners as Meyerhold, Artaud, Ionesco, Brecht, Beckett and Littlewood could be described, albeit through a different lens, as 'physical theatres'.

However, notwithstanding sporadic sightings of the term in the 1970s, it is not until the mid-1980s that the phrase begins to gain some momentum and becomes a fashionable designation for a range of emerging practices. Although the *DV8* website still employs *physical theatre* in various contexts, it is no longer a term that Lloyd Newson finds useful because 'of its current overuse in describing almost anything that isn't traditional dance or theatre' (www.*DV8*.co.uk). We look at *DV8* in more detail in Chapter 4, but at this moment we may note that since its launch 20 years ago, Newson has talked of the company's work as 'breaking down the barriers between dance, theatre and personal politics' and of 'taking risks, aesthetically and physically' (ibid.), saying that this mode of description is not untypical of how other companies begin to identify their practice.

Théâtre de Complicité, renamed Complicité in 2006, and founded three years before *DV8* in 1983, has never claimed the term to describe its practice, and indeed has been hostile to having its work labelled in this way. None the less, Complicité, for better or worse, has often been regarded as the quintessential 'physical theatre' company to emerge in the mid-1980s. Complicité describes its principles as 'seeking what is most alive, integrating text, music, image and action to create surprising, disruptive theatre . . . what is essential is collaboration. A collaboration between individuals to establish an ensemble with a common physical and imaginative language' (Complicité website: www.complicite.org).

David Glass has been performing internationally – initially as a solo mime artist – from a base in the UK since 1980, but established his own ensemble in 1990. Glass describes his practice and that of the ensemble as 'committed to imagination and collaborative theatre, rooted in the alternative traditions and skills of physical and visual theatre' (David Glass Ensemble website: www.davidglassensemble.com). In 1979, Desmond Jones established in London what he initially and unapologetically described as a 'mime school', but from the mid-1990s this had become a 'School of Mime and Physical Theatre'.

By 1989, five years after its launch, *MAGazine* – the journal of Mime Action Group – had metamorphosed into *Total Theatre* (*The Magazine for Mime, Physical and Visual Theatre*) and this banner very quickly began to take visual precedence over 'Mime Action Group' in most of the organisation's transactions. Today Mime Action Group is the 'Total Theatre Network', and claims to be the 'UK's lead body for physical and visual performance' (Total Theatre website: www.totaltheatre.org.uk), but also has an international membership. Total Theatre Network claims to represent and articulate the interests of 'clown and other circus performance, dance theatre, mask, mime, puppetry, and street theatre' (ibid.). Thus, over a comparatively short period, mime is supplanted – willingly or not – by 'physical and visual theatre' and is relegated to stand alongside, for example, puppetry, mask and street performance. In the mid-1980s, for David Glass and – especially – Desmond Jones this represented a diminution and a weakening of everything they believed mime represented. Jones took these arguments into the pages of the MAG newsletter and the early issues of *Total Theatre* in a number of witty, joyful but scabrous polemics against those who would dilute the art of mime for what he believed was a nebulous and bland 'physical theatre':

I am convinced that Mime will change the face of the speaking theatre in the next 25 years. Maybe not mind-numbingly staggeringly, but significantly. People will come to us, are coming to us to learn our techniques . . . . We do mime. No pissing about. If we are strong people will come to us. We are going through an identity crisis, certainly . . . Krakatoa was a squib compared to what has happened in Mime in the last 9 years.

. . .

I do Mime

What do you do?

Stand up and be counted.

(Jones, *MAGazine*, Spring 1985)

We could extend this type of mapping exercise to hundreds of companies, agencies and theatre practitioners emerging in Europe, Australia or North America during the 1980s and 1990s and find similar constellations of key words and phrases. In Australia since the 1980s there has been an equally burgeoning theatrical movement which seems to have embraced the physical theatre appellation with less awkwardness than its UK counterpart. Our book regrettably cannot do more than signal these energies in Australia and observe that there is a study in waiting which might usefully explore the cultural and dramaturgical particularities of Australian physical theatres. For now we can note the useful section in Heddon and Milling's *Devising Performance* (2006) on Australian physical theatre practices. Heddon and Milling observe throughout their book that late twentieth-century devised theatre has consistently been preoccupied with the shifting politics of personal and cultural identity, and that this has been especially the case in Australia. They suggest that physical theatre practices there have sharply articulated a celebration of diversity in Australian social life, a diversity that has partly been driven by a developing desire for distance from many of the smothering and colonialising cultural forces of Europe and Britain in particular. 'Today', as Heddon and Milling remark, 'this body-based devising draws more fully on Asian and Pacific Rim cultures and practices, most fully exemplified by the popularity of Butoh and the use of Suziki training' (Heddon and Milling 2006: 164). Formally, circus and dance conventions impacted strongly on many of the earlier Australian physical theatre practices, although today – as in Europe – many of the new companies are perhaps more likely to look towards the propositions of contemporary visual arts.

In North America the explicit naming and claiming of physical theatre was significant by its absence until the 1990s, although today it is often to be found as a strap line to identify the direction and aspiration of many young companies determined to resist the embrace of mainstream realism and naturalism. However, of course, there is a roll-call of iconic North American companies and artists over the past four decades whose work has often been strongly and self-consciously physical and movement based. Within performance conventions ranging from contemporary dance theatre, mime and popular theatre, carnival and street theatre, *Happenings*, live/performance art and the modernist avant garde theatre traditions, companies or artists such as Mabou Mines, Bread and Puppet Theatre, the Open Theatre, San Francisco Mime Troupe, Living Theatre, Robert Lepage, Richard Foreman, Robert Wilson, Anne Bogart and SITI, the Wooster Group, Goat Island, the Adaptors, Dell'Arte and Pig Iron Theatre all might appropriately be examined though the multiple lenses of a physical theatres perspective. The works of Anne Bogart (Chapter 4) and Goat Island (Chapter 3) are examined in more detail later in this book.

As we have argued earlier, these descriptions – or aspirations – in themselves offer little by way of analysis of the practices they depict, nor do they signpost particular dramaturgies or compositional approaches. However, together they reveal a matrix of interests, dispositions and codes which tell us something significant about the cultural contexts of the times in which they exist. The inclination to employ any one of a raft of similar phrases – for example, visual theatre/performance, movement theatre, body-based theatre, gestural theatre, dance dramas, dance theatre and (even) modern mime – so as to signpost the shape and direction of contemporary work outside the mainstream, discloses significant information about late twentieth-century Western cultural preoccupations and interests. We elaborate upon the relationship between these emerging theatre practices and their wider theoretical and cultural contexts later in this chapter.

Physical theatres and devising

Aside from this project's interest in physical action *within* text-based theatre, we need at this juncture to acknowledge the critical interrelationship between the emergence – and naming – of a plethora of physical performance practices, and the growth in *devised*, collaboratively authored works of theatre. Indeed, it has been argued that any account of contemporary forms of body-based theatre is at the same time a history of devised work generated through various models of collaborative practice. Arguably, the key line of distinction between the range and nature of physical actions within text-based theatre, and those forms we might with some confidence label as 'physical theatre', lies around notions of authorship, authority and the creative role of the actor/performer. In a previously unpublished essay (1997) but now carried as an extract in *PT:R* ('MAG: The Next Five Years, 1997–2002') Franc Chamberlain explored distinctions between the actor with physical and gestural skills whose task is still predominantly to *interpret* – usually with the help of a director – a playwright's text, and the actor/performer who becomes part of a creative partnership in authoring the emergent theatre piece in question. Of course, such actors may be one and the same person and it is the process of identifying and realising the text that is different.

The actor whose abilities are restricted to a glorious vocal range on an unexpressively lifeless body is easy – especially perhaps in Britain – to caricature, but, as Chamberlain points out, virtually all developments in twentieth-century actor training were physically based. From the later work of Stanislavsky on physical actions, through Meyerhold, Copeau, Artaud, Brecht, St Denis, (Michael) Chekhov, Grotowski, Decroux to Brook, Barba, Lecoq and Pardo, one can trace an insistence on practices of embodiment, physical expressiveness and corporeal fluency. Of course, these practitioners may have differed radically from each other in terms of philosophical assumptions, paradigms of the body and the theatrical objectives which their training regimes were to serve.

The central issue as identified by Chamberlain (1997), and later in a different context by Hans-Thies Lehmann in *Postdramatic Theatre* (2006), is not in itself whether there is a pre-existent text upon which to construct theatre making, but *how* actors, director, scenographer, movement choreographer and others work on such a text. What do they *do* with the text? Chamberlain distinguishes between 'working' a text and a process of learning, and then staging it. Simon McBurney, director of Complicité, insists that he brings the spirit and strategies of devising into all the company's projects whether working from a play text, a short story, a novel or a blank sheet of paper. Thus, if our investigation is to edge towards conditional acceptance of difference between physical theatres and text-based theatre forms, it lies in:

- the nature of the relationship with pre-existent text (if there is one)
- the creative – i.e. authoring – role of the actor/performers
- a distinctiveness, rooted in the performer's body as starting point, in the compositional and dramaturgical strategies employed in the composition of the emerging performance text.

Although devising practices really only begin to surface in the post-Second World War period – and do not take off until even later – devising arguably has its deep roots in some of the European avant garde movements between the two World Wars. The challenge to theatrical conventions as manifested by the Dadaists, Surrealists, Futurists, and particularly in the rhetoric and practice of Artaud, are crucial indicators here. The emphasis these movements and individuals placed on spontaneity, creative freedom, the power of image as opposed to spoken word, and the necessity of theatre to engage with the senses and not simply the intellect, are a kind of seed-bed, or prefigurative form, for the startling growth in devised work in the 1960s and 1970s.

None the less, it is important not to elide the processes of devising, as we recognise them today, with early and mid-twentieth-century European experimentation in theatre forms. While there may be a common anti-establishment impulse here, the experiments of the Modernist avant garde were largely writer (for example, Jarry, Genet, Ionesco and Stein) or director/writer led (Meyerhold, Copeau, Artaud and Brecht), and had their main purpose in subverting the dramatic traditions of the 'well-made play', and challenging Aristotelian precepts of dramatic form and audience response. Devising, however, as defined by varying degrees of collective authorship in the theatrical process, but not excluding the presence of a director, is indeed a phenomenon of the past four decades of the twentieth century. Heddon and Milling firmly locate its emergence in the political context of the 1960s and within the rhetoric of (re)claiming democracy and collectivity:

(Heddon and Milling 2006: 17)

> As the ideology of 'participatory democracy' took international root, it was evident that for theatre to play its role in the formation of any new society, the praxis of participatory democracy should also be implemented within the theatre. Set beside the model of hierarchy, specialisation and increased professionalisation in the mainstream theatre industry, devising as a collaborative process offered a politically acceptable alternative.

A critical dimension of understanding the emergence of physical theatre practices is to locate them historically within the devising paradigm and its politics of *process*. The histories of physical theatres and devising are certainly not identical with each other, but there is a productive and symbiotic relationship between them that is impossible to ignore.

A word on mime

Mime has a history dating back to Greek antiquity when in the fifth century BCE Sophron of Syracuse composed the first mime plays (Pavis 1998). Its legacy survives through adaptation and re-invention via wandering troupes in the Middle Ages, the *commedia dell'arte* in the fifteenth/sixteenth centuries, pantomime and harlequinade in nineteenth-century Europe, the burlesque films of Buster Keaton and Charlie Chaplin, the re-invention of French theatre at Jacques Copeau's Vieux-Colombier in the early twentieth century, and culminates in the radical experiments of Etienne Decroux, Jean-Louis Barrault and Jacques Lecoq in France from the 1940s.

Within Chapter 2, 'Roots: Routes', we consider the influence of the French mime tradition on contemporary physical theatre practices, but it is significant to note at this juncture that mime as both label and practice has an awkward (recent) history, especially within Britain. Paradoxically, given the proliferation of body-based theatre forms over the past three decades, in 2006 there are few UK practitioners and companies within the landscape of physical theatres who would proudly proclaim either to be mimes, or to be representing a practice with that particular description. Even an artist like David Glass who for many years was pleased to describe his work as 'mime', or 'modern mime', no longer uses the word on his website. Until the early 1990s Jacques Lecoq's Paris establishment had 'mime' as part of its title, but since then has described itself as an 'International Theatre School'. In continental Europe, however, there seems less reluctance to avoid the mime word, especially from artists who trace their lineage to Etienne Decroux. For example, the Paris-based company, Le Théâtre du Mouvement, describes its work as 'mime and visual theatre'. A rare example of a British organisation confident enough to stay with mime is the London International Mime Festival, now into its twenty-eighth year and run by Joseph Seelig and Helen Lanaghan. The British difficulty with mime is that it has often conflated 'mime' with 'pantomime', and is perceived to delineate a very narrow range of theatrical endeavour, epitomised by the illusionary mime of Marcel Marceau, although at its best, highly skilled and technically virtuosic. Jacques Lecoq, whose influential teaching we shall consider in Chapter 4, 'Preparation and Training', notes wryly that many contemporary mimes:

> express themselves in a way far removed from silence, via gesticulating as though crying for help or pulling a face in order to remedy a lack of speech and to make themselves understood. These poor mimes have caused the genre to be viewed as a strange zoological phenomenon which one should observe from behind a glass screen – a kind of theatrical malady.

(Lecoq 1987: 96)

Mime as 'theatrical malady' is a perspective probably widely held by artists and theatre academics. While this is clearly unfair when applied to the kind of work represented by the Théâtre du Mouvement, or that offered by Seelig and Lanaghan in their annual and highly respected international festival, it illustrates none the less the power of Marceau's legacy – and his legion of white-faced surrogates – over the public imagination. It is, too, a view which does scant justice to the complexity and richness of the mime tradition and the range of practices that practitioners and teachers have embodied within this designation. Jacques Lecoq and Etienne Decroux differed significantly on how mime should be theorised, reframed and practised for artists and audiences in the second half of the twentieth century, but both had an unswerving commitment to a form of mime which they believed must lie at the heart of a vibrant, regenerative and *contemporary* European theatre. For Decroux, it was mime itself that was the radical art form which would ultimately displace dance and theatre as the 'total' performance of the future. Lecoq, however, offers a very different proposition, namely that any theatre which lacked the corporeal sensibility and deeply embodied structures – the 'driving motors' – of mime would never have the power to engage contemporary audiences.

Acting and performing in physical theatres

The mapping, identification and analysis of contemporary forms of physical theatres take place in this book within, across and between a number of axes – or tensions – which are central to our understanding of the mutable nature of modern Western theatre practice. These include:

- literary drama and postdramatic theatre
- acting and performing: character and 'performance persona'
- theatre and performance
- task and psychology
- presence and representation.

We regularly return to all these issues as they thread their way through our narrative. At this point, however, we rehearse the acting–performing dynamic and consider how this tension intervenes throughout our examination of contemporary forms of physical theatres. Over the past 30 years, what constitutes 'acting' has been investigated and problematised by a range of commentators (e.g. Auslander 1997, Birringer 1991, Carlson 1996, Fuchs 1996, Kaye 1994, Lehmann 2006 and Zarrilli 2002). A common starting point for all these writers is that there is no such thing as 'natural' acting. All acting is culturally encoded and subject to historical conventions; it is shifting territory, continually to be contested and negotiated:

(Pavis 1998: 8)

> To advocate the natural, the spontaneous and the instinctive is only to produce natural effects, governed by an ideological code that determines, at a particular historical time and for a given audience, what is natural and believable, and what is declamatory and theatrical.

Within the widely accepted relativism of this position there remain many possibilities as to what constitutes acting. One particular fault line engages with acting as representation of character (further elaborated in Chapter 2) – playing the role of another, usually prescribed by the writer and interpreted through rehearsal by a director – and the actor as a performer of him/herself. Both positions wrestle with notions of the 'real', but offer a range of strategies for reaching and communicating this elusive – and perhaps, illusory – state. Many examples of contemporary physical theatres distance themselves from the 'acting as representation of character' model, and instead strive for an experience of the *real* through task, action and refusal of illusion. Here, for example, actual tiredness or exhaustion through performers' energetic or repetitive actions removes both spectators and actors from the realm of pretence into 'an intentionally unmediated experience of the real (time, space, body)' (Lehmann 2006: 134). Alternatively – and sometimes contiguously – rejection of 'truthful' character acting is replaced both by heightened physical theatricality, or pleasure in the self-conscious play of extreme exaggeration, and a Brechtian revealing of the tricks and machinery of acting. An example of the latter might be Wooster Group performer Willem Dafoe's explicit use of glycerine to depict John Proctor's breakdown in *LSD (. . . Just the High Points)*.

The paradigm of the actor as 'performer of him/herself' raises questions as to who or what the 'self' is that is being invited to perform. The often heard director or workshop leader's injunction to 'just be yourself' is at one level an easily translatable code towards honesty, economy, simplicity and eschewing mannered overacting. However, it also covers a complex range of issues surrounding the nature of identity, and proposes that 'the self' is an unproblematic and autonomous foundation for acting. An unquestioning acceptance as to what constitutes self is one of the building blocks of much twentieth-century acting (theory and practice) and remained largely unchallenged until developments in philosophy and critical theory through the work of thinkers such as Ferdinand de Saussure (1983) and Jacques Derrida (1990).

Within theatre, concepts and assumptions about the nature of self are often articulated by the notion of 'presence' which in turn directs us to the performer's body and how it is apparently constructed. Here, it may be argued, we are in the world of *charisma*, of corporeal qualities which transcend rational or acculturated explanations, and of mystique and mystery. In theatre forms which privilege the performer's body, and in dance, the language of 'presence' can become blurred with beliefs that there is something immutably and timelessly authentic about bodies and movement in a way that is less true for language and the spoken word. In debates and conversations about contemporary physical theatres it is sometimes suggested that there is an authenticity and truthfulness about these forms because they retain the potential of being untainted and unmediated by the sophistry and deceit of language. The aphorism ascribed to choreographer and dancer Martha Graham that 'the body never lies' precisely encapsulates such statements of faith. In her book on the French mime tradition, Myra Felner (1985) writes about Copeau, Decroux, Barrault, Lecoq and Marceau, and considers what these practices say about how we know and make sense of the world. In contrast to much contemporary philosophical analysis which proposes that it is only through language that we can comprehend the world, in Lecoq's work with the neutral mask, for example, he is trying to return students to a condition where they only *know* the world through gesture, movement and touch, all of which in his analysis originally preceded the word:

Gesture precedes knowledge   (Felner 1985: 150)
Gesture precedes thought
Gesture precedes language

For the fundamentalists, 'presence' is beyond signification, ahistorical and acultural. (We interrogate these possibilities further in Chapter 6.) When possessed, presence offers the performer a universal quality that may be sensed, perceived and understood by anyone regardless of identity: class, race, gender, ability and education. While few Western theatre academics would hold to this position in its pure form, variations on it are part of the daily vernacular – the shorthand – of acting and professional theatre. At the other end of this continuum lies a position which argues that the tools of semiology offer us all we need to analyse and 'read' theatrical or dramatic discourse. The most fruitful conversations have been located between these two end-points and are those which acknowledge that the body in performance seems in some ways to defeat or exceed signification. The transaction between actors and spectators cannot simply be understood by the theoretical framework and toolkit of semiotic analysis. A space therefore opens up between the language of pure presence on the one hand, and semiotic reductionism on the other. Strategically, or unconsciously, many physical theatre practices can be located in this space and profit from being analysed within such a framework. We elaborate on these issues particularly in Chapter 4, 'Preparation and Training'.

Physical theatres: cultural and philosophical contexts

As may already be apparent, throughout this book we have a dual trajectory:

- to focus on the matter and forms of physical theatres, to understand their claims and intentions, and to make explicit the kinds of relationships these practices have with other theatre territories, both culturally and historically
- to offer commentary, insights and analysis on the 'bigger picture' – the social, cultural, ideological and philosophical contexts – which physical theatres inhabit.

Preoccupation with the second of these two strategies is not simply because the authors have their own interests, agendas and histories beyond theatre and performance, nor is it because we believe our readers need a good dose of philosophy and cultural theory to stiffen and brace their eclectic and fluid artistic practices. Rather, it is to hold firmly to a position which argues that theatre practices can only effectively be understood and engaged with through a focus that Susan Bennett describes as 'inner and outer frames' (1997: 1). Neither of these frames exists without the other, and cannot therefore be used productively in isolation.

The inner frame requires close examination of the actual stuff of theatre: who makes it; how it is composed; what the main protagonists do; what conditions, styles and forms shape its practices and so on; while the outer frame invites us to connect to the world beyond, the world brought into the theatre by its audiences, and the histories and other contexts that inform the work in question. Above all, the 'outer frame' obliges us to acknowledge that the meanings and senses we take from theatre do not simply flow *outward* from the piece we are witnessing (scenography, acting, text, music, choreography) to us as passive consuming spectators, but are produced – collaboratively – by both audience and the work in all its manifestations. Our understanding, definition and invocation of the 'outer frame' inform how we grasp and analyse the business itself: both outer and inner frame are symbiotically interdependent.

What follows is predicated upon the reasonable assumption that our readers either already possess some working knowledge – even if rudimentary – of the most prominent examples of cultural or critical theory of the past 50 years, or can find their way to texts which will provide the necessary explication. Believing strongly that the world does not need further potted summaries of the 'usual suspects' – semiotics, phenomenology, post-structuralism and deconstruction, psychoanalytic theory, feminism and gender theory, reception theory and cultural materialism – we have decided not to offer more of these in this account, but to simply provide an indicative map of how some of these theoretical approaches can connect to – and illuminate – the diverse practices of physical theatres. Any of the following, in varying degrees of detail, deal with the theoretical frameworks which can – at best – illuminate and locate theatre and drama practices: Aston and Savona (1991), Auslander (1997), Counsell and Wolf (2001), Eagleton (1983), Elam (1980), Fortier (1997), Lehmann (2006), Schechner (2002), Schneider (1997), Williams (1973) and Zarilli (2006).

What is noticeable about many of these accounts is that, insofar as they explicitly invoke or focus upon theatre, it is largely an analysis predicated upon the paradigm of text-driven drama. 'Dramatic literature', rather than theatre or performance practice, is both the main object and preoccupation of these narratives. Concern with the production of language – and occasionally its performance – is privileged well beyond other theatre methodologies and forms. While all these writers are explicit in their awareness that an analysis of written drama – typically the play text – is a very different exercise from a detailed scrutiny of that text's realisation on stage, few of these figures have specifically applied their theoretical frameworks to devised performance where models of authorship, acting, dramaturgy and form may be radically different from traditional 'dramatic theatre' (cf. Lehmann 2006).

Although there is a disposition within most theoretical frameworks to presuppose (performed) theatre as the dramatisation of literature, the human body has been relentlessly subjected to theoretical inquisition over the past four decades. The body as both object and subject, and as something culturally inscribed rather than as physiologically and genetically given, has been central to contemporary theories of identity and within discourses of, for example, feminism, gender, sexuality, consumerism and popular culture. In what follows we provide a sketch of how selected theories offer potentially productive explanations and reflections on both the practices of physical theatres and the acting body in mainstream theatre.

Reading gestures: the significant action

While semiotics has been an extremely influential – and the dominant theoretical – tool in analysing theatre for over 30 years it can only offer a partial account of the nuances and complexities of the theatrical transaction, especially in relation to movement and physicality. Rooted in an emphasis on language and aspiring to provide a coherent structure within which all theatrical activities can be read for their signification, semiotics has a difficult relationship with theatre. However, where semiotics is helpful is to remind us that sense making cannot simply be reduced to the level of the individual spectator's reception of what s/he experiences from the stage. In place of the unique individual constructing their own personal edifice of meaning from the business in front of them, semiotics argues that we can only exist in the world – and make sense of it – through a shared understanding of a complex matrix of codes and conventions. This 'shared understanding', however, is not a universal disposition, but – in varying degrees – conditioned by compound cultural factors. Theatre and its audiences buy into these signs which become both the language and trade of performance. Live theatre and performance presupposes a 'contract' between makers, performers and spectators which will allow enough of a mutual recognition of these codes and structures of meaning for the theatrical event to 'work'.

Kinesics is that branch of semiotics which attempts to provide a code for translating and interpreting the movement of the body on stage; in other words, how an actor's movements, mobility, gestures, facial expressions and postures can be constructed and controlled so as to communicate the meanings which are intended by script, director and performer. Clearly, at a basic level within – and to a certain extent across – cultures we operate with an accepted code which allows us to register and understand what a scowl, a smile, a raised eyebrow, the clenched fist or the pointed finger conveys within the daily discourse of human communication. A sophisticated kinesic analysis, however, highlights the 'gestural fallacy' of assuming that a gesture or physical action can be understood as a discrete unit without recourse to a possibly complex range of other signs and contexts.

As we know, a smile can cover a range of meanings, and may convey emotions quite different from the affirming and welcoming emotion suggested. The smile may, of course, be an attempt to hide jealousy, boredom, frustration, and even – perhaps – murderous intent or suicidal despair. Kinesic analysis aspires to offer a method of reading the gestural physicality of a theatre piece without reducing this to over-simplistic notions of 'body language'. Keir Elam in *The Semiotics of Theatre and Drama* (1980) explains kinesic analysis and reviews the literature on this branch of semiotics. While Elam is at pains to stress that the single action or gesture cannot be understood as a discrete sign vehicle – in other words, cannot be satisfactorily read in isolation – his analysis is so anchored within the paradigm of semiotics that he is unable, or unwilling, to acknowledge the rich complexity of the transactions between performers themselves, and with their audience. At its most limited, semiotics substitutes a rigid and mechanical structure of reading meanings for a more fluid model which incorporates the physicality – the viscerality – of the spectators' experience (see Chapter 2), and an acceptance that it is not possible to control the plurality of meaning-making activities among a potentially diverse group of theatrical spectators. Lehmann puts it like this:

Despite all efforts to capture the expressive potential of the body in a logic, grammar or rhetoric, the aura of physical presence remains the point of theatre where the disappearance, the fading of all signification occurs – in favour of a fascination beyond meaning, of an actor's 'presence', of charisma or 'vibrancy'. . . . The body becomes the centre of attention, not as a carrier of meaning but in its physicality and gesticulation. The central theatrical sign, the actor's body, refuses to serve signification.

(Lehmann 2006: 95)

Subjectivity and feeling: the phenomenologist's case

In many respects, phenomenology seems to offer a mutually incompatible theoretical perspective to that of semiotics. Here, an emphasis on individual consciousness and a preoccupation with essential truth appear at odds with the language-centred character of signification in semiotic analysis. For the phenomenologist, the human body is not *in* space but *of* space, a crucial perception from which it follows that an individual's relationship with the world is manifested not as a series of linguistic signs, but as sensory, somatic and mental phenomena. Phenomenology proposes methods for intuiting the materiality of the real world within the arena of our own inevitably embodied experience. At first glance, phenomenology might seem to offer fruitful insights into theatre practices which foreground the actor's body, movement and physical expression. For the phenomenologist, our knowledge of the world comes primarily from the senses. Here, knowledge and understanding are generated – and continuously reproduced – as our bodies encounter the world and its matter, re-inventing it, as it were, on a moment-by-moment basis.

For practitioners and theorists of physical theatres, phenomenology therefore seems to offer a rather productive way of beginning to grasp the deep structures – or driving motors – of their practices. For example, although Jacques Lecoq never described his approach as 'phenomenological', his pedagogy of the neutral mask, which may be traced back to Jacques Copeau's early twentieth-century experiments at Le Vieux-Colombier, invites students to experience somatically the living, natural and material world afresh. Through the neutral mask students rediscover a *sense* of the world, apparently unmediated and unfabricated by the censoring and selecting processes of mind, intellect and socialisation. From Meyerhold and Artaud, through Julian Beck and Judith Malina's 'Living Theatre' and Peter Brook's theatre of cruelty experiments in the 1960s to the work of *DV8*, Lloyd Newson, Wim Van derKeybus, Franco B and Brith Goff, theatre has aspired to communicate itself viscerally and sensually, working on the bodies of living actors. And this 'working on' is not merely as conduits or representatives for writer and director, but as forces which somehow capture a spirit of life through rejection of the word, and instead embrace pain, love, loss and mortality: a theatre, which at least in part answers to Heiner Müller's plea for the 'rebellion of the body against ideas' (Müller 1982: 65).

For the phenomenologist there is a presupposition that as humans we can have an experience of the world which precedes reflection and thought. Alan Read feels that phenomenology offers theatre a particularly fruitful method of investigation:

(Read 1993: 93)

The relevance of phenomenology for theatre arises with its attempt to describe our 'situated experience' as 'body subjects' who creatively experience the world before ever analysing it in abstract terms.

At its most useful, phenomenology seems to offer a way of understanding the deep feelings and processes of physical theatres and the physical *in* theatre that acknowledges the limitations of a semiotic approach. Its starting point is the live bodies of the performers, what it *feels* like to undertake this series of actions, or that sequence of movements on stage, and how audiences may experience these beyond the intellect, beyond employing the usual toolkit of interpretation. Phenomenology challenges us not to reduce any aesthetic representation to its 'message'. Lehmann, writing about the work of German theatre maker Einar Schleef, notes the physical effect on the spectators:

(Lehmann 2006: 97)

They often have to experience very directly the players' sweat or physical exertion; they feel the pain and extreme demands on the voice in an awkwardly direct manner. . . . The physicality of the theatrical event stands out in the hard, even physically dangerous actions of the players.

What Lehmann is suggesting here is that as spectators of Schleef's work we are taken beyond an experience which is explainable – reducible to the normal discourses of theatrical representation. Here, semiotics is not enough, and Lehmann proposes that:

(Lehmann 2006: 97, emphasis added)

what the bodies in Schleef's theatre did when they tested their strength and stamina, naked and drenched in sweat, did not 'demonstrate', 'show' or 'communicate' the presence of a past political catastrophe or the possible future of a thoughtless and unscrupulous sportive, virile military body, but instead *manifested* all this.

Lehmann's response to Schleef's work could be invoked when looking at many other examples of physical or 'post-dramatic' theatre. Whether it is a *sufficient* explanation of the transaction between performance and spectator, however, is questionable. Phenomenology is useful in that it draws us into territories of understanding which invoke feeling, consciousness, the immediacy of experience and viscerality. Its serious shortcoming lies in its attempt to keep internal experience 'pure' and free of the social blemishes of language and experience. Cultural theorist and philosopher Terry Eagleton is highly critical of this endeavour, arguing that phenomenology:

(Eagleton 1983: 61)

promises to give a firm grounding for human knowledge, but can do so only at a massive cost: the sacrifice of human history itself. For surely human meanings are in a deep sense historical: they are not a question of intuiting the universal essence of what it is to be an onion, but a matter of changing, practical transactions between social individuals.

Cultural materialism: framing the bigger picture

An undogmatic, meditative Marxism

We have to learn and to teach each other the connections between a political and economic formation, a cultural and educational formation and, perhaps, hardest of all, the formations of feeling and relationship which are our immediate resources in any struggle. Contemporary Marxism, extending its scope to this wider area, learning again the real meanings of totality, is, then, a movement to which I find myself belonging and to which I am glad to belong.

(Raymond Williams (1989: 76), *Resources of Hope: Culture, Democracy and Socialism*, Verso)

The theoretical insights and perspectives of cultural materialism take us in a radically different direction from phenomenology, but have the potential to add extra layers of understanding to the over-structured mechanisms of semiotics. The paradigm of cultural materialism insists that theatre – indeed any art form – is *of* the world and not simply *in* it. Thus, a crucial dimension to understanding and explaining any artistic practice is to place it, to see it, to hear it and to 'unpack' it in such a way as to reveal social and cultural imprints on its form and content. An intelligent cultural materialism does not claim that revealing the social and cultural marks on a particular theatre practice tells us *all* we need to know about that process, but it refuses to accept that any art form can be understood simply in its own terms.

Raymond Williams (1921–1992) has been most associated with refining and developing cultural materialism as a tool for understanding theatre and drama. For Williams, cultural materialism stresses the inherent complexity and plurality of performance texts, and thus their potential for paradox and change. While Williams' writing in this area is largely preoccupied with the translation of dramatic literature into performed theatre, the questions he poses are as appropriate for application to contemporary physical theatres as they are for studying the plays of Ibsen or Chekhov. Certainly, Williams never applied cultural materialism to the subject areas of this book, but he would have wished to identify the precise social and historical location of new and emerging (physical theatre) practices. For Williams, innovations in any art form are not simply about the technical and aesthetic preferences of the artists concerned, but mark wider shifts in thought and social consciousness. Shifts in the conventions of theatre making articulate changes in the way we see, feel and experience the world. They are intimately bound up with each other and both artists/practitioners who make the work, and the audiences who receive it, are subject to these shifts in consciousness which Williams calls 'structures of feeling'. For Williams 'structure of feeling' is a wider term than ideology, largely because of its preoccupation with the senses, with feeling and with embodiment. He writes:

(Williams 1977: 132)

> We are concerned with meanings and values as they are actively lived and felt, and the relations between these. . . . We are talking about characteristic elements of impulse, restraint and tone; specifically affective elements of consciousness and relationships: not feeling against thought, but thought as felt and feeling as thought . . . practical consciousness of a present kind, in a living and inter-relating community.

If there were not some degree of a shared sense of these new 'structures of feeling' the emerging artistic practice would never have any purchase on or engagement with an audience. In terms of trying to understand why physical theatres – arguably – began to emerge, or be named, from the mid-1980s we have to attend to the wider cultural and social forces ('structures of feeling') which gave birth to them.

In relation to this project, physical theatres may be understood at many different levels and through various perspectives. However, following Raymond Williams, we believe that the rise of physical theatres reveals significant insights into wider cultural and social phenomena towards the end of the twentieth century. Williams, in a lecture at Cambridge University in 1974, put it like this:

(Williams in O'Connor 1989: 11)

> I learned something from analysing drama which seemed to me effective not only as a way of seeing certain aspects of society, but as a way of getting through to some of the fundamental conventions which we group as society itself. These, in their turn, make some of the problems of drama quite newly active.

More concretely, the lens of cultural materialism suggests that the following types of questions might be productive in any quest to understand physical theatre forms and practices:

- What models of the body are proposed in training, composition and dramaturgy?
- What relations of power and collaboration, between the different protagonists involved, are suggested by devising and rehearsal processes?
- Where do the practices of physical theatres fit within the contemporary ecology of theatre making?
- To what extent do physical theatre practices offer ideologically liberating, resistant or transgressive responses to culturally accepted norms and behaviours?
- Where do contemporary physical theatre practices sit within performance histories?
- What cultural, economic or ideological factors might explain the rise and development of these forms at this particular historical juncture?

Feminism, sexuality and gendered bodies

She stamps, she thrusts, she ex-poses

For here we have a female performer whose aura continues a lineage of theatre dance that figures the body as a transgressive, subversive site. In particular, she resists the encoding of the female dancer as feminine. She stamps, she thrusts, she ex-poses herself, she does not contain herself, she is sensuous and seductive, she takes the gaze out to meet the gaze of those 'others', her audience. Her work speaks of the forbidden aspects of being in the flesh, and is at the same time proud to be flesh. As a performer she meets the gaze of the audience not with mute blankness, but with an active reciprocating look which invites her audience in to her co-authored space of invention. She is perceived differently, not as an object of a desiring gaze, but as the subject of invention.

(Carol Brown writing on Liz Aggiss in Liz Aggiss and Billy Cowie (2006: 7), *Anarchic Dance*, Routledge)

Feminism and feminist theories – the plural seems crucial here – have a particularly useful contribution to make in locating and understanding the possibilities of physical theatres and the body in theatre. That feminist and gender theories have emerged within broadly the same time frame as the naming and development of the practices of physical theatres is not coincidental. Often consciously and explicitly, preoccupation with gender roles and sexuality has driven, framed and provided content for modes of physical theatre. Although there are significant dimensions of essentialist thinking in some corners of the landscape of feminist theory, an assumption that is central to most preoccupations with gender and sexuality is the differentiation between biological sex, and the cultural construction that is gender. An understanding of gender as something 'made', mutable, produced and performed through relationships of power is a particularly salient paradigm for physical theatre practices to play with and make strange.

If most feminist theories demand that we challenge traditional representations of our bodies, and acknowledge that they are sites which articulate our histories, our struggles and our living in a – patriarchal – world, then this becomes territory rich with possibilities for theatre makers concerned with the languages and vocabularies of physicality and movement. If the body and its representation is one of the most important sites for feminist interrogation and critique then it is a small step to recognise how physical theatre modes of performance making have the potential to become highly appropriate vehicles for the articulation of gender and sexuality.

A particularly influential contribution to feminist theory is Judith Butler's work on gender as performance. Here, Butler radically moves the idea of performance from the context of the 'performing arts' and argues that as men and women we *perform* gender (and other) roles. These are not biologically or genetically given, and hence an expanded and revised notion of performance, Butler proposes, is the most productive way of understanding how we act out roles of being man or woman. The rules governing this performance are bound by historical moment, and cultural factors such as class, race, sexuality and education. Our performance of gender is highly corporeal and not simply articulated by a collection of inner beliefs, thoughts and attitudes. Indeed, Butler proposes that it is only through physical gesture and expression that we can understand and respond to the signs and codes of gender and, 'even when done unconsciously or by habit, these gestures result in a performance that is as stylized and as choreographed as a ballet' (Zarrilli *et al.* 2006: 138). Richard Schechner, however, puts it like this:

(Schechner 2002: 131)

> Each individual from an early age learns to perform gender-specific vocal inflections, facial displays, gestures, walks and erotic behaviour as well as how to select, modify, and use scents, body shapes and adornments, clothing, and all other gender markings of a given society. These differ widely from period to period and culture to culture – indicating strongly that gender is constructed.

Immediately, it is possible to identify rich and fruitful connections – and applications – here between the performative qualities of gender and explorations within the arenas of physical theatres. Both theoretically and practically, Butler's ideas provide forms and strategies for physical theatres interested in exploring gender both as subject matter and as an inescapable and integral part of the devising and dramaturgical process.

Another critical contribution of feminist theories has been to interrogate the parameters and properties of what may be deemed to be 'political'. While these challenges may be traced far further back to the suffragettes, and to early feminists such as Mary Wollstonecraft (1759–1797), the notion that 'the personal is political' became a mantra of 1970s feminism and associated movements. Here, the presumption that politics is solely the domain of the still (largely) male-dominated world of political parties and governance is replaced by a more inclusive approach which argues that, for example, the home, intimate relationships, families and the workplace are arenas of power, political tension and unfinished negotiation. Although at its extreme, the personal being political might be accused of strategic naivety, or of rendering the political almost meaningless – if everything is political then nothing is political – it has been fruitful ground for devised and physical theatre makers. Here, 'permission' to open up and review how political theatre is defined, and to explore the politics of gender and sexuality, suggests that theatre forms which privilege physicality and movement-based dramaturgies are potentially just as appropriate vehicles for such discourses as more traditional word-based literary drama.

Devising, as collective authorship of theatre, contains the conditions of invention for performative explorations of gender which are appropriately embodied, and which harness visual and movement-based dramaturgies. Similarly, performers' ability at and disposition for physical transformation and expression would seem to be a fitting vehicle for investigating the fluidity of gender. If contemporary theories of gender and sexuality insist on the mutability of identity, then the arena of theatre – particularly a physically based one – is perhaps a very appropriate space for established norms and expectations to be played out, subverted and transgressed. The following companies, writers and performers, within diverse theatrical languages, have all sought to explore matters of gender and sexuality: Pina Bausch, *DV8*, Gay Sweatshop, Split Britches, Women's Theatre Group, Joint Stock, Caryl Churchill, Lois Weaver, Annie Sprinkle, Orlan and Karen Findley.

Perceiving theatre: the contribution of reception theory

In a number of crucial respects, the four short sections (semiotics, phenomenology, cultural materialism and feminism) which precede this all engage with the question of how theatre is perceived and received. What they have in common is the unswervingly held belief that the construction and communication of meaning in a theatrical event is not one-way traffic. The notion that meaning is foundational or self-enclosed in the art object – in our case, live physical theatre and performance – and that these meanings flow outward to the spectator/listener, who passively ingests them, has been challenged and problematised from a range of positions over the past 50 years. Reception theory is an overarching term covering a number of different propositions and perspectives. In relation to theatre and performance, reception theories do not, of course, dismiss the work itself, but are concerned with how people, other than the writer, director, actor and scenographer, for example, help to construct the meanings of the piece in question.

All theories of reception suggest that there is inevitably a cultural fluidity in the way in which theatre is perceived. There are many variables ranging from the mode of the theatre piece itself, the spatial contexts and rules of its location, and the socio/cultural/ psychological composition of its spectators. A corollary of these propositions is that no one spectator experiences and perceives the work in question in exactly the same way as another. However, this is not to suggest that there is no 'community' of spectators, and clearly if the reception of a theatre piece was purely an individual transaction, then it would be impossible even to talk about theatre, let alone theorise it, in any meaningful way. Furthermore, without some sense of a 'contract' of shared expectations between the event and its protagonists *and* potential audiences, theatre, or indeed any arts practice, could not function culturally or in any other way. As we have already seen, Raymond Williams' 'structure of feeling' is a helpful conceptual framework to examine that 'contract' of shared expectations, however complex this may be.

Cultural and other factors will clearly have a bearing on spectators' reception of work. Class, gender, ethnicity, age, education, knowledge of the piece and its references, for example, will be influential in clustering perceptions in particular ways, but this can never be reducible to one factor alone. A working-class audience may share a number of class-engendered predispositions about going to the theatre, or possess a degree of shared knowledge about the piece in question, but this 'community' of thought and feeling is likely to be problematised, fragmented and interfered with by other cultural factors such as gender, sexuality, race, education and age.

A recurring theme within modes of analysis concerned with audience reception has been a preoccupation with the impact that architecture and space have on spectator perception and understanding. Here the notion of site is crucial and commentators have argued that the spatial context in which a piece of theatre is made and presented is critical to an audience's framework of expectations, and their subsequent perception of what they see and hear. The cultural context of a performance in the gilt and gold plush of an Edwardian theatre contrasts significantly, in terms of anticipation and experience, with going to see theatre in a black box studio, a community hall, a street, a circus tent or a derelict warehouse, regardless of what the work itself is speaking.

The writings of Roland Barthes have been extremely influential in the transactions entailed in reading literature, but have productively spilled over into the territories of theatre and performance. In his well-known phrase, 'the birth of the reader must be at the cost of the death of the Author' (1977: 148), Barthes articulated the keystone of reception or reader response theory, namely that readers or – in the case of theatre, spectators – construct meaning and understanding as part of a complex web of interactions of which the original art work itself is only one component. Barthes' explication and contrasting of 'readerly' and 'writerly' texts is highly relevant to physical theatres and performance. For Barthes, the readerly text is a relatively closed one where the possibility of audience or reader invention and creativity in response to the work in question is comfortable, but limited. The writerly text, on the other hand, is one that is less likely to follow the conventions of the linear narrative structure and opens up the possibility of a response that is beyond a narrowly semiotic set of codes and interpretations. In our own context of physical theatres, Barthes' insistence on the possibility of sensuality, bliss and *jouissance* in the transaction between the art work and its spectator is relevant and insightful. Susan Bennett elaborates in relation to Artaud and Peter Brook:

(Bennett 1997: 60)

> Barthes's descriptions of texts of bliss recall Artaud's desires for a theatre that abolished masterpieces and sought an immediate physicality. The text of pleasure coincides with Peter Brook's concept of 'deadly theatre', the text of bliss with the envelopment possible in 'immediate' theatre. Both Artaud and Brook put the emphasis on contact with the individual spectator and desire to break through the comfortable reassuring complacency of the audience as group.

Central to an escape from 'reassuring complacency' in the performer–spectator transaction is an exchange which goes beyond the cerebral and intellectual understanding of the work, and takes us into a territory that is sensual and visceral. The importance of the image and the (moving) body in achieving Barthes' *jouissance* cannot be overestimated. Of course, we would be guilty of a similar reassuring complacency if we were to claim that physical theatres automatically generate and achieve in their audiences the bliss of which Barthes speaks. None the less, we would argue that physical theatres, at their most challenging, productively disrupt received notions of how spectators perceive and respond to work of this order. Indeed, the whole notion of 'perception' is reframed to include a transaction that paradoxically is dynamic and creative precisely because of its unsettling nature and its willingness to plunge the audience into a state of loss and uncertainty.

Afterthoughts on contexts

One of the main thrusts of this book is to argue that physical theatres and the physical *in* theatre must be understood and located within a 2000-year history of theatre forms. At the same time, however, the dramatic increase in theatre practices which articulated modalities of physical theatre during the past two decades of the twentieth century in Europe, Australia and North America remains unexplained. The question of why such an 'explosion of form' (Daldry 1992: 4) at this historical moment needs addressing in another book, but to conclude this chapter we signal a range of contextualising cultural factors that deserve further consideration:

- a changing cultural climate which serves to reconfigure the conditions of invention of theatre making
- a decline in deference to the structures of authority that have traditionally characterised Western theatre production
- as a corollary to this decline in deference the rise of collectively authored devised theatre practices
- an embedding and strengthening of a dialectic between theatre making *and* visual literacy and visual culture
- a preoccupation within both academic discourses and forms of popular culture which privilege and foreground the human body and its movement
- the rise of the politics of identity and an appetite for articulating and playing out such concerns through the diverse practices of contemporary arts
- the rise of performance studies and other critical discourses which have demanded a reframing and expansion of the landscape traditionally inhabited by theatre
- an internationalisation of theatre production which has facilitated forms of exchange through practice, education and performance
- cyclical and dialectical patterns of Western theatre production which generate alternative responses to the traditional hegemony of the play text as the main driver of performance composition.

The articulation of *doing*

Over the time that I have been working with Complicité what happens in the rehearsal room has changed enormously, yet certain elements are always present. The constant fooling around; the immense amount of chaos; pleasure as well as a kind of turbulent forward momentum. Nothing is off limits apart from not turning up . . . When rehearsing a piece I do not have a method, no single approach. Ultimately the material dictates each rehearsal.

We always begin with a text. But that text can take many forms – I mean it can equally well be a visual text, a text of action, a musical one as well as the more conventional one involving plot and characters. Theatre, says Aristotle, is an act and an action. Action is also a text. As is the space, the light, music, the sound of footsteps, silence and immobility. All should be as articulate and evocative as each other . . . What people DO must be as clear as what they SAY.

(Simon McBurney, Complicité website, www.complicite.org)

CHAPTER 2

Roots: Routes

Moving into theatre

Aeschylus, the first great playwright of the Western world, was also a choreographer: one of the few facts known about him is that the movements of his chorus were meticulously devised and directed by the master himself . . . . But physical theatre, over the centuries, has both flourished and languished, formed – at times – the backbone of a robust popular tradition – at other times – been almost forgotten. Today we see a vast and thrilling revival of interest in theatre which uses the full range of human expressiveness: shapes, sounds, silences, and this form; the human body itself.

(Richard Eyre in J. Keefe (1995), *Moving into Performance Report*, Mime Action Group)

As this book has evolved it has become clear that we are confronting certain principles of theatre(s). Principles that are neither 'timeless' nor metaphysical 'essences', but which run as essential tropes or through-lines across the forms and histories of theatre, and which are then manifested in specific ways (culturally, socially, politically, artistically).

In this chapter we seek to play with and tease out these principles of practice and process in theatres; as well as setting out the cognitive, neurological and cultural roots and/or routes of mimesis, empathy and play which shape and influence physical theatres/the physical in theatres.

The chapter is divided into two main sections: 'Deep traditions: classical and popular', where we identify the roots of the physical in theatres, and 'Hybrid pathways', where 'text' (see Chapter 5 for discussion of this term) is often discarded or is a supplement to the body. Without claiming to be comprehensive we range over a wide variety of material to provoke perspectives, to identify and reflect the traces of these principles in their many and varied manifestations in physical theatres. Thus there will also be a small number of 'byways' where we outline issues distinct from our main theatre routes, yet which propose a complementary lens through which to understand the routes/roots of physical theatres.

Deep traditions: classical and popular

Words, signs and actions

We've come to the end, then – the world's end . . . | (Roche 1964: 23)

This is the world's limit we have come to . . . | (Grene and
Lattimore 1968: 65)

These words, spoken by Might, open Aeschylus' *Prometheus Bound*; they act to place us, the spectator, precisely at a very imprecise place. Geographically in the desolation of the Scythian country, but conceptually at the 'endplace' of civilisation, at the beginning of the human existential fear of being cast out. Might continues: 'Hephaestus, it is you that must . . . nail this malefactor to the high craggy rocks in fetters unbreakable' (ibid.: 65).

While theatre is visual before it is oral (we see the bare stage, the set, the actor before we *hear* him/her), here the words spoken tell us where we are, what is to happen to Prometheus. They are a spoken text delineating the physical text – action – to be carried out by the actors-as-characters in a story familiar to its audience. Such drama is conventionally taken as the beginning and roots of the European-Western traditions of theatre which have their genesis in the performance of play and ritual.

As we suggest in the Introduction, all theatre is physical in the combinations of its elements. At the centre is the body of the actor – as empirical, as perceived, as constructed, as trained, as ostentation; a **somatic** whole of gesture/ movement/stillness/ voice/silence. This is the actor as *actant*; the functional (to present and signify) as well as representational role of the stage figure.

Physical theatres are also phonic – the making of sounds, the speaking of words, the listening to these sounds and words. But in addition, they are scenographic – the physical and visual signs of setting, props, costumes and stage space. These elements are combined towards a specific purpose; to re-enact or present (or represent) and thus conceptualise and confront the everyday through specific practices removed from the habitual everyday.

Theatre is an event within *real* life that exists at one remove from *everyday* life, yet is symbiotically and symbolically attached to human life in all its social, cultural and historical modes.

We suggest that theatre is dialectical in structure and content:

(Keefe 1990,
unpublished
teaching notes)

Theatre is a complex network of interactive, autonomous, and specific sign systems in a dialectical relationship to each other and which together comprise a performance text itself in a dialectical relationship with the spectator-audience.

This is a formulation developed over many years which derives from Brecht (1978), Elam (1980), Kowzan (1968), Pavis (1982), and the Prague School. It may seem dry and unromantic, but states with unadorned clarity the means and material by which theatre is constructed. Veltrusky explains very simply, but profoundly, in 1940: 'all that is on stage is a sign ... The actor's body ... enters into the dramatic situation with all of its properties' (Garvin 1964: 84–85).

[T]he **polysemic** nature of theatre, ie. its ability to draw on a number of sign-systems which do not operate in a linear mode but in a complex and simultaneously operating network unfolding in time and space.

(Roland Barthes in E. Aston and G. Savona (1991: 99), *Theatre as Sign-system*, Routledge)

In itself the term 'physical theatre' is simply one aspect of this polysemic complex that embraces body, voice and scenography. It is a rhetorical lens or frame that privileges certain practices, fashions and ideological-aesthetic aspirations.

A path backwards

We may map a (very) partial route for this rhetorical through-line:

1984   'Mime increasingly appears to be seen as incorporating a wide sweep of movement or physical based theatre, ranging from Mime Corporeal to Clowning, Mask theatre, Circus, and Commedia styles of presentation. As such, grouped under the banner of Mime we find important traditions which go back to the very roots of our theatre (mummers plays, masques, jester & clowns, C19th pantomime, circus, etc.)' (Jamison 1984: 2).

1975   'Nancy Meckler ... has been generally recognised as the most successful exponent in this country of the US-inspired style of "physical theatre" which was perhaps illustrated most succinctly by her adaptation of Sophocles' *Antigone*: Royal Court Theatre, 1970' (Ansorge 1975: 23).

1968   Kowzan articulates a taxonomy of theatre sign-systems which puts the actor's expressive body and voice at the centre of the stage picture (Kowzan 1968: 73).

1934	On the Theatre of Action's production of *Newsboy* . . . : 'Using symbolic figures, stylised movements, orchestrated chorus speaking, it moved at great speed' (Goorney 1981: 7).
1932	'The idea of agitprop suited me. A bare platform, everything created by the actor – tempest, sun and rain, swimming rivers, drowning in storm-tossed seas' (Littlewood 1995: 92).
1905	'No; the Art of the Theatre is neither acting nor the play, it is not scene nor dance, but it consists of all the elements of which these things are composed: action, which is the very spirit of acting; words, which are the body of the play; line and colour, which are the very heart of the scene; rhythm, which is the very essence of dance' (Craig 1980: 138).
1599–1600	'Suit the action to the word, the word to the action . . . [to show] the very age and body of the time, his form and pressure (*Hamlet* 3:2).

And so on; the route has a trajectory back from Edward Gordon Craig arguing that theatre consists of all its components – action, words, line, colour, rhythm – being equally important but with action at the centre, to Aristotle proposing that imitation is 'natural to man' and that tragedy is the imitation of an action which involves human agents shown by spectacle, verse and rhythm (Aristotle 1967: 29, 35). (This line also shows us that the provocation of roots or routes is equally the intertwining of roots and routes; see Pitches in *PT:R*.)

At the centre of this trajectory is the body in action: whether as still, silent yet remaining dynamic; whether as the gesturing hero or bumbling buffoon; whether the clown or the dancer; whether the juggler or shaman; whether the actor or performer. If the term 'physical theatre' may be located in the latter part of the twentieth century, then the 'timeline' takes us back to the fundamental tropes of theatre: of meaningful physical actions exemplified by Craig and Aristotle.

To return to Prometheus. Here the play text is its own blueprint for the physical stage action it requires; it is its own word picture of verse and physical action. The dialogue and stage directions are a 'oneness', and not the hierarchical separation implied by the terms '(chief)text' – dialogue – and '(beside)text' – stage directions (see Aston and Savona 1991, Ingarden 1973).

What is also striking in this trajectory is the sameness of ideas and principles, however articulated and however overlooked in the fashions of theatre. The making of theatre is a dialectical set of relationships between practices (Kowzan's sign-systems). It is always *syncretic* (within the piece itself); always **synchronic** (within the prevailing customs and conventions of any era or style; and always **diachronic** (across changes in history).

Freedley and Reeves (1941) give a history of theatre that starts with the Egyptians: the *Pyramid Texts*, the *Coronation Plays*, the *Passion Plays*, the *Medicinal Plays* which they date back to 4000 BCE. In hieroglyphic form there are directions for action, and indications of stage figures and their dialogue, at times with a character name preceding the speeches. It is argued that these may be seen as directions for staging, for acting.

The same 'text-embedded' style we are familiar with from Greek drama is used: speech identifying the speaker, speech identifying the action to be portrayed. The *Abydos-Osiris Passion Play* is the best known of these 'texts in stone', describing the death, dismemberment and resurrection of Osiris with evidence of it having been performed up to the sixth century BCE. Freedley and Reeves point out that these plays in one form or another were presented in festivals until AD 391 when the *serapeum,* or place of performance, was burned down as Christianity became the official religion.

The overlaps and pre-echoes with Greek theatre are to be noted first: the special place in which the performance was presented, the equality of speech and action implied by the embedded staging instructions, the use of masks, the portrayal of holy figures by the priests. These are the physicalising in drama and ritual of both an ***agon*** (a spiritual and moral conflict) and a reconciliation between the corporeal and transcendent, the corporeal and spiritual. Not as duality but a bridge between modes of existence, and thus occupying **liminal** or threshold space.

Drawing on the conventions of performance, the body here is presenting the physical actions of invocation, the dramatic actions of ritual as a form of pre-dramatic theatre. It is highly unlikely that these were realistic portrayals in Aristotle's sense of imitation (see *PT:R*) but perhaps may be regarded as a pre-dramatic mimesis of the human and the god presented through physical actions which draw on the everyday but are reframed as outside the everyday.

Mimesis and empathy

We focus now on three terms – mimesis, empathy and play – which, it is argued, run as human tropes through all theatres. We resist the suggestion that theatre is not mimetic; rather it is the form(s) of imitation that differ, be they more abstract and stylised, ritualised or conventionally realistic. Thus perhaps we can reread Lehmann's distinction between mimesis (embodied imitation or reality) and *mimeisthai* (representing through dance) (Lehmann 2006: 69) to suggest that the latter term is the physical action of the pre-dramatic theatre of ritual. If we use Lehmann's reading of 'drama' (ibid.: 3) – despite the limitations inherent in any definition of theatre – then the theatre of Egypt is pre-dramatic, but still of the dramatic as it plays out its rituals as a bridge between corporeal and cosmic existence.

All theatre rests on an *actant* or functionary and on a transformation into some other figure; whether through the use of mask or costume, or through the mass hypnosis of the ritual, or through the displaying of an apparently 'impossible' act of physical attainment. (Away from theatre itself, we enter the discussion of performance and ritual, of social performance, of the presentation of self in everyday life and at special occasions (see Bial 2004, Schechner 2002/2006; also *PT:R*).)

But all that needs saying here is the deep-rootedness of the human desire to perform, to act and play outside of the everyday; as a special occasion outside the habitual realm and yet intimately and existentially connected to it, be it to appease nature or for simple pleasure (see Eliade 1987, Keefe 2003).

Thus, as suggested above, in both invocatory performance and theatres, the physical actions of the body still remain those of the everyday body. These may be stylised or contorted or otherwise heightened but the body remains the same somatic, corporeal 'thing' that it can only be. The physical actions it performs are those of – or derived from – the everyday in physiological and neurological terms and are recognised as such whatever their purpose. The actions are mimetic of the everyday but *outside* the everyday or habitual. At the risk of labouring the point, the human agent can only do what the body is capable of whatever the farthest reaches of such capability are; such action will always be a form of mimesis or extension of human physical action.

This is the root of physical theatre/physical in theatre; the transformed mimetic actions of the actor or performer – whether clown, acrobat, priest, shaman – accepted via the active imagination and suspended disbelief of the spectator.

It is because of this rootedness in what we recognise of and from the everyday that we have empathy with what we see on stage, in the performance space. As we 'see' through the words of action, Prometheus being 'fixed' to the rocks at the world's end, we share his pain through our own recognition of what pain is as we have suffered it. As we 'see' Osiris being dismembered in a pre-dramatic ritual we still have the same recognition of pain as that evoked by the drama. The mimetic element rooted in our own bodies remains the same.

We have the imagination (but see below) to 'feel' his pain as it is enacted by word and action through our own body and mental memory of pain, just as we would similarly 'feel' the pain when witnessing an execution or physical punishment. Such feeling may be vicarious but, as Greek writers recognised, it is by this empathy that the desired effect of **katharsis** (a moral purging and thus learning) is achieved by playwright and actors. Georgias puts it like this: 'By means of the discourse (the audience) feels a personal emotion on account of the good and bad fortune of others' (Gorgias in Taplin 1985: 168).

It is part of the human condition to feel emotion physically and thus to understand the same human conditions in others, however portrayed. But any proper *katharsis* is not dependent on feelings alone; as discussed elsewhere we feel ideas and think feelings. The discourse is presented through dialogue and actions; the performance text to which we respond as a *katharsis* is of mind, body and emotions acting on each other.

Tragedy and the spectators' emotions

It is not in the tragic characters that pity and fear manifest themselves – but rather in the *spectators. Through those emotions the spectators are linked to the heroes . . .* because something *undeserved* happens to a character that resembles themselves.

(Augusto Boal (1979: 29–30), *Theatre of the Oppressed*, Pluto Press)

Thus Brecht's rather strained attempt to distance his theatre from that which he labelled 'Aristotelian', or dramatic theatre, may be read with sympathy given his political-theatrical aims. But if we open ourselves to the full impact of that final image of Mother Courage, now alone, straining to move her solidly immobile cart, we must both be critical of her – remain distanced and estranged – but at the same time feel her pain and loss – have empathy for her as a fellow human (see Chapter 5).

In his contrary way Brecht recognised this centrality of empathy while trying to (re)define it for his own purposes. Thus the oppositional list of differences between 'dramatic' and 'epic' theatre from 1930 (Brecht 1978: 37) becomes a more nuanced view by 1940.

Figure 2.1
I Miss You
(2002) Franco B,
Malmo, Sweden.
Photo: Manuel
Vason

Figure 2.4 *Waiting for Godot* (1964) (Samuel Beckett), Theatre on the Balustrade, Prague, Czechoslovakia.   Copyright: JK/Magnum Photos

Figure 2.5
Haunted,
Daunted and
Flaunted (1997)
Wendy
Houstoun.
Photo: Chris Nash

[S]kimmed through the MESSINGKAUF. The theory is relatively simple. it deals with the traffic between stage and auditorium, how the spectator must master the incidents on the stage. The theatrical experience comes about by means of an act of empathy; this is established in aristotle's (*sic*) POETICS . . . criticism is stimulated with reference to the way empathy is generated, not with reference to the incidents the spectator sees reproduced on the stage . . . it consists in the reproduction of real-life incidents on the stage in such a way as to underline their causality and bring it to the spectator's attention. This type of art also generates emotions; such performances facilitate the mastering of reality; and this it is that moves the spectator.

(Brecht 1993: 81)

It is of a different kind, a political as well as moral *katharsis,* but the theatrical moment still rests on our being able to have such empathy. As Fierling's muscles strain and the cart remains still, we understand/feel her foolishness, her courage, her humanness.

Empathy (as with mimesis) has become rather unfashionable in much theatre theory and discussion, perhaps because it has become debased in the easy, banal sentimentality and bathos of so much drama that is written and produced. But empathy works at every level, as Brecht knew and found so uncomfortable because of the possibilities of debasement or sentimentalising.

For every Prometheus or Fierling who moves us, so we have an equally powerful and visceral response as Dorothy sings of her rainbow in the *Wizard of Oz*, or we see the trunks of Dumbo (Disney, 1941) and his imprisoned mother straining and stretching to touch tips and entwine (as always discovered when showing this clip to university film students, who respond in the same manner as a 5-year-old). In other words we cannot help but be moved by the greatest range of ideas, images and actions.

The cognitive and neurological roots of mimesis-empathy-play

By rerouting this discussion towards an outline of the physiological and neurological roots of empathy, of body and mental memory we find some rather more radical origins of what later become these tropes of physical theatres. But we will start with a wider but none the less complementary theory concerning the interactive development of human culture (objects and signs) and the human brain. Thus Geertz:

(Geertz 2002: 67–68)

> The Ice Age appears (to be) . . . a time in which were forged nearly all those characteristics of man's existence which are most graphically human: his thoroughly encephelated nervous system, his incest-taboo-based social structure, and his capacity to create and use symbols. The fact that these distinctive features of humanity emerged together in complex interaction with one another rather than serially . . . suggests that man's nervous system does not merely enable him to acquire culture, it positively demands that he do so if it is going to function at all.

This may be taken into a more specific area for our purposes where in *On Origins: behind the rituals* (see also *PT:R*), David George reflects on the cognitive roots of human self, performance and action as play. This is where play and its symbols are not a frippery but a fundamental requirement of the human functioning as human via our social brain and behaviours.

(George 1998: 7)

> Acts are intentional and provide a basic sense of self because they make us discover a physical world which resists them. A sense of self and a first cognition of an objective world are complementary. . . . Within this model, an infant becomes almost immediately aware of a world of events occurring; it then acts in that world . . . . The whole syndrome is creative, voluntary, imaginative and active: we perceive, record, compare, adjust, improve. . . . This fundamental syndrome then becomes, of course, the basis of play – arguably a better origin for theatre than ritual, not least because it offers deep cognitive parallels.

We then see what the neurological sources of empathy are, a necessary concomitant of play and other social behaviours:

> **Mirror neurons** are pre-motor neurons that fire when the monkey performs object-directed actions . . . but also when the animal observes somebody else . . . performing the same class of actions. . . . In contrast, the present data show that the intentions behind the actions of others can be recognised by the motor system using a mirror mechanism.

(lacoboni *et al.* 2005: 529–32)

It is both arresting and enlightening to sense that we are 'hard-wired' to see others as we are ourselves, a necessary counterweight and complement to our equally potent enculturation and socialisation; that we recognise and identify with others because of common ground in reciprocity and mutuality of behaviour, feelings and ideas. It is in these cognitive and neurological-physiological roots that we find our empathy for others, not just in the actions of real life, but also in the actions of represented life in the theatre.

Similarly with emotions; at the onset of a trigger event the brain and body are engaged and affected by signals sent via chemicals in the bloodstream and in the neuron pathways to produce a 'change-in-state' of the human organism.

Emotions, signals and the brain

1   Engagement of the organism by an inducer of emotion, for instance, a particular object processed visually, resulting in visual representations of the object . . .
2   Signals consequent to the processing of the object's image activate all the neural sites that are prepared to respond to the particular class of inducer to which the object belongs . . . [these] have been preset innately but past experience with the thing . . . modulates the manner (of response) . . .
3   As a result of step 2, emotion induction sites trigger a number of signals toward other brain sites . . . and toward the body . . .

The combined result of steps 1, 2, and 3 is a momentary and appropriate collection of the responses to the circumstances causing the whole commotion.

(Antonio Damasio (2000: 67–69), *The Feeling of What Happens*, Heinemann)

This understanding of the cognitive and neurological foundations of mimesis, empathy and emotion underlines the intersubjectivity of the *actant*-character-spectator. It is these deep foundations that allow us to 'feel' the pain of Osiris, of Prometheus and of Anna Fierling: the fundamental *physicality* of theatres, in acting or performing.

To repeat David George's words:

> This fundamental syndrome then becomes, of course, the basis of play – arguably a better origin for theatre than ritual, not least because it offers deep cognitive parallels.

(George 1998: 7)

In terms of the mimetic parameters and the empathetic neurons that appear to underlie such play of physical theatres, the deep traditions go deeper than we perhaps wish to acknowledge. It is a sense of such roots in our deep self that gives us an understanding of the human which is felt through various articulations in mind and body (for discussion of other – arguably esoteric – non-cognitive readings of mimesis see Taussig (1993) and Kear (2005)).

Of course, these roots and their ramifications must be qualified by the counter-actions of humans when not empathetic or reciprocal, but selfish and violent. These poles do not cancel each other out, but merely point us to the uneasy tension between these indivisible polarities of the human figure and behaviour.

We now turn to a different, often parallel, but also symbiotic route which leads us – through mimesis and empathy for other forms of play – into the popular traditions of theatre.

Popular playing

The *Oxford English Dictionary* (OED) gives an etymology of 'popular' rooted in Latin and Old French concerning 'the people as a whole'; this may be the whole population of citizens who identify with or who are identified with their city ('polis') or, as becomes increasingly the case, the 'ordinary people' (OED: 1573) or the 'common people' (OED: 1771).

It was the ordinary people who attended both the tragedies and comedies of Classical and Renaissance theatre. Such theatre had an appeal, a compulsion for the whole citizenry to attend, making the same demands on each spectator whatever their class or social status, and thus their qualified reading of the drama. But in modern theatre we see a shift from forms which appealed across the whole of a society, however stratified and satirised all of those strata might be, to theatres and entertainments which themselves become layered and divorced, with an often uneasy and messy migration of practices and material between the forms.

As John McGrath argues, the meaning of theatre differs from group to group, class to class, and, as it is nearly impossible to evaluate theatre from 'within several frameworks' (McGrath 1981: 2), a point of view is universalised, becomes hegemonic and therefore 'normalised'. This hegemony distorts our understanding of theatre. (Of course, the issues of class and hegemony contained within McGrath's six talks are to be found throughout the roots and routes of this chapter, and within all the forms of theatre and performance covered in this and other books.)

Ironically, the (re)presentation of human concerns can be more profound in popular theatres as multifarious paradoxes and contradictions are exposed. It is the popular or semi-legitimate which may say more about the messy complexity of our worlds than the official and legitimate. Too often the popular is derided or given a sneering tolerance as being only suitable for the commons. It may, however, be reified or romanticised as anti-aristocratic or anti-bourgeois by those who wish to plunder and (ab)use the popular for their own cultural or political purposes. Audiences become patronised by the demographics of advertising, or the categorising of theatre seasons and television schedules. They may be conceptually excluded by the continuing baleful influence of (R)romanticism and elitism in art. Likewise, the popular may now be defined merely in terms of box office sales or television ratings; a financial criterion which privileges numbers over quality.

Thus the routes through the popular are paradoxical and treacherous as generalisations are confounded; as one historical or theoretical position is immediately countered by an opposite example or fact from the history of theatre.

> The spokesmen for Puritan London described the audiences as riotous and immoral . . . the City fathers found . . . not only Gentlemen, and servingmen, but lawyers, clarkes, countrymen . . . knightes.

(Gurr 1970: 141)

> Other points generally agreed are that they were local and working-class, well-behaved but vociferous in their reactions.

(Barker 1979: 31)

> On 15 September 1896 over 30,000 people gathered in a field at Crush, Texas to witness an actual train crash . . . the railroad announced 'we are now at work on thirty privilege stands, to be arranged in Midway Plaisance style, like the Chicago (World's Fair) plaisance. In these places will be located all amusements of the ground'.

(Moy 1978: 60)

What we may call popular is more far-ranging in taste, style and content than the theatre of serious drama, and for those very reasons is despised as a threat to good taste. So often either romanticised or despised, it remains distrusted because of its bodily and visceral roots. Nevertheless, we would propose that 'the popular' in drama and performance offers examples of the physical in exaggerated forms that take further our understanding of the mimetic and empathetic dynamics of theatre.

Drama versus the dramatic

Our starting point is to reaffirm the distinction between popular drama and popular performance or entertainment. The latter may be part of theatre and may be dramatic but it is not drama; it is in the world but does not represent the world nor is other than itself.

Likewise we can talk of the popular drama as that which appeals, or is deemed to appeal, to the greatest number, or the use of devices or conceits derived from the popular drama in more serious work as either comic relief or as satire, irony or pathos. For example, the figure of Autolycus (whose ancestor is the minstrel named as the 'far traveller' in sixth-century *Widsith*) in Shakespeare's *The Winter's Tale*; the out-of-service ballad singer who has his role in the plot, but is also a mimetic figure from popular entertainment.

Looking first at drama, perhaps one of the most revealing aspects is the migration of ideas, techniques and physicalities between forms of theatre and the everyday.

The Second Shepherd's Play (fifteenth century)
Lord, but this weather is cold, and I am ill-wrapped,
My hands in frost's hold, so long have I napped;
My legs they fold, my fingers are chapped . . .
But we are simple shepherds that walk on the moor,
Are soon by richer hands thrust out of door
For the tilth of our lands lies as fallow as the floor
As you know.
We are so lamed,
Overtaxed and maimed
And cruelly tamed,
By our gentlemen foe

(Rose 1961: 178)

These are the hands and bodies and lives of working people across the centuries and across all class-feudal structured societies. As the spectators watch the Wakefield cycle, they listen to the words and watch the annunciation to the shepherds while recognising the conditions of their own lives in empathy with the circumstances of the 'mythical' shepherds.

Within a deceptively simple style of language and action, we are being confronted with the universal and the archetype, not as high art, or removed ritual, but as part of the prevailing consciousness which links the travails of the everyday with a perceived state of higher being within a particular ideological context.

(Coult and Kershaw 1983: 1)

We try to find the archetypes that are universally shared, and present them in an idiom accessible to a broad audience. This search for myth and its enactment, could become elite and introverted, and unrelated to the complex, messy culture that we live in. Welfare State, however, works from the assumption that myth and archetype are functional operations of human consciousness.

As they create their festivals and celebrations, so do the UK-based theatre company Welfare State also use the tools and physical actions of the everyday working world. We see the wires and rods of the giant puppets, the scaffolding that supports the structures and booths and figures, signs which make myth and archetype part of everyday spiritual-secular existence. The approach of Welfare State is also a celebration of the desire expressed by Brecht and Neher that the physical artefacts of theatre be as central to the *mise-en-scène* as the actor, the character and the dialogue. The spectator can recognise the outcomes of theatre constructed with the same tools they use at work or at home; these are not hidden or denied.

We then see the same techniques of the vernacular being used to portray the Passion itself as both popular and spiritual:

The Crucifixion (fifteenth century)

1 Soldier:	Strike on then hard, for him thee bought
2 Soldier:	Yes here is a stub will stiffly stand;
	Through bones and sinews it shall be sought . . .
3 Soldier:	It fails a foot or more;
	The sinews are so gone in . . .
1 Soldier:	Why carp ye so? Fast on a cord,
	And tug him to, by top and tail . . .
2 Soldier:	Lug on, ye both, a little yet
3 Soldier:	I shall not cease, as I have sele
4 Soldier:	And I shall fond him for to hit . . .
	Ho now! I hold it well
1 Soldier:	Have done, drive in that nail
	So that no fault be found.

(Cawley 1974: 148–49)

As the audience watch the representation of the crucifixion being carried out by the nail makers of York, they will recognise not only the grimness and the dark humour of the trade being put to such a purpose, but also the craft competence of pinners and painters for such a task. The physical skill in handling the tools, the cords and the body will be familiar from managing gear and meat in their own lives. This is the power of such distanced familiarity.

It is the same precision of detail that fascinates us in the techniques of sleight-of-hand or juggling seen below, the same precision of detail in a gesture, a stance, an angle of the head that holds us in the work of Chekhov or Beckett (to be examined in Chapter 5).

While evidence points to a form of brutal, stylised 'realism' it is, more importantly, the basic physical elements of acting that give a picture to the audience. Without the photographic realism we are used to, we have rather the mimesis of the everyday that allows the spectator to 'see' the nails going into flesh, the cords stretching the body. It is an image that arcs back in popular traditions of theatre to the 'fixing' of Prometheus evoked in another form of play.

As Richard Schechner reminds us, 'in ancient Athens, the great theatre festivals were ritual, art, sports-like competition and popular entertainment simultaneously' (Schechner 2002: 26/2006: 32). Just as we have suggested the validity of play as the original driving impulse of theatre, it seems equally arguable that play is the origin of entertainment. On Greek vases from the Classical period we see images of comic theatre; a servant, phallus hanging, filching and hiding food from under the eyes of his master – a simple piece of comic acting that becomes the basis of all farce and slapstick.

The Trickster's play

But it is also play – a 'look at what I can do and get away with' moment that is at the heart of child's play. Hiding (and seeking) is played as a theatrical moment. It is the root of the dexterous manipulation of objects that becomes conjuring, or juggling, or that athletic manipulation of the body which becomes tumbling and balancing. We see how popular physical entertainment that rests on such manipulation of objects and body for the sheer delight of the spectator necessarily shares with dramatic theatre the fundamental use of the body and its physicality.

From the seventeenth-century book *Hocus Pocus Junior, The Anatomy of Legerdemain*, we read of the tricks of the trade which we can safely surmise were passed down over many eras and which stand for the craft of the entertainer.

(McKechnie undated: 14)

> First he must be of an impudent and audacious spirit. . . . Secondly, he must have a nimble and cleanly conveyance. Thirdly, he must have strange terms and emphatical words, to grace and adorn his actions. . . . Fourthly, and lastly, such gestures of body as may lead the spectators' eyes from a strict and diligent beholding his manner of conveyance. For the effecting of this feat you must have a blade for the nonce, made with a gap in the blade. . . . You must conceal an inch with your finger, and then wring it over the fleshy part of your nose, and your nose will seem as if it were half cut off with the knife. Note that in such feats as this, it were necessary to have a piece of spunge with some sheep's blood in it to be retained privately.

This is the exaggerated mimesis of the everyday turned into a playful and somatic sleight-of-hand. We recognise the 'manner of conveyance' which these physical actions rest upon, yet cannot see it in the trick – the hand is faster than the eye and we take pleasure in the hoax and applaud as we simultaneously recognise its deception. We are willing collaborators, not passive spectators, in the collusion of knowing it to be trickery, but enjoy the play of hand nevertheless. We simply enjoy the play.

More honest than the dance of veils

It's the directness of its address that drew Forced Entertainment to variety . . . 'theatre addresses the audience sideways or through subterfuge . . . in variety the audience is right there, dealt with . . . there is no pretension that you are there to give them anything other than what the audience want . . . this directness of variety is more honest than the theatre's subtle dance of veils'.

(Tim Etchells in Dorothy Max Prior (2006a: 11), 'Old Dogs, New Tricks', *Total Theatre* 18)

Just as we are active collaborators in the illusion of the drama by our willingness to suspend disbelief, so we are complicit in the joy of the trick of the conjuror as we suspend our dismissal of it as mere deception. Similarly, we enjoy the exaggeration of gesture, the motions of the body in the recognition both of the mimetic gestures and of our inability to do such things without entry into the craft, into the training. Hence the pleasure we take in the physicality of the tumbler, the juggler, the clown, the aerialist, as an exaggeration of the everyday mimetic.

We always speculate for an hour about what is the difference (between the theatrical and the clown) and we have many answers. One line of thought says the difference is logic. The clown follows the logic of the unconscious, that is the things we all think of but never do, and the actor the logic of the conscious by outwardly portraying characters that everyone can relate to.

(De Castro 2000: 4)

While agreeing with the spirit of De Castro's distinction, it is flawed in one respect in that we also relate to the clown – like the actor – as an *actant*, a function and role. The clown is a human and we relate to him/her as such; that is why we have empathy for clowns in whatever sorrow or joy or zaniness we see them. Hence we may learn as much from the comedy of Aristophanes as from the tragedy of Shakespeare as from the tragi-comedy of Chekhov or Beckett, as from the television sit-com *The Office,* or the bewildered body of the street clown. The routes take many paths and we reject any hierarchies – except of merit – here. When we watch the distortions of the clown in slapstick we are watching a deformation – via exaggeration – of human corporeality, and in this we find a strange form of empathy.

As mirror neurons and play are at the root of *katharsis* out of empathy and recognition, then is it also these same roots that allow us to enjoy the sheer physical entertainment of the conjuror or the juggler. It is shared somatic pleasure enhanced by the awe at another's technical ability, while recognising it for what it is. In this sense we need to rework some further observations of Boal on Aristotle:

Aristotle's coercive system of tragedy survives to this day thanks to its great efficacy. It is, in effect, a powerful system of intimidation . . . the objective of which is to eliminate all that is not commonly accepted. . . . His system appears in disguised form on television, in the movies, in the circus, in the theatres . . . it is designed to bridle the individual, to adjust him to what pre-exists.

(Boal 1979: 46–47)

This is true so far as it goes, and it is the same impulse that drove Brecht to search for a 'new' poetics. It is a truism that all kinds of theatre – tragedy as well as bread and circuses – can, by intention or default be coercive, dulling and a perpetuation of the status quo.

But equally theatres may be an impulse for change using the existing poetics for new or other ways of seeing the world. Propositions such as Boal's are in danger of bypassing the human capacity not only for revolution, but for ignoring or ridiculing that which is presented by those theatres. To argue otherwise is to deny the potential of human agency in changing its affairs, its life. The roots of empathy in our cognition and neurons allow us also to recognise make-believe or spectacle for what it is; to enter its world momentarily while remaining aware of its status. (Thus in another discussion one would wish to look at our empathetic reactions to the distortions of the anthropomorphic body in cartoon animations such as *Tom & Jerry*; an enjoyment of destruction so outlandishly unreal precisely because we recognise it as such.)

Aerial dancing

I started to create new work, out of the circus arena (called aerial dance). . . . In its simplest form we could say that traditional dance is like traditional circus where strength, stamina, skill and innovation are admired . . . contemporary dance is freed from these chains and is creating movement for movement's sake, the interpretation lying in the eye of the beholder. . . . So what is aerial dance? Is it dance that reaches for the sky via aerial techniques and equipment? Is it aerial that reaches down to earth for its ideas and dancers for its choreographic endeavours?

(Tina Carter (2001), 'Angelic Upstarts', *Circus Arts News* 6)

Official and everyday bodies: conflicts in culture

In this first section we have seen the centrality of the body to these parallel theatre traditions which are both separated and intertwined. A history of attitudes to the body is beyond the scope of this book, but may schematically be placed in two categories – what we can call the 'official or codified body' and the 'everyday body'.

The first is that identified by religion and ideological culture as one to be denied, hidden, reified in scripture, verse and prose while at the same time its visceral corporeality is demonised. This is in tension with the 'everyday body' – a body with its own codes but one that has bodily functions, procreates, suffers without pain relief, has pleasure, works; the one that is *directly* experienced through day-to-day living (and dying). Although the attitudes of the 'official body' condition and shape the everyday body, these are in conflict with this body as it is lived and experienced (perhaps the *habitus* of the body: see Chapter 1 and *PT:R*, or the *Hyle* of the body: see below). It is the conflict and tension between these 'bodies' as the messy human reality that we see played out in the physical dimensions of classical and popular traditions of theatre, in official-unofficial culture.

Stools from Samuel Pepys' Diary

Having taken one of Mr Holliard's pills last night it brought a stool or two this morning and so forebore going to church. (24 May 1663)

She gone, I up and then hear that my wife and her maid Ashwell had between them spilled the pot upon the floor and stool and God knows what, and were mighty merry making of it clean. (25 May 1663)

Early in the morning my last night's physic worked and did give me a good stool, and then I rose and had three or four stools, and walked up and down my chamber . . . and by and by comes Mr Creed and he and I spent all morning discoursing against to-morrow before the Duke. (28 June 1663)

(Samuel Pepys (1875–1879), *Diary*, transcribed by Bright Mynors, Bickers & Son)

Hybrid pathways

This intertwining and at the same time separating of popular theatre and art theatre and the concomitant intertwining of the 'official and everyday body' is exemplified by the hybrid pathways that physical theatres have taken since the nineteenth century. We are looking at these via three particular routes of physical theatres that emerge from the roots and histories outlined above, and which have their own interlacing and over-lapping of practices and ideas. These routes draw on what we call 'the mime tradition', 'the dance tradition' and 'the avant-garde tradition'. They will be treated under these terms for the sake of coherence and to acknowledge their discrete features, but without losing sight of the overlaps and commonalities – the blurred edges.

Miming bodies

Of course the principles of theatres are always diachronic, but the modern mime tradition has a particularly coherent quality (see also Chapter 1). At the risk of over-simplifying, there is a kind of generational line from teacher to student (and onward in this way) which may be found in this area of work that is more usually detectable in classical music or dance.

Training is as much at the centre of this work as is public performance, and is the formal equivalent of the unofficial and usually unrecorded lines of training in the crafts of theatre which characterise the popular forms outlined above. As teachers, the work of some key mime practitioners touched on here will be discussed in more detail in Chapter 4. But this acts as an example both of the way in which ideas reappear in different guises and of the way in which ideas and practices migrate from informal to formal theatres. Indeed one of the key characteristics of the mime tradition (as of many others) is its rediscovery of certain earlier theatre practices which fall outside hegemonic conventions. Perhaps in this sense the work and reputation of this tradition still carries an aura of the dangerous, the unconventional, despite its influence on the mainstream of theatre from the late twentieth century.

We are looking at the miming body particularly in its 'French manifestation' for the sake of coherence. But we must also acknowledge the ambivalence of the practitioners discussed here towards the practices known under the terms 'mime' or 'physical theatre' and their variants. Such ambivalence has its own irony given the centrality of this work to the rhetoric and practice of 'physical theatre' itself.

Lecoq and mime

Lecoq says that the term 'mime' has become so reductive that we have to look for others. This is why he sometimes uses the term *mimism* . . . which is not to be confused with *mimicry*. Mimicry is a representation of form, *mimism* is the search for the internal dynamics of meaning.

(David Bradby, note in Jacques Lecoq (2000: 22), *The Moving Body*, Methuen)

This section will look at some key ideas on movement, gesture and corporeality represented through the approaches of Copeau, Decroux, Barrault, Marceau and Lecoq: what the roots of their ideas and work may be and the routes they have opened up. Simon Murray notes that:

(Murray 2003: 3)

> he [Lecoq] was a central figure in a loose movement of practitioners, teachers and theorists who proposed that it is the actor's body – rather than simply the spoken text – which is the crucial generator of meaning(s) in theatre . . . during a period when many young European theatre-makers were creating work which they – or the publicity departments of theatres and art centres – wished to describe as physical theatre, movement theatre, body-based theatre, visual performance.

Tom Leabhart (1989) and Myra Felner (1985), for example, provide a comprehensive history and overview of the European mime traditions, and it is not our intention to give a potted reiteration of these and other writings. But historically mime and pantomime seem to be terms that are often used interchangeably, as are their defining characteristics. Nicoll (1931) traces a European mime tradition to the sixth century BCE; Leabhart cites the mime plays of Herondas dating from the third century BCE; Nagler (1952) includes descriptions of Roman pantomime from the second century BCE. We may also look at the use of dumb show in Shakespeare's *Hamlet* or *A Midsummer Night's Dream*. In all these and other cases we find a mixing and co-mingling of words, sounds, music, silence and the expressive body. The *silent* mime seems an invention of the nineteenth and twentieth centuries.

However, it is the coming together of the *commedia dell'arte* (Rudlin 1994) and the silent pantomime of the Italian Players in Paris from 1700 (Leabhart 1989: 4–5) that mark the accepted origins of modern European mime forms, in particular the traditions of white-face mime associated with Jean-Gaspard Debureau and his successors who influence Jacques Copeau. From these two sources come the central characteristics of the French tradition: the expressive (often silent) body; the mask; the objective mime. It is on issues around these three themes that we will now concentrate.

Expressive bodies

Such a body is quite clearly at the centre of all world theatre in all its roots and routes. But in the nineteenth century it becomes a topic that starts to take on particular resonances and ramifications for acting and performing, as part of a general changing of views, attitudes and interest in the body in general. The body is both idealised and sentimentalised as *Nature*, and demonised in its animalistic or brutal *nature* in both the individual and the crowd-mob. In either case the corporeality of the body is made the victim of a psychological-social-cultural hierarchy of highly simplistic dualisms. The body is to be feared, vilified, denied, or admired as some 'other' from a safe distance in the gallery/ theatre/circus ring, or lusted after in the pornography of the photograph or freak show. The body is made object in ways quite distinct from earlier eras.

Film and motion

This objectifying is also true of the body in motion in the investigations of Muybridge and Marey (see Mannoni 2000). While capturing the physiology of movement in remarkable sequences of pictures, the camera paradoxically objectifies the body of the subject while revealing it to our voyeuristic gaze. We see how expressive and aesthetic the body is in its everyday actions as, at the same time, it is framed – captured – for us to look at.

It is worth proposing that Muybridge and Marey are as important to this focus on physiology, movement and action as Craig, Appia, Jacques-Dalcroze, and Duncan. Can we trace a line from Muybridge, Marey, Melies and other early film-makers glorying in the physicality of the body to the explorations of Barrault and Decroux in 1931 to 1933?

We would argue that it is this double (paradoxical and contradictory) attitude from both theatre makers and spectators towards the body that is a further trope characterising physical theatres. A double attitude because such revealing of the body is also being explored, for example, in the development of the gymnastics movement in Europe, the codification of movements and gestures into various dance forms and the gradual systematising of actor training:

> after years of working with actors, I have come to the conviction that the problem of the actor is, at base, a corporeal problem. The actor is standing on stage.

(Copeau in Rudlin 1986: 93)

For Copeau – as for Jacques-Dalcroze, Appia and Craig – the actor's body was both problem and solution. How was the actor's body to be made distinct from the everyday body? How was the spectator to see that body and which body was to be seen – the actor's or the character's? If it's the actor's body that we see then surely the actor becomes in fact a performer, foregrounding his/her body at the expense of character?

We would argue that this is a false dichotomy because the actor's craft depends on complicity with the audience; they will suspend their disbelief to 'see' the character. Consequently, the audience are accepting another of the many double qualities that characterise theatres – that actor and character are present simultaneously in distinct but symbiotic ways.

This dilemma of the actor–character relationship may be resolved in a number of ways: via a philosophy of training and staging which allows the acting to be seen as part of the character; placed 'side-by-side' as in crude Brechtian theatre; 'hidden' as in crude Realism; sublimated as in crude Ritual theatre; separated as in non-acting, i.e. performing.

> I believe that acting should be simple rather than natural, because acting should seem natural but not be so. The question is how to make it appear that way. The old school methods do not make for naturalistic acting, and the naturalistic school of acting is a horror.

(Copeau in Katz 1973: 163)

(Marshall 1957:
61–62)

The acting at the Vieux-Colombier was, in a modern play, at first sight completely realistic. . . . But watching more closely one realised that gesture was being used sparingly and selectively, so that each gesture was given unusual significance . . . the acting had a balletic quality which so many producers attempt to achieve though the result is generally no more than a series of self-conscious posturings . . . one was never conscious of a producer composing effective groupings for their own sake; they seemed the natural result of the action of the play just as the movement about the stage had an ease and fluidity.

This is not photographic psychological-emotional realism. Rather we have an acting of character not seeking to reproduce a character as if lifted from the street, but presenting the essential qualities of the character and their actions. The audience, in their complicity, complete the picture, an issue we shall return to in Chapter 5.

Masked bodies

Marshall recognises that the skill and quality of masked acting comes from a particular training regime (one that is quite distinct from that of Stanislavsky's system). This approach aims for the articulate, expressive body that is to be found and developed by the actual process of using the mask (see the photo-essay in *PT:R*):

(Leabhart 1989: 26)

The students called the class 'the mask', since for it they wore expressionless masks (at first, only a scarf wrapped over the face), the body as bare as decency would allow. Diminishing the potential of the face to communicate meant that the rest of the body would need to take on that role in addition to its own.

In training and rehearsal students are forced to remove themselves away from a reliance on the face. As Decroux recollects: 'for, once the face was obliterated, the body needed all of its parts to replace it' (Decroux 1985: 4). It should be emphasised that we are not talking of mask theatre here, the 'expressive' or 'character' mask covering and replacing the animated powers of the actor's face and working with its own theatrical conventions and traditions. Rather this is a means of discovering the physically expressive body which thus becomes an articulate *equal* to voice and face, instead of being reduced to a vehicle for carrying face and voice around the stage.

In training this means using various forms of neutral mask, whether the simple scarf used by Copeau, the more sculpted balanced mask of Lecoq, or a mere bag over the head, the aim is to release the body into its expressive potential.

Once the face is covered the hitherto inanimate object that is the neutral mask becomes animated by the gestures, angles, inclinations, postures of the body creating mimetic archetypes and stereotypes of human emotions, actions and gestures that are read empathetically by the observer. When such a neutrally masked head, remaining still and silent, evokes such archetypal states by a simple tilt or angling of the covered head we are watching and responding to a piece of 'pure' physical theatre.

The challenge is to retain that physical articulacy when face-voice-body are reconnected outside the training studio. Once on stage, when the mask has played its central task in releasing the body, face, body and voice have to remain connected. When the face is revealed it is the actors' integrity and skill which are required to maintain this complete articulacy of body-face-voice; of total theatre.

Illusionary bodies

This section considers what would now be known as objective or illusionary mime, where:

> all objects are imaginary. The imagined existence of an object will become real only when the muscular disturbance imposed by this object is suitably conveyed by the body of the mimer.

(Barrault 1951: 27–28)

It is a style which at its best is based on formidable technique, exemplified here by looking at a key scene from Marcel Carné's iconic film *Les Enfants du Paradis* (1945). Played by Jean-Louis Barrault, Debureau, a pantomime performer at the Théâtre des Funambules, is witness to an incident of pick-pocketing outside the theatre. When the woman he loves is falsely accused he proceeds to give an eye-witness account of what really happened. 'Eye-witness' is crucial here as he gives evidence without speaking, depending on his skill as a mime and the eyes of the crowd to interpret his illustrations to 'speak' the truth. We, as further members of the crowd, also see this truth as it is articulated through the face and body. Just as the crowd in the film, we become an audience to this piece of street theatre. We are active.

Debureau speaks: 'Me – I saw everything' and then gives his account, 'describing' the figure of the woman, the fat victim, the moustached thief; he then 'separates' his own arm and hand from his body to become the thief, letting 'his' fingers crawl across the stomach of the Debureau-victim to 'take' the watch from the waistcoat pocket; the thief 'flees', the accusation is made and Garance is cleared. The watch, the figures, the thief's hand are created by the muscular disturbance imposed by the objects and the expressive articulacy of the mime's body. It is the way that Barrault creates the thief's hand and fingers from his own body, aided by the masking-curtaining effect of his drape-coat that make this such a supreme illusion. It is the skill of the mime that makes us believe we are seeing the other's fingers take the watch – plus, of course, our willingness to suspend disbelief for the duration of the performance. It is a supreme example of the skills of what Anne Dennis calls the *physically articulate actor* (Dennis 1995), here without voice. The fingers tell the story while the face adds the emotions that go with the situation.

The irony is, of course, that we are not seeing Debureau, but Barrault personifying the historical figure; it is Barrault's physical articulacy that we are witnessing and admiring in performance. It is an irony recognised by Barrault himself:

(Barrault 1951:
156–57)

> We don't even know exactly what Debureau's style of pantomime was like. We can only guess at it across the pantomime we sometimes saw in our childhood thanks to Séverin and, more recently, George Wague.

This is a physical theatre of recollection, traditions and inheritance of a mimetic art; an inheritance that comes to us via both formal and informal routes. The formal rescuing of techniques and the reworking of these by Copeau, Decroux, Barrault and Marceau; the informal routes of popular entertainments as passed on through music-hall, vaudeville and in the filmic echoes of Chaplin and Keaton.

**B
Y
W
A
Y

2**

Gestural language

As a form of communication (usually) without 'voice', the miming body depends on a theatrical vocabulary that we may think of as a universal gestural language. Whether wearing a mask as such, or a moustache which serves the same focusing function as the clown's red nose mask, we see the mime using his body and face without words to express and communicate the archetypes and stereotypes of basic human emotions and ideas. This is based on a tradition of physical theatre which stretches back to Greek comedy and tragedy with expressive conventions that remain broadly the same, and which can be read by any audience that has a common cultural inheritance.

> [Birdwhistell] describes his original impetus and purpose as confidence that 'it would be possible to isolate a series of expressions, postures, and movement that were denotative of primary emotional states'. He was concerned, like Delsarte, with an attempt to 'isolate universal signs of feeling'.
>
> (Kirby 1972: 64)

It is when we move away from such universality that we are confronted with subjective mime. This will not be discussed as such, but for Decroux it becomes synonymous with an expression of deeper truths about the human spirit and beauty rather than a surface representation. For our purposes it serves to exemplify the distinction between that which is a recognisable mimetic representation and that which is an abstract mimesis of human line and form.

Both are constructions, but this distinction between the non-abstract and the abstract may be seen as a fault line in twentieth-century arts practices, but perhaps more usefully could be regarded as another spectrum, a dialectic between two poles of execution and perception.

Dancing bodies

Dance audiences are mainly interested in dance. And physical theatre doesn't sound like dance. They tend not to ask what physical theatre is.

(Eve Wedderburn (2006: 20), 'Borderline Cases', *Total Theatre* 18(2))

When researching this chapter we were struck by a key assumption in virtually all the writing on dance: that the term 'dance' is to be equated with performances of what we might call 'art dance' – ballet/free/modern/contemporary/new dance. Thus Haskell calls his book *The Making of a Dancer* but discusses only ballet dancing, partially defined as 'a system of physical education that enables the dancer to be expressive in every type of movement' (Haskell 1946: 37).

Or Emilyn Claid: 'dancing – I mean *dancing* as an artistic codified expression, as an articulate language' (Claid 2006: 140). Here, dance is equated with a form of theatre or entertainment whereby one set of people – the practitioners – perform in front of another set of people – the audience – who will read what is being expressed or communicated from their knowledge or interpretation.

But unlike the theatre forms already discussed – defined by the necessary presence of an audience – dance has another manifestation; the social dance whose primary purpose is participation – an entertainment for and by the dancers themselves. These participants may become onlookers (not a conventional audience) from one moment to the next but the point is to *do*, not to watch. The demonstration dancers of *Come Dancing* or *Hi De Hi* are merely an exception to this basic rubric.

As we have seen already, the art form becomes detached from the popular form and sets up another hierarchy by which one is elevated, and the other is relegated to be dismissed, plundered or romanticised. The irony is that ballet, the first of the modern Western art dances, is taken and then removed from the popular. Growing out of the Italian court spectacle,

Ballet, as we know it, originated at the court of Louis XIV in France. It was made up of the dances of courtiers, peasants and the acrobats and tumblers from the fairgrounds.	(Haskell 1946: 37)
He (Noverre) created the *'ballet d'action'* . . . he sent his pupils into the streets, market-places, and workshops in order that they should study the movements of their contemporaries.	(Laban 1963: 3)

This desire to create a dance from the people is redirected to become the *danse d'école*; the removing and theatricalising of ballet and other modern art-aesthetic dance forms for a paying audience. But underneath this the social dance of the ballroom, the disco and the club continues.

Thus, in opposition to such narrow definitions, perhaps dance can best be understood as:

- a set of codified movement patterns or sequences of a fixed duration for particular purposes (with or without music);
- a form of expression through either narrative or abstract movement which may engage the full range of human emotions and psychologies without using words;
- a participatory entertainment based on folk traditions and social mores.

In ways not available to dramatic theatre or popular performance, social dance is a means by which the everyday participant (with minimal learning) uses the whole body as a means of enjoyment; not a physical theatre, but a popular 'bodyplay', or whole body sensation (*somatics*). In this sense social dance is nearer to amateur sports in that the participant and spectator are usually one and the same person turn and turn about, not a distinct and separated category of groups.

A piece such as Pina Bausch's *Kontakthof* (1978) plays with this categorisation in its mixing of art and social dance while using the latter to display the body. When revived in 1998 with a cast of non-professional, mostly over 60-year-old social dancers, it becomes also a confronting of age discriminations as well as an exploration of the body as merchandise.

(Judith Mackrell, *Guardian*, 27 November 2002)

> In order to perform the work, however, these ordinary men and women had to learn to strip themselves metaphorically – and sometimes literally – naked. During the work's three hours the cast pair into couples, dance together and compete in solo routines. . . . All this is hard enough for seasoned performers with perfectly honed bodies. For anyone with a complex about being unfit or overweight, or for the shy, it is agonising exposure.

Debates over the (dance) body in recent decades have oscillated between considerations of the body as in some way 'constructed', and what Foster has called 'the return of the real' (Foster 1996). With all respect to the thinking this phrase represents, the real never went away, and never goes away. Such debates can become facile in their danger of removing the real from discourse, experience from rhetoric; making the lived experience of the body a mere plaything for theoreticians' ping-pong. (See also the discussion of these issues in Chapter 3, 'Contemporary Practices'.)

The body as an anatomical, physiological concrete phenomenon is a fact that is with us until death. Thus the body as such is not constructed (although it is altered through social and cultural factors such as class, lifestyle, diet, training/education, surgery and so on); it is our perceptions of the body which are manufactured. The 'real' body is read or perceived through social and cultural shaping but only insofar as our cognitive processes rework such shaping. The physical is again the root of the routes being traced here.

The cognitive operations called thinking are not the privilege of mental processes above and beyond perception but the essential ingredients of perception itself. . . . There is no basic difference in this respect between what happens when a person looks at the world directly and when he sits with his eyes closed and 'thinks'.

(Arnheim 1969: 13)

The perceiving body processes both actual and represented experiences in the same way. Therefore the lived experience of theatre can fuse non-verbal cultural memory with present experience.

(Di Benedetto 2003: 102)

What needs to be reiterated here is the ongoing influence of the spectators' lived and continuing (auto)biography. How the represented experience (itself, of course, an actual physical experience at the time of viewing) will be read and understood. As spectators, we know that it is a represented experience, which we treat as 'real' through varying degrees of suspension of disbelief.

The lived body

Husserl's concept of *Hyle* (hi-le) refers to the body at the basic level of conscious experience; the lived, embodied consciousness. Depraz argues that a Husserlian awareness of body and its processes is not prior to consciousness but is a hyletic body, what Husserl calls the 'Leib' or 'lived body'. Not merely the corporeal body but the body which has intentionality, motivation and which senses-feels itself, has awareness of itself as the spiritual here defined as 'that which is foreign to the I but which deeply inhabits me' (Depraz). . . . This hyletic body is the body of Michael Chekhov's *Psychological Gesture*; it is the body of Husserl's 'Leib' in which our lived-bodies share the same experiences and behaviour as empathy and reciprocity.

(John Keefe (2005), 'Chekhov: The Psychological Gesture and the Fantastic PG; Stage Action or Stage Metaphysics', Conference paper, *The Theatre of the Future*, Dartington College of Arts)

We would suggest that just as the body is a fact, then so it is a fact – albeit of a different order – that the body is understood and perceived as an outcome of the individual and collective socialisations and enculturations that each of us experiences as we move through our lives. Thus to state the obvious, the body as physical fact is not (re)altered or (re)constructed except by physical intervention. This intervention may come from an external source or be the consequence of desire, itself the result of conditioning and other social pressures. Such physical intervention is part of the ethos of certain live/performance art which seeks to offer a confronting real body being cut or displayed in a raw, 'unmediated' manner, as we shall see below.

The body is (re)constructed or (re)altered in a social or cultural sense only as perception. Our reading or perceiving of the body, or a desire to change it, comes from an ongoing process of conditioning, prejudice and indoctrination. Of course, such processes affect our behaviour and attitudes towards our own and others' bodies, and may lead to an impulse to abuse a body, or a desire to change it. Such impulses may come from credulity, be ingested from a range of sources and have a variety of (undesirable) outcomes.

But unless the intervention becomes physical the body remains the same, yet is 'constructed' – and continues to be 'reconstructed' – in our perceptions. This is a necessary and unavoidable tension, but also an inescapable dialectical intertwining, between what we experience as a physical phenomenon and how we perceive or wish to be perceived. Perceptions (however powerful) do not substitute for the actual experience of a real body, nor can they become a dominant part of the tension between the concrete and the perceived at the cost of human agency.

(Winnicott 1974:
13–15)
> From birth, therefore, the human is concerned with the problem of the relationship between what is objectively perceived and what is subjectively conceived of . . . that the task of reality-acceptance is never completed, that no human is free from the strain of relating inner and outer reality.

B Y W A Y 3   Gazing and looking

Dance as a primarily visual form allows us to consider what it is to look at another in the specific circumstances of theatre. Just as dance compels attention to questions of body perception so it has forced – with cinema – the question of 'the gaze' on to the cultural agenda. From Laura Mulvey's original theory (1975) we are to understand that to look is to possess, especially from a male point of view. Male attitudes dictate how we all 'gaze' at others, especially women. While concerned primarily with how film is watched, the theory can be translated to the theatre experience, but in both cases the hypothesis has only partial validity in that it cannot account for the pleasures of same-sex watching, the agency of the watched, and the pleasure of being watched. The theory seems to leave the watched merely as victim and, as with certain 'body theory' (already indicated), it fails to allow for human agency, however constrained, in the affairs of each individual's body and actions (see Chapter 1).

More productive is Gaylyn Studler (1984) who by rooting her theory in the oral stage of child development, rather than Mulvey's genital stage, allows for the common experience of both men and women in the centrality of the mother at the earliest phases of our development as infant. In this, Studler echoes David Winnicott, again in his placing of the centrality of the oral stage, whereby the breast is regarded psychologically as part of itself by the infant; under its magical control. It is this 'loss of control' that marks the beginning of the infant's awareness of an external world, and the tension that is 'reality-acceptance'.

Both Winnicott's and Studler's work allow us to make the vital distinction between looking and gazing (taking the latter as standing for a process of negative objectification).

Loss of the world as 'ours' is also what allows us to look at the world and at others as we ourselves are being looked at. What Winnicott calls the 'problem' and the 'task' is in fact the necessary condition of simply being an agent in the world that is outside us. As an agent we both look and are looked at, and get pleasure and knowledge from both. In this way playing is looking and looking is playing: both essential activities in the development of reciprocal being in and learning about the world.

We seem to be, via yet another route, at the same roots of human behaviour, grounded in cognitive and **proprioceptor** factors, which are shaped by and shape our biographies, experiences and desires.

> Seeing comes before words. The child looks and recognises before it can speak. But there is also another sense in which seeing comes before words. It is seeing which establishes our place in the surrounding world; we explain that world with words, but words can never undo the fact that we are surrounded by it. The relation between what we see and what we know is never settled. . . . Soon after we can see, we are aware that we can also be seen. The eye of the other combines with our own eye to make it fully credible that we are part of the visible world.
>
> (Berger 1972: 7–9)

The issue remains of distinguishing between such inevitable looking at another as object (at the same moment as we are looked at as object), and the possessive gaze that arises from hierarchies of power which objectify the other and thereby diminish their agency.

The dancer, as with all other forms of theatre, is faced with the same question: How is the world to be shown; what do I want to show with my body? The dancer, the actor, the performer goes on stage to be looked at for a specific set of purposes. One of these purposes is for art to be a 'bridge' (see Williams, *PT:R*, p. 239) between ourselves and the world, between our own inner and outer reality. Art performs the same function as looking and play in our cognitive and experiential development. What follows from Berger and Winnicott is that the 'gap' should not be characterised as simply a negative one; rather that understanding and working with this 'gap' is what characterises us as human. It is an ethical and creative 'gap' that helps drive, motivate and develop us.

Theatres are as much visual as physical and vocal; so when we watch any forms of theatres do we look or gaze? Or is it unavoidably both? Not all looking is gazing, but all looking carries a degree of gazing; it carries a measure of the erotic, of desire, as well as an inevitable social, cultural and politically conditioned dimension. If any dance or other stage act becomes seen as merely an act of gazing then it reduces the innate importance of looking to mere objectification. It diminishes the act of theatre as an affirmation of identity as we empathise with the human behaviour being (re)presented before us as a real event in our lives at that moment of theatre.

How do we distinguish between gazing based on objectification and aggression, and the necessary pleasure of looking/being looked at? If we go back to Pina Bausch's *Kontakthof* (1998 version), we see a group of non-professional social dancers wishing to display themselves on a new stage just as they have been doing in their everyday dancing for pleasure. It is 'agonising' to so expose themselves but they come to the audition to so do.

The importance of 'body theory' and 'gaze theory' in recent decades is to expose and help us understand the imposition of perceptions (sexual, mediatised, ideological) which thus socially and culturally 'construct' the body, and our attitudes towards it.

A discussion that began in dance MIME has taken us beyond dance MIME itself as a form of (physical) theatre into the deeper roots of human physicality and psyche, and the impact these have on each other, those further principles which are at the centre of all physical theatres. As a form, predominantly without words, dance forces to the foreground the visual quality of 'physical theatre' and the ways the stage body may be looked at.

Self-destruction and survival

'My work is made up from my insecurity, my feelings of inadequacy. . . .' In some ways Franko B's performances express a self-destructive drive which is shared by many. 'The performance is to do with survival. What I do in performance makes me feel totally free.'

(John Daniel (1998: 15), 'Baying for Blood', *Total Theatre* 9(4))

Avant garde bodies

The impact of this visual quality in physical theatres is seen in more brutal and raw ways when we consider the avant garde in live/performance art. This will be examined through a series of mini case studies illustrating modern extremes of the theatrical body.

Shattuck gives the dates of 1885 to 1918 as marking the convictions and practices that define the avant garde (Shattuck 1968: 31), and we will use some examples of work and ideas from this span. But beyond a specific period in European art, the notion of an 'avant garde' is always with us. The rhythm and impulse of creative rejection that produces new work out of the status quo may – sooner or later – itself becomes the new convention. In this sense the avant garde is often both an impulse to the new and a victim of the shifts it brings about. Thus the tendency of always desiring the new which can become little more than the momentary riding of the wave of the latest fad or fashion in arts and ideas. How, then, is the substantial new to be distinguished from the hollow and faddish novelty?

Such a tension did not seem to be an issue at the end of the nineteenth century when the desire to remake art and the world as a rejection of bourgeois, industrialised capitalism was the dominant radical ethos. Thus Shattuck characterises the avant garde through four traits which stand for this rejection (see Shattuck 1968: 31–37):

- the cult of childhood, or showing and seeing the world through the child's view
- the humour of ridicule, absurdity, irony and the surreal in order to describe the world as it is in contrast to how it should/could be
- the use of dream techniques to release dreaming consciousness, the unrestricted intuitions of the sub-conscious to reach other worlds
- a sense of ambiguity or equivocation in meaning not as *meaninglessness* but as expressing multiple meanings in any given signifier.

What is fascinating in looking at these traits is the extent to which these still characterise so much of what is considered radical in art throughout the past century.

From roots in Jean-Jacques Rousseau and in Romanticism's idealised conceptions of the Child and of Nature, as well as from Wagner's notion of the *Gesamtkunstwerk* ('the total work of art') we see interweaving strands of theatres which draw upon such roots and traits: theatre and performance practices which are still working with the same visceral responses to the body, and against the dominant values of bourgeois society. These responses are themselves usually characterised by an overt or covert nihilism which differentiates such modern movements from those of earlier periods; perhaps a fifth trait that will run through this section.

Destroying the theatre of the present

(Craig's) theatre could not be realised until the great incubus of the present theatre is destroyed leaving clear space.

(Isadora Duncan (1911) quoted in Christopher Innes (1983: 4), *Edward Gordon Craig*, Cambridge University Press)

Ubu Roi (Jarry, 1896)

Shattuck (1968: 206–9) gives a chilling description of the first performance of *Ubu Roi* in 1896. This account gives a marvellous sense of the sheer physicality of Jarry's and Gémier's theatrical creation, but what has been created is an oversized child throwing tantrums in the shape of an adult. From his delight in obscenity, through the scatological humour of an excrement-covered toilet brush to the violence of a young person picking wings off flies, we view the opposite of the idealised child. Rather we see the adult who has not resolved the relationship between the objective and subjective worlds; who, in Winnicott's terms, still sees the world as his breast. Not only the child in the adult, but the infant in the child. *Ubu* is a stage version of Henri Rousseau's *Pour fêter le bébé*,

1903 (Shattuck 1968: plate ix) but presented in grotesque terms. In hindsight this is an unintended irony on Apollinaire's 'new spirit' of innovation. What cannot be destroyed is made into a dream world of Ubu's own distorted 'utopia'. The physicality often overwhelms the words, but both are essential to understanding Jarry's nihilism and escapism.

The jerky movements used by Gémier for Ubu's physical character may be likened to those of the marionette, here to become a mockery of human grace by reducing the figure to a childlike lack of control. In its own way it is a rejection of the human body which must be replaced by a marionette, or to force it into an almost transcendent state so as to meet some aesthetic-spiritual ideal.

(von Kleist 1810/1972: 22–24)

> Each movement, he said, will have a centre of gravity; it would suffice to direct this crucial point to the inside of the figure. The limbs that function as nothing more than a pendulum, swinging freely, will follow the movement in their own fashion . . . that each time the centre of gravity was moved in a direct line, the limbs would start to describe a curve . . . a kind of rhythmic movement that was identical to dance . . . he dared to venture that a marionette . . . could perform a dance that neither he nor any other outstanding dancer . . . could equal . . . such a figure would never be affected . . . these puppets possess the virtue of being immune to gravity's force. They know nothing of the inertia of matter, that quality which is above all diametrically opposed to the dance.

This is the striving to overcome gravity that is the aspiration of both ballet and the modern dancer, a struggle which seems to be demanded by the aesthetic of the art form, and the purist spectator. This reduction of the dancer or actor continues in Appia's attempts to recast the actor as a lesser part of the total *mise-en-scène*. In *The Staging of Wagnerian Opera* (1895):

(Bablet and Bablet 1982: 33, 37)

> the music should govern all the elements involved in the production and group them according to the necessities of the dramatic action . . . training in diction and in pure music must be complemented by training in 'loosening up' . . . this aim . . . is renunciation. The actor must give up his entire being, so as to become strictly musical.

Or Craig:

(Craig 1980: 54–84; emphasis added)

> Acting is not an art. It is therefore incorrect to speak of the actor as an artist. . . . Art arrives only by design . . . we may only work in those materials with which we can calculate . . . as *material* for the Theatre he is useless. In the modern theatre, owing to the use of the bodies of men and women *as their material*, all of which is presented there is of an accidental nature . . . all are at the mercy of the winds of his emotions . . . it should commence by banishing from the Theatre this idea of impersonation, this idea of reproducing Nature; for, while impersonation is in the Theatre, the Theatre can never become free. . . . Do away with the actor. . . . No longer would there be a living figure to confuse us into connecting actuality and art. . . . The actor must go, and in his place comes the inanimate figure – the Über-marionette we may call him. . . . The Über-marionette will not to compete with life – rather it will go beyond it.

At the end of this essay (*The actor and the Über-marionette*, 1907) Craig claims that 'once more' there will be a 'Theatre' where 'Creation [will] be celebrated . . . and happy intercession made to Death' (ibid.: 94). This seems to be a life that is transcendent and which by its nature is at odds with the corporeality of human life. Thus, again, a distrust of the physical body in theatre. We see in avant garde theatre a body that is both to be discarded and transformed, either in the actor or in images evoked by the actor using techniques of the body.

Erwachen/Awakening (Stramm,1915)

SHE: (clasps her hands together and whispers looking up to him) Husband!
. . .

HE: (strokes her hair and lets his hand rest on her head, gently happy) Wife! (the last red glow is extinguished, it grows dark outside. Ethereal night mists waft in through the gap in the wall and dim the room. The Star flares up brilliantly. He and She turn round slowly and arm in arm look up to the star in close embrace)

(Ritchie and Garten 1980: 48)

After two words we see He, the Nietzschean 'superman', take the (virgin) She into a new world represented by the star, an allegory staged in visual-physical terms which represents a rejection of sexual corporeality. The implication is that this theatre demands a stylised or heightened physical style in both acting and scenography to show the leaving behind of the banal everyday. For Ubu it is an escape into dreamland, while for He and She it is a flight into the cosmos.

Our aim here is not to trivialise or denigrate practitioners such as Appia and Craig. Some of their ideas and practices are vital to extending our understanding of the possibilities of the physical in theatre especially through the plastic body, scenography, space and rhythm. But they also reflect contradictions in attitudes towards the body and its place in the world; that is, a rejection of the creative tensions which lie in the gap identified by Winnicott and Berger in favour of the seductions of the body as spiritual commodity. Here they are shown as disconnected from messy, sexual reality, or the body as corporeal commodity to be represented as abused, broken and distorted.

Moreover, we are not seeking to reject the avant gardes per se, but to suggest a necessary caution about the romanticised and seductive routes that these projects also stand for alongside an honourable critique and ridiculing of the smugness, hypocrisies and narrow-mindedness of bourgeois society and its values. This caution is necessary when we recognise the rejection of both the theatrical body of the actor/dancer – to be discarded as imperfect or incapable of showing a transcendent art – and what the theatrical body stands for in relation to its role as bridge between actual and perceived worlds.

This ambivalence towards the body, the desire to have an audience submit and the political challenge which is yet a form of theatrical seduction, may be seen in two examples which follow from avant garde work by the Living Theatre.

Further definitions

To reiterate some earlier definitions, Goldberg defines 'performance' as 'a way of bringing to life the many formal and conceptual ideas on which the making of art is based' (Goldberg 1979: 6). The need for working yet valid definitions is exemplified by an article about the National Review of Live Art (NRLA), in Glasgow on 2006 (Max Prior 2006b: 20–21). The NRLA is described as 'live art in all its manifestations'; it embraces practices of performance actions, screenings, inter-medial installations and performances, theatre, dance and projections.

Thus to reiterate the difference already intimated above, we wish to make a distinction between non-theatre performance (for this see Schechner 2002/2006; which allows the use of theatrical metaphors of 'social or ritual acting' and 'social or ritual performance') and theatre performance, placing the latter within the broad understanding of 'physical theatres'.

In Chapter 1 we explored distinctions between acting and performing and here we may elaborate this further, based on the status of the actant's body as an event in itself, always present. Thus by talking of physical theatres, we allow that many practices fall within this as a broad field, but also give definition to our central concern with theatre acting, this latter being the presentation of the double body of actor and character, and theatre performing where we are offered the single body of the performer. In this sense we would disagree with Bert States who claims that:

> One way of approaching the phenomenology of the actor is to consider him as a kind of storyteller whose speciality is that he is the story he is telling.
>
> (States in Zarrilli 2002: 23)

This is to confuse actor with performer; it is the latter who is the 'story' being told, with the actor telling another's story. Thus physical theatres embrace the physical in acting, and the physical in performing, as well as the physical in theatre.

The concept of performing then embraces a number of practices, each with a status of rough understanding for practitioners and theorists; physical theatre, performance theatre, visual performance, performance art, some forms of non-character dance, stand-up comedy and so on. Often these come across as manifestos, usually sharing many characteristics; for example, so-called 'street theatre' is more often street entertainment – not acting but a mixture of circus skills, installations, performance art, illusion. In other words, a hybridity that is both rich and infuriating in various measures, but which at root displays the ambivalences of the avant garde.

Visceral theatre

This hybridity is a characteristic of the Living Theatre in its mixture of Artaudian 'cruelty' towards body and audience, a political activism which verges on the romanticised, and a theatricality which challenges the conventions of the proscenium arch.

The Brig (The Living Theatre, 1963)

The Brig is in some respects a piece of text-based theatre using actors. Set in a naval prison it shows the incarceration and treatment of marine inmates, the play being a form of protest about ill-treatment, and a metaphor for our society. But words are secondary here – it is the overwhelming physicality of the production that is striking. In the way the actors take on the roles of guards and inmates, it becomes almost a staging of experiments in obedience-control and psychological suggestion carried out by Milgram in 1961 and Zimbardo in 1971.

In watching the play we seem to see the actors playing the guards go beyond acting and 'becoming' such guards in the way they brutally treat the 'prisoners'. It takes the conceptual ideas of Artaud and places these into a form of heightened, visceral, hyperrealism, not of psychological character, but of the physical which provokes the emotions of revulsion being sought by the company. We are driven to see the brig's dehumanisation and control by the visceral physicality of the acting. The simple scenography becomes a platform for acting that overwhelms the audience; it remains acting rather than performing, but with the characters given only in outline.

Prometheus at the Winter Palace (The Living Theatre, 1978)

Here, we see something quite different; the viscerality of the acting-performing is taken much further, the material presented is more ambitious – a *mélange* of the mythical archetype of Prometheus, the revolution of 1917, the betrayal of revolutionary ideals, a cry against imprisonment and authoritarianism of all kinds. The published text (*Performing Arts Journal* 5:2, 1981), however, shows nothing of the style of the production, only indicating some lines of text, the historical figures, events covered and outlines of various episodes. It is a scenario, a **score** from which the actor-performers devise and improvise the events of and on the stage.

When seen, the production displays the actor-performers tied to chairs, hanging from scaffolding, the re-creation of the storming of the Winter Palace using the audience as groups of Bolsheviks, anarchists, etc. Workshops are held on stage to prepare the audience participants for these episodes. There is the use of nudity to evoke the human and mythic archetypes. This is a physical theatre of spectacle and overt participation (see Chapter 5).

Thus when performed in London in 1979, the audience were invited to create Part Three of the play in the streets, walking from the Roundhouse to a silent, candle-lit vigil at the Holloway-Pentonville prisons. As audience we literally left both our seats and the theatre to become part of a theatrical and para-theatrical event, with one shading into the other. Acting becomes a form of action. The gestures are stylised and rhetorical, the movement veers between the choreographed and the ecstatic.

This is physical theatre and the physical in the theatre that extends beyond the building itself, and in this respect it also goes beyond the original aims of the avant garde. Jarry never invited his audience to participate in any overt sense, although both flirt with the nihilistic. Jarry discusses this while the Living Theatre evoke it in physical and visual terms.

Artaud's concept of 'sharing breath' may be applied to the degrees of *complicité* found in all theatre, but Artaud is seeking something more spiritual and atavistic in his idea of a submission that leaves the theatre for ritual. The Living Theatre remains theatre but, like Artaud, represents a striving to a form of 'beyond' quite different to that imagined by Appia, Craig or Decroux. The body is not denied, nor is it made a temple, but becomes a vehicle of confrontation and abuse with – strangely – its own form of visceral *katharsis*. We are returned once again to the fundamental *hybridity* of theatre-performance.

This abuse of the body combined with nudity as a theatrical device marks our next examples.

Striptease + 13 Distinguished Pieces and More Distinguished Pieces 97 (La Ribot, 1998)

Appearing in the London International Mime Festival, La Ribot used her body to confront us, the audience, with our own impulse to look and desire to gaze. By placing us in the position of what in other circumstances would be voyeuristic, she played with that ambivalence of looking versus gazing which we have already identified. Ribot both absorbs and reflects our theatrical looking. It is a physical exchange of the eye as she looks at us looking at her in a return and exchange of theatrical looking.

In *Striptease* she sits in a chair and in a parody of striptease disrobes as if shedding skins by reaching nudity – nakedness? As the lights dim she intends to play with our looking-gazing (it is impossible to separate these as the difference remains in tension).

In sets of *Distinguished Pieces*, both nudity and semi-nudity are again used to confront us with the question of who or what is looking, who or what is gazing. Images of familiar paintings are evoked, the body is wrapped in plastic, smeared with 'blood', painted, exposed and hidden; not especially shocking and not overtly erotic. Here we are less concerned with meaning, but rather to exemplify the way the body is used, not for acting but as itself as the site of theatre performance.

The performer makes her body into the object of our attention, utterly different to but resting on the same principle as the trapeze artist – not presenting a character but the artist her/himself as the object of our attention, awe, desire. This self-objectification clearly has different aims in different theatres, and has reached us by different routes, but these roots are the same. The body as physical being is placed before the audience in costume but in La Ribot's case the naked body is its own costume by virtue of theatrical context. But there is no character for us to have empathy with as it confronts or awes us. We are again being forced to ask: What exactly is physical theatre?

The non-idealised body is again shown to us in the next example.

A brief history . . . (Silence) and The Visitation (Fisher/Spackman, 1997)

These pieces were created and performed by Ernst Fischer and Helen Spackman. Much more strongly influenced by DaDa and contemporary body theory, they were billed as containing images which some might find offensive. We are seeing theatre which wishes to use physical and visual shock, again to confront us with what the body can stand for, but here in more brutal terms. The performers' own body is turned into some physical 'other' (utterly unlike the 'other' brought into being in Debureau's narrative through the skills of Barrault). Here the performer is detached from his/her own body and what is being done to it. As the body is cut, objects suspended from genitals, eggs broken and smeared, the performers' blood appearing on clothing and underwear, we see not acting, but again the body as site of its own performance as it is used and abused.

This is not the idealised body discussed above, but the rejection of the body itself in literal terms. It is hard to think of this performance in terms of empathy, although such a response is still present. Empathy is a robust as well as complex human phenomenon that allows us to laugh at pathos and cry at the sentimental. We are taken back to echoes of the body in classical and popular traditions. Just as we empathise with the pinned body of Prometheus, the crucified body of Jesus as enacted, so we are being asked to empathise here with the abuse of the body in real terms. As theatre it is on a cusp, akin to the real re-enactments of the Crucifixion in certain Easter ceremonies, but it none the less remains a piece of physical theatre rather than ritual by virtue of the context of its presentation.

Finally, even as a raw visceral experience, such theatre-performance still draws on the same principles of construction and signifiers as all the work examined in this chapter. Even as we respond to the 'felt' moment in all its vitality, we must not forget that it is a piece of work, constructed from physical processes, engagements and signs that are the principles of all theatres.

Into the millennium

In 1994, the *Performing Arts Journal* produced a special section on the 'ages of the Avant-Garde' inviting a number of practitioners and writers to reflect on where the avant garde could go as the millennium drew to a close. One of the most striking of these came from Allan Kaprow (see *PT:R*):

> Today, after a generation of 'deconstruction' in serious discourse around the arts, the Euro American vanguard appears to many to have been at best a naïve continuation of Western elitist values. . . . In contrast, sophisticated art and theory today are mainly retrospective, looking to the past for explanations of our current malaise, self-consciously anxious, angry, or parodistic . . . it is called postmodernism . . . but theories are just theories . . . that makes for an unbalanced situation. It's all head work, just thoughts. There is no actual experience, and experience resides in the body (not in discourse about the body). Unembodied thoughts are only mental toys.

(Kaprow 1994: 51–52)

We may call this 'applied theory', 'physical, thoughtful invention' or the need for embodied thought as well as action. The body remains at the centre; as in the case of the 'feelies' in Aldous Huxley's vision of dystopia, *Brave New World*. Sitting in 'pneumatic stalls' the audience feel the plot:

(Huxley 1932/1955: 135) the stereoscopic lips came together again, and once more the facial erogenous zones of the six thousand spectators in the Alhambra tingled . . . [he] fell on his head. Thump! What a twinge through the forehead! A chorus of *ows* and *aies* went up from the audience.

The actions of the plot are transmitted to the hands via the metal knobs on the stalls; they are felt though the tactile medium of the hands as the senses are empathetically stimulated. We no longer leave the theatre to stand vigil at a prison in order to participate, but remain in our seats to have the vicarious made real.

Is the future of physical theatre to be via a technical avant garde, in which we no longer rely on enactment triggering a 'mirror mechanism', but on a performance where we literally feel another's pain or pleasure? What then happens to the physical skills and responses that are the manifestations of the many routes that are still grounded in the roots of all theatres: empathy, recognition, mimesis, play; the physiological-psychological-emotional-sensual responses of the human body to the human body?

Afterwords

We have endeavoured to trace what we see as the roots, routes and underlying conditions of the physical in theatres-physical theatres. We offer neither closed nor open definitions, but have aimed to give frames of references and readings by which these practices and processes may be understood, an agnostic yet (understated) passionate invitation to understanding what these theatres were, are, and can be.

We do not see physical theatre as a 'confrontation of the stage' except insofar as all theatres both confront and use the stage space; rather as particular forms of empathetic and mimetic play which are read, recognised and completed as images by the audience. From these antecedents an examination of contemporary work follows in Chapter 3. The issue of the integral and active role of the audience will be looked at further in Chapter 5.

When the x-ray was invented, late-Victorian modesty was outraged by the prospect of being able to see what lay beneath a lady's clothes. . . . Today, imaging technologies are commonplace. Our insides have become a digital spectacle – we are glass bodies, transparent beings who can hide nothing. What does that do to our sense of self? . . . What does that do to our imaginations?

(Lyn Gardner (2007), review of 'Glassbody', *Guardian*, 13 March)

CHAPTER 3

Contemporary Practices

Shifting together like a flock of starlings . . .

People talked of the choreography, but it wasn't choreographed; instead through innumerable improvisations the actors physically learned to shift together like a flock of starlings. They learned to dip and wheel and found a fantastic pleasure in it. This required enormous physical discipline and they worked extremely hard every day; it is this discipline of body and voice that is fundamental in my work.

**(Simon McBurney on directing Street of Crocodiles,
in G. Giannachi and M. Luckhurst (eds) (1999: 74), On Directing, Faber & Faber)**

Some warnings on writing theatre

This chapter attempts to map a number of tropes of contemporary Western physical theatre practices. We have used this analytical term before (in Chapter 2) and for our purposes it is worth reiterating that 'trope' may be recognised as a way of identifying regularly repeated and returned to qualities of form, so that it is possible to propose some fluid typologies that seem to be present among and between different bodies of work. 'Trope' seems to us to be looser than 'category' and far more open than 'definition'. It is important to acknowledge the schematic and porous nature of trope in the way we are using the term.

In this account we have regularly come up against difficulties and shortcomings in the strategies to describe and delineate the physical practices that are the subject of this book. It must be clear by now that we feel there is no closure or resolution to this state of affairs, rather an uneasy preparedness to live with such messiness and uncertainty. This chapter, rather more than the others, also takes us into the elusive territory of how to write *about* performance, how to convey through words on a page some attempt at an accurate distillation of an artist's or company's work. We might momentarily wish to reflect on these difficulties.

Accuracy

1   The state of being accurate; precision, correctness. M17.
2   The degree of refinement in measurement or specification, as given by the extent of conformity with a standard or true value. Cf. PRECISION *n.* 2c. M20.

(*New Shorter Oxford English Dictionary*, 1997)

How 'accurate' can such accounts be, however assiduously researched and observed? Accuracy and truth are elusive and slippery goals in the context of performance writing, raising awkward questions about ownership, perspective, singular or plural viewpoints and time frames as well as, perhaps, with the adverb 'about' as in 'writing *about* performance'. 'About' can mean either, and together, a sense of getting to the heart – the centre – of your subject matter, or more productively maybe in the sense of 'round and about', skirting, circling, getting close to and moving away. 'About' as in 'she's about somewhere', not here (in the centre, beside me) but somewhere in the vicinity: that kind of 'about', rather than 'it's about *this*'. This chapter embraces a spirit of the 'roundaboutness', 'aroundness' and 'throughness' in our attempts to write practices of contemporary physical theatres.

There are other difficulties, too, that seem to raise awkward questions about 'expertise' – the expertise of the writer in relation to the expertise of those who are being written about. The meeting point, the nature of the conversation – or the clash – between different expertises. Here, questions of epistemology insist on being considered. What sort of *knowing* is possible about a performance, a production, a company and its practice? How does the *knowing* we are striving for come about? How can the academic writer's analytical toolkit help – or hinder – the *knowing* of the work, the practice and the performance? These difficulties also encompass questions and complications around the role of intuition: understanding the function and nature of intuition in the theatre-making process, and in the myriad ways writers and commentators, like the authors of this book, respond intuitively to the material they have in front of them.

It is important, however, not to become over-apologetic or defensive about these difficulties. Any articulation of the messiness, the contingencies, the uncertainties, and of this failure to *know* everything somehow resonates productively and truthfully with the lived making process of devised physical theatres; indeed with the construction of any theatre. Too often the telling of how a particular piece of performance was made and performed suggests a confident and seamless linearity to the process, omitting, conveniently – but often genuinely – forgotten experiences of chance, coincidence and intuition: the rows, disputes, sulkings, exhaustion, boredom, mistakes, failures, misunderstandings and collapses of concentration and focus that are airbrushed, like some 1950s photograph of the Soviet Politburo, from performance history in countless conference papers, lectures to students, essays and books such as this.

In what follows we offer a number of case studies which fall within that framework of practices we are considering as physical theatres. The first collection of practices which propose a trope for physical theatres are those that claim, or are ascribed, a formal or rhetorical connection to dance. The second four studies are gathered under the heading we have chosen to call 'physicalising narrative'. Together, these eight exemplars of contemporary physical theatres articulate forms and dramaturgical strategies which extend into other tropes not examined here. Theatre is proudly a mongrel art form, but nowhere more so than in these contemporary visual and physical theatre/ performance practices. Clearly, these eight studies are in no sense formally representative of the whole cosmology of physical theatres, nor do they correspond to some notion of geographical or cultural spread. The practitioners presented here have their base in Germany, the UK, France, North America and Italy, but all these companies are resolutely international both in their composition and cultural 'mission'. As we remarked in an earlier chapter, part of the hybridity of contemporary physical theatres lies in the cosmopolitan and multicultural character of the key protagonists and in their aspirations.

Theatre in dance theatre, dance in physical theatres

Looking for reality. . . . No more ballet slippers.

(Reinhild Hoffman in Bergsohn and Partch-Bergsohn, 1997)

When you work on a piece something comes from the side, something important to you.

(Pina Bausch in Bergsohn and Partch-Bergsohn, 1997)

The thing is the thing.

(Etchells 2004b)

Dance theatre is almost as difficult to circumscribe and delineate as our own subject matter, *physical theatres*. Historically, we can identify a dance theatre lineage to German *tanztheater* and *ausdruckstanz* (expressionist dance). Both have their roots in Germany between the two World Wars and consequently have a relationship with Hitler and Nazism, an association which at one extreme was heroically and honourably resistant, and at another murkily complicit in the catastrophic journey towards the Holocaust. (See Kant and Karina 2003.)

It is not the task of this chapter to trace and interrogate the roots and routes of contemporary dance theatre, but merely to note that while ballet has a genealogical umbilical cord to nineteenth-century Russia, *modern* dance to post-Second World War America, the deep archaeology of Western dance theatre leads us to the early twentieth-century German *tanztheater* of Marie Wigman, Rudolf Laban and Kurt Joos, and several decades later to the immensely influential practice of Pina Bausch and the Wuppertal Dance Theatre. Until the recent new wave of dance theatre, or perhaps more appropriately labelled, *performance dance* (which we return to below), the dominant paradigm of Western dance theatre has been indelibly marked by cultural conditions – *structures of feeling* – stamped, shaped and nurtured by the mid-twentieth-century experience of fascism, war, mass destruction, unparalleled slaughter, Holocaust and Diaspora.

Twentieth-century European dance theatre challenges the hegemony of dance as codified, technically accomplished, flowing and wordless movement. Here, both the technical virtuosity (and narrative banality) of ballet, and the aesthetic formalism of modern dance (dis)integrates into theatre, live art, performance, installation and song. Here, initially at least, dance is struggling to find dialogue with the conventions of theatre – and particularly the principles of a Brechtian theatre – but later this conversation becomes refocused towards frameworks more engaged with contemporary (visual) art practices than with the imperatives of drama and theatre. Here, a celebration of form and aestheticism is subverted, giving way to the credo articulated by Pina Bausch, Lloyd Newson and many of their disciples in dance theatre: 'I am not interested in how people move, but what moves them' (Pina Bausch in Bergsohn and Partch-Bergsohn 1997). Here, in the territory of dance theatre, we are more likely to encounter some of the following:

- a physical articulation of personal politics
- a theatre of physical presence
- ways of moving that are personal to the performers
- an unabashed celebration of political message
- ethical preoccupations
- real time, real tiredness, real exhaustion
- attempt structures to engage with the real
- playful flirtation with and disintegration of virtuosity
- boredom and disdain for the question: 'Is this dance, or is it theatre?'
- 'this dance is of the world and the world belongs to everyone' (Vuyst 1998)
- performance as mosaics of movement and sound
- dancer-performer as author-creator
- the play of tenderness and violence
- 'gestures, rearranged, enhanced, overlayered and often sped up' (Kiernander 1995: 10).

In what follows we will consider elements of the iconic work of Pina Bausch and Lloyd Newson, so as to exemplify a number of the most recurring features of their practices which seem to speak for many 1980s and 1990s dance and physical theatres. We will then scan some of the formal and more discursive qualities of the work of Liz Aggiss and Jérôme Bel to illustrate a range of other departures and endpoints from practices that seem to be emblematically *Bauschian*.

Pina Bausch and the Wuppertal Dance Theatre

It is impossible to overestimate the influence that Pina Bausch has had not only for dance/dance theatre practices, but also across the whole landscape of visual/physical theatres and contemporary performance. While it is hardly surprising that a choreographer like Lloyd Newson should invoke the influence of Bausch during the emerging years of *DV8*, it is almost more significant that such diverse figures as Peter Brook, Simon McBurney, Matthew Goulish and Tim Etchells in the cosmology of contemporary theatre/performance making should also testify to her impact on their own practices.

It is almost as if Bausch has defined the benchmark or template against which late twentieth-century Western dance and physical theatres can be considered, but it is noteworthy that a younger generation of European performance dance makers such as Les Ballets C de la B, Jérôme Bel, Xavier le Roy, La Ribot (see Chapter 2) and Jonathan Burrows are proposing something significantly different – or additional – in their work from that which we are accustomed to expect from Bausch and her immediate contemporaries.

Any starting point to consider the work of both Pina Bausch and Lloyd Newson has to be their respective reactions to the abstraction and – some would argue – vacant formalism embodied in the practices and circumscribed by the territories of modern dance. Rhetorically, if not in exact detail, Bausch and – slightly later – Newson were reacting passionately to the position exemplified by Yvonne Rainer's well-quoted manifesto for modern dance:

'No' to spectacle . . .

(Tulane Drama Review,1965, 10(2): 178)

No to spectacle no to virtuosity no to transformations and magic and make-believe no to the glamour and transcendency of the star image no to the heroic no to the anti-heroic no to trash imagery no to involvement of the performer or spectator no to style no to camp no to seduction of the spectator by the wiles of the performer no to eccentricity no to moving or being moved.

Bausch took over the artistic directorship of Wuppertal's dance ensemble in 1973 and so the sheer longevity of her work might suggest that attempts to summarise this career are doomed to banal and questionable generalisations. Yet, as many commentators would affirm, there are a set of consistent choreographic and dramaturgical questions and propositions which characterise her productions over a 30-year period. There are a number of centres to her unfolding practice that speak for and against the structures of feeling of the era in which she has been making work. Aesthetics that constantly reaffirm the importance of a performer's personal history and identity as the content of work, but which are always physically articulated through an unyielding commitment to communality and ensemble. A return – again and again – to the pains and ecstasies of desire, sexuality, love, loss, death and relationships. Of attempts and failures. Of failures and attempts. Of the body as both temple and prison, as an (unreliable) repository of values, ethics, power, woundings, triumphs and – above all – sheer dailyness. Bausch's dancers repeatedly embody entrapment, but also the fleeting possibilities for escape, transformation and redemption through movement, collaboration, contact and humour.

Choreographically, Bausch returns again and again to walking, running, falling, crawling, shuffling, dragging, chasing and embracing: an obsessive cyclicality of gestures placed in and out of context, gestures broken, fragmented and discontinued. In addition: the tossing head, the bowed head, the stroking of hair, the on-stage undressing and changing of clothes, the genuine exhaustion, the popular song, the operatic aria, the social dance, the manipulation of limbs, the sleepwalking, the direct audience address, the confessions to microphone, the moving through auditorium and audience, and – above all – the eternal human tango between aggression and tenderness.

Bausch takes quotidian physicality and gesture and turns them into something extraordinary, awful and sometimes sublime through precision, repetition and exaggeration. No matter the extremes of emotion represented, actions are performed with dexterity, deftness, commitment, lightness and always embodied within an extraordinary sense of ensemble and collaboration. What Neil Bartlett has called 'a sexualised athleticism and precision' (*Guardian*, 10 February 2005). To convey a sense of this language and her choreographic vocabulary we will present authorial readings/descriptions of two iconic and emblematic scenes from an early piece of work, *Café Müller* (1978). *Café Müller* is in some respects more dancerly than much of her subsequent work. It is a bleak but utterly compelling piece, without obvious humour and speaking apparently of a life growing up around her father's café, where she spent many hours watching adults trying to survive in a devastated and dislocated world. Compared with much of her work, it is short (about 40 minutes), but seems to offer a statement encapsulating the form, direction and sensibility of Bausch's dance theatre.

**S
C
E
N
E

1**

Problems with chairs in Café Müller

Staged as an empty Café Müller, populated only with wooden tables and bentwood chairs. Back stage glass doors reveal further revolving glass door. The space is (deliberately) underlit and music from Henry Purcell's 'The Fairy Queen' and 'Dido and Aeneas' frames the action. This section of the piece – lasting 10 minutes – contains a number of recurring movement motifs, described here, not in sequence, but so as to capture the most dominant images within the scene:

- At different moments two female dancers, eyes closed, somnambulists or without sight, move across the space, arms outstretched, hands imploring, walking between tables and chairs, knocking into them, flinching, changing direction.

- Bausch herself, mostly at the back of the set, a desolate, solitary and gaunt figure dancing in heart-breaking, slow movements.
- Early in the scene another female dancer enters through glass doors, wearing curly blond wig, coat and high heels. She takes small stuttering steps, moving rapidly between tables, arms raised, changing directions and exits.
- Somnambulist dancers have loops of falling/sinking to floor, or down the side wall, recovering to upright, undulating movement of head as long flowing hair covers and uncovers face.
- Male dancer, wearing glasses, enters, watching somnambulists and begins urgently to remove tables and chairs from their path. This repeats more desperately as tables/chairs are scattered around the space. Between these episodes he waits, anticipating the next call for action.
- Scene reaches an urgent climax of falling, sinking, collisions with furniture, scattering of chairs/tables. It quietens as one somnambulist returns to side wall and the other moves more calmly through chairs. Male dancer has now lost his glasses through insistent chair/table moving. The pace slows. The stage is in turmoil, chairs and tables upturned.

This second scene follows in real time from the one above. The loop of embracing, falling and being picked up are among the most emblematic of Bausch's choreographic signatures. The scene is described here by Adrian Heathfield in his penetrating essay on contemporary dance theatre and performance dance.

Interlude on writing Bausch

The author of this essay writes the following words while watching an often-recited clip from Bausch's *Café Müller* in which dancers, Jan Minarik, Dominique Mercy and Malou Airaudo, enact an increasingly frantic trio. Airaudo, drifting blind across the space, has come to rest, intimately facing Mercy. Minarik enters from behind and purposefully places the couple in a loving embrace that he evolves into a tableau of Airaudo carried in Mercy's arms. Minarik leaves to exit and Airaudo falls through Mercy's arms, collapsing to the floor. She then immediately resumes her initial pose of disconnected facing. Minarik returns and precisely repeats this failure-bound gestural sequence in loops of increasing speed and desperation until there is a transfer of impetus and it becomes apparent that Airaudo's compulsion towards Mercy is driven not by Minarik, but by her own volition. This volatile cycle eventually stills and Airaudo drifts away unheld. Mercy appears unmoved.

(Heathfield in Kelleher and Ridout 2006: 193)

SCENE 2

Of course, both of these readings have to be experienced within the contingencies identified at the beginning of this chapter. They are far from the full story. Bausch's dance engages with the conventions of theatre at a variety of levels, some self-evident, but others more complex and nuanced. Many commentators have particularly identified Bausch's engagement with propositions and discourses around the 'real' as being among the most significant elements of her continuing conversation with theatre and the theatrical. Usually the raw materials which Bausch choreographs are the motions, tasks and gestures of daily life, the 'realistic' actions of the quotidian. Through repetition, the presentation – or 'showing' – of these actions to her audience, and their assembly through the principles of montage, alteration and decentring Bausch is quite consciously engaging with Brechtian doctrines of '**gestus**' and '**epic theatre**'. The choreographed movements and gestures performed by the Wuppertal ensemble are frequently emotionally charged and/or aesthetically pleasing, but these qualities or effects are not what impel Bausch's choreography. Rather it is an attempt to expose the politics and social realities behind everyday actions that are the driving forces of her work and philosophy of performance. Neil Bartlett expresses it like this:

(Bartlett 2005)

> And underneath all of this, underpinning it like industrial steel is the sense that Bausch has not finished yet. That she's putting in front of us an attempt to show what can't be spoken. For want of a better word, what Bausch puts on stage is politics; a raw unaccommodating account of who does what to whom these days – what the memories and gestures of our time look like, feel like. No theatre was as brutally or as elegantly in the present tense as Bausch's, no women are more powerful than hers, no men more tender, no steps, slaps, looks or touches were ever as real.

Like Brecht, and so much of contemporary performance which is only in the loosest sense 'Brechtian', Bausch's work does not seek to offer consolation, or an Aristotelian catharsis through recognition. For Bausch pain is the corollary of living, loving and desire. It is also an existential condition born out of the monstrosities of fascism and the Holocaust. We may weep at a Bausch piece, but we are not crying for the fate of an individual character, or the tragic twist of narrative: 'not the easy, pleasurable "having a good cry" of the British stage, but deep, unexpected, snot-down-the-face weeping' (ibid.). Rather, the shocking tears that flow from *witnessing* something sublime, or horrifically momentous. Perhaps only Forced Entertainment within the landscape of contemporary British theatre gets as close to constructing these conditions of performance.

Bausch's movement theatre does not speak its contents in a didactic fashion, through the Brechtian *fable*, but certainly embraces and re-invents the 'gestus' for contemporary dance theatre choreography. Here, as Norbert Servos proposes:

(Servos 1981: 58)

> Her theatre derives 'everything from the Gestus'. . . . It neither supports nor contrasts something spoken; rather it 'speaks' by itself; it is the mode, but also the subject of the performance.

In Bausch's work an embrace, slap, kiss or female performer draped around a man's neck like a scarf all speak the social and ideological conditions and specificities which have driven these embodied behaviours.

Three things about Pina Bausch

One: dance is not a question of athletic performance or complex gymnastics at an Olympic level, it is rather a collection of 'indicative signs', replacing or supplementing the purely verbal for which we all too quickly (and easily) reach.

Two: the fear and incapacity of people to communicate with each other is the ever-recurring theme in each of her works, and my concern is to transpose this sort of theme into visual terms.

Three: The division between audience and stage should be made as minimal as possible. And yet this division is there, because what is shown is shown on the stage. In other words what is shown may deal with reality but it is not reality.

(Unpublished text by Alain Platel intended for his colleagues (1982), www.lesballetscdela.be)

Lloyd Newson and *DV8*

Lloyd Newson's significant role in identifying physical theatre, both as a set of parameters for practice and as a label to distance his work from modern dance, has already been flagged in Chapter 1. As we have seen, Newson has little interest today in either invoking or discussing the merit of the term. None the less, such is *DV8*'s long-standing association with the idiom, the query 'what is physical theatre?' features on the 'frequently asked questions' page of *DV8*'s website. Newson responds to this question by reiterating his ambition to make work with 'meaning', and by retorting that the question is really no longer very relevant and – in any case – best left to people who *analyse* work rather than *make* it.

In an interview (Giannachi and Luckhurst 1999: 108–114) Newson acknowledges Pina Bausch as his principal influence, but goes on also to cite Anne Teresa de Keersmaeker, Pete Brooks/Impact Theatre and Tim Etchells. The connections to Bausch may initially be configured around an explicit rejoinder to the Rainer manifesto quoted on p. 77. From the outset of his career Newson has said he wants to make work 'about something', but this aspiration is particularly articulated in response to the (not so) hidden sexual politics of modern dance and ballet. When criticised for his unapologetic preoccupation with sexual politics in works such as *Never Again*, *Dead Dreams of Monochrome Men*, *Strange Fish* and *Enter Achilles*, Newson has exasperatedly questioned whether the commentator has failed to recognise, for example, the oppressive gender politics of point shoes, tutus and arabesques in classical ballet. Like Bausch, Newson has regularly returned to social, gender and sexual orientation issues in his work, constructing and choreographing the physical language of his pieces from the individuals with whom he works. He says:

(Ibid. 110)

> What fascinates me is who the performers are, and the style of the company will vary depending on the amalgamation of those performers. None of us move in the same way: I want to acknowledge the differences and what they mean, not eradicate them. It is this approach, I believe, that allows us to see and understand individuals over form.

Enter Achilles (1995) was inspired by Newson's own experience of snapping his Achilles tendon, and, while in hospital recovering from an operation, observing the differing behaviour patterns between his male and female friends who visited him. These reflections initially focused around the apparent inability of even some of his gay friends to express emotion in this context. However, the process then developed into a meditation on the complications and ambiguities of masculinity which are over-simplified, Newson felt, by stereotypical generalisations around the emotionally 'constipated' male. *Enter Achilles*, a physical theatre of manners, exhibits many of Newson's choreographic and dramaturgical signatures:

- a physical vocabulary of everyday (male) gestures and corporeal habits as choreographic material
- an exploration of the relationship between movement and space (architecture) – in this instance a bar and its immediate surroundings
- a shifting and looping between a choreography of daily movements and those which are more readily codifiable as dancerly, athletic and virtuosic
- an exploration and celebration of ambiguity, mutability and uncertainty as subject matter in terms of the relations between the men
- an explicit acceptance, exploration and celebration of the sensuality and erotics of dance and dance/physical theatre as form and dramaturgy.

Enter Achilles marks one staging post on Newson's particular journey – again, not dissimilar to Bausch – which continues to explore the contours of contemporary identity and relationships. Newson's work wrestles with the tensions between bodies defined by sex and physiological construction *and* the ways in which identity is endlessly mutable within a complex power matrix of gendered and other culturally induced relations. *Enter Achilles* moves persistently between the blokey, joshing pack mentality and move-ments of a group of – largely – heterosexual men in a bar, and moments of uncertainty, vulnerability, grace, humour, tenderness and insecurity. The piece invites us to note the precariousness of identities which often seem so energetically fixed into a particular gendered (male) mould, while at the same time demanding that we witness and question the incipient aggression and violence that lurks beneath the camaraderie and bonhomie of these men.

In terms of physical language, Newson explores both the choreographic potential of daily corporeal behaviours, actions and gestures – for example, a man performing a very skilful but gracefully meditative solo with a beer glass in *Enter Achilles* – and a repertoire of movements through fast and dangerous contact work, far removed from the manners, habits and rituals of the quotidian. Particularly in his earlier pieces, Newson's work would contain a catalogue of falls, jumps, lifts and rolls, often performed at furious pace, and requiring a substantial degree of technical skill and courage from his dancers. However, unlike much modern and contemporary dance from the 1970s and 1980s, this inventory of highly skilled and energetic routines was always in the service of the socio-cultural contexts Newson was exploring at the time. Newson's choreographic vocabulary is offered neither for display nor as an expression of mathematical abstraction. In the devising process, however, Newson has been prepared to use strategies employed by some of his fellow dance makers, but for very different purposes:

> I have done workshops with Twyla Tharp, Cunningham and Cage – just using mathematical formulae to make movement, using retrograde, inversion or random chance. . . . and I use those processes [but] in themselves, they are just means to find, or structure material. So many people in dance are working with formulae alone, and no matter how intricate that is, to me it always feels vacuous and empty.

(Newson 1998)

Throughout his working practice Newson harnesses the physical vocabularies and technical skills enjoyed by his dancers, but uses them in a process more typical of devised theatre making than contemporary dance. For example, the concrete mechanics and structure of contact improvisation – a duo involving encountering another, sharing weight, co-authoring movement, collective flow in ways impossible for a solo performer, etc. – are exploited here for their metaphorical charge. Contact is often ruptured or impeded in Newson's work, and the blocking or failure of connection, and the subsequent collapse into an isolation where contact with another is desired but impossible, accrue both narrative and political import (in *Dead Dreams of Monochrome Men*, for example). In *Enter Achilles* Newson experimented with a range of improvisational strategies based upon acceptable notions of male contact and physical behaviour. However, he insists that these improvisations are driven from the specifics of behaviour known and experienced by the performers, rather than from an abstracted generalisation of apparently masculine conduct. In this way Newson is trying to nurture the individual performance vocabulary of his dancers while harnessing their technical skills developed through years of professional training.

Tim Etchells on *DV8's* early work

One was struck by their obsessive essentialism – the desire to strip away the twin veils of decoration and technique. Leaving only the body in extremis. There's a constant sense in the work, which finds close parallels in theatre performance of the time, that what we are watching is the physical and psychological equivalent of peeling an onion – layer after layer pulled away until there's almost nothing left. The aesthetic of DV8 in these works is a kind of back to basics of the body ... the self here is elusive. Located in the body and desire, but always shifting, disappearing, out of reach; the body observed, the body in struggle, the body blindfold, the body in exhaustion, the body thrown, the comfort of the catch, the fear of the fall, the rejection of the drop, the body itself as witness, the body as dead weight.

(Tim Etchells (1994: 116), 'Diverse Assembly: Some Trends in Recent Performance' in Theodore Shank (ed.) *Contemporary British Theatre*, Macmillan)

Liz Aggiss and Divas Dance Theatre

Liz Aggiss has collaborated with Billy Cowie under the flag of Divas Dance Theatre for over 25 years. On where and how their practice might be located, Aggiss writes: 'our need is not to resist classification, but to re(de)fine our own' (Aggiss and Cowie 2006: 1). This neatly encapsulates how most artists would relate to the issue of classification of their work: a lack of interest in the outcome of any debate over taxonomy; rather a cognitive and embodied preoccupation with finding a practice that effectively articulates the needs and aspirations of their processes. We consider Aggiss' work in this context, partly for the pleasure of scrutinising a practice that seems idiosyncratically singular in the contemporary landscapes of dance-based physical theatres, but also because her collaboration with Cowie proposes a language of performance possibilities which distances them from the purities of modern dance. Aggiss says:

(Ibid.)

> Our work is driven by content, explores body politics and the performer as subject, and makes commentaries on language, word-play, age, death, love, power, Thatcher, diversity and difference. The choreography is collaged, cut and sited within dramatic visuality. We aim to . . . blur the boundaries between high art and popular culture.

Immediately, despite Aggiss' work *looking* very different from much contemporary dance theatre, we can recognise in her statement elements of those tropes identified at the beginning of this chapter: 'driven by content', 'performer as subject', collage, exploration of identity and body politics, and a playful relationship with technique and virtuosity. Thus in some significant respects Aggiss inhabits similar territory to Bausch and Newson in terms of making dance 'about something' and a preoccupation with the politics of identity. In addition, after discovering in 1981 the work of the legendary 1920s German dancer, Valeska Gert, Aggiss has quite explicitly drawn from – and played with – the expressionist traditions of German and Austrian *tanztheater* and cabaret between the two World Wars. *Grotesque Dancer* was made by Aggiss in 1986, but then reconstructed by her 13 years later in 1999. Although Aggiss' repertoire extends well beyond this exploration of the fantastic and the monstrous, *Grotesque Dancer* seems emblematic of a number of key preoccupations which characterise her practice. As in all her work there is a high degree of mischief making about the piece. Aggiss is extremely playful with the conventions and principles established by Gert 50 years earlier.

At one level, *Grotesque Dancer*, using a complex mix of dance, mime, music, song and spoken text, is a highly skilful reappropriation of a style and the cultural critique offered by Gert. But it is far more than simply a virtuosic archive piece. Behind the pleasurable overstatement which grotesquery enables there is an almost sinister playfulness with her audience, seducing them/us into an uncritical gratification of what this ridiculous (and monstrous) figure apparently represents. Just who are the objects of Aggiss' mockery? The choice of this material in mid-1980s Britain – a year or so after the ruthless defeat of the miners' strike by Margaret Thatcher's Conservative government – offers Aggiss an oblique opportunity to comment on parallels between the disintegration of Germany just after the First World War and life under Thatcher's regime of right-wing populism. As Marion Kant puts it in her essay on Aggiss and grotesque expressionism in *Anarchic Dance*:

> [Aggiss] explodes the familiar genres. Her movement registers, which are on a tremendously large scale, yet at the same time meticulously executed, hover just above the understandable, doable and acceptable.
>
> (Ibid. 32)

In *Grotesque Dancer*, as in much of her subsequent work, Aggiss was embodying a transgressive, refusenik response to the new dance aesthetic of the 1980s. 'It disobeyed the current vogue of breathy-gentle-touchy-feely-considerate tactile dance language that was infusing the contemporary dance world' (Aggiss quoted in Claid 2006: 187). And this takes us to two other critical elements of Aggiss as dancer/performer and choreographer, which might be articulated as (1) Aggiss as feminist, and (2) Aggiss as clown. Fellow choreographer and dancer Emilyn Claid (2006) clearly locates Aggiss within a group of contemporary dance practitioners who celebrated the 'presence of feminist androgyny in the body image, expression and physical language of women dancing . . . a muscular, unbound, expansive, I'm-looking-at-you power' (Claid 2006: 75). Claid remembers Aggiss dancing *Grotesque Dancer* at Dartington College of Arts in 1986, 'her knobbly knees exposed as a statement against conventional beauty. No pretty steps here' (ibid. 187). That 'I'm-looking-at-you power' seems to recur throughout her work – not aggressive, but insolent, wry, cheeky, active, and inviting reciprocation.

And the connection to expressionist dance, which radically challenged notions of the classical body and the performance expectations that went with it, now becomes transparent. Much of Aggiss' work has been with other female performers, few of whom fit the expectations of age, ability and size typically associated with contemporary dance. And with Aggiss there is a constant shifting, sliding and slithering between identities, between visiting personas; for, as Carol Brown suggests, 'as a contortionist, a fabulist and a caricaturist, the agility of Liz Aggiss to inhabit a series of different identities and yet remain inimitably her-self refuses a reductive singular identity' (Brown, in Aggiss and Cowie 2006: 6).

Here, as is already evident, Aggiss is slipping inevitably into (and out of) the language of theatre, performance, stand-up comedy, and even vaudeville, rather than the dry, formalist, often mathematical and solipsistic configurations of modern dance notation.

But then – and completely connected – there is nonsense, physical clowning, self-deprecating humour, spoof lectures, burlesque, and an almost childlike delight in mockery and caricature. Here, we are reminded of the *bouffon*, that re-invention for twentieth-century theatre by Jacques Lecoq and Philippe Gaulier of the subversive and wickedly funny power of the medieval outcasts who had absolutely nothing to lose by their grotesque parody of the powerful, the self-satisfied and the arrogant. Aggiss takes pleasure in performing ridiculous activities and injunctions – often around how women are expected to behave – with great seriousness and a stern (but mock) gravitas. In *die orchidee* (1989 and 1999) Aggiss' language tutor instructs us, for example, first in German and then in English, that:

- inter city is the train for the men, there and back
- They come also with secretaries
- Dusseldorf is a very discreet town
- I am eating pig's liver.

Each verbal injunction is followed, as the lights go up, with a tightly choreographed sequence of mimetic, bump-and-grind dances by women (1989) and men (1999) clad in bright orange lederhosen, and performed to groupings and patterns of words and music. As Valerie Briginshaw attests, 'the intense seriousness of the performance, which inevitably mischievously suggests the stereotype of a certain Teutonic dourness, together with the physical exertion, makes it very funny' (In Aggiss and Cowie 2006: 69).

In all of Aggiss and Cowie's work we can find an edgy and witty interplay between political seriousness, order and disorder, movement/dance skill, and an endlessly productive interrogation of dance and theatre forms and histories. Aggiss plays again and again – through text, dance and movement – with the conventions of the tragic, sinister and grotesque clown. The clown who induces a shudder rather than a simper; the clown more likely to generate a sense of melancholy than side-splitting laughter; and the clown who through a revelation, display and celebration of her own physical idiosyncrasies mirrors back to the audience images of its own vulnerabilities, desires and prejudices. Deborah Levy, delightfully, likens Aggiss to the comedian Tommy Cooper (1921–1984), suggesting they share some of the same vocal inflections and 'rhythmic oddness' as Aggiss declaims Cowie's text in *Absurdities* (1994), wearing only a silver minidress with matching shoes and knickers:

My my my
My my my
My my my
My my my
My my my
My my my
My my my
My my my
My mother said
I never should
Talk to the animals
In the
'Would that I were in England
Now that Spring is'
Here's a funny thing
As I was walking down the road
I met a man
Whose insincerity showed
I could see it in his eyes – everything he said
He was lying

(Aggiss and Cowie 2006: 19–20)

Jérôme Bel and performance dance

Some dance poetry . . .

At the still point of the turning world. Neither flesh nor fleshless;
Neither from nor towards; at the still point there the dance is,
But neither arrest nor movement. And do not call it fixity,
Where past and future are gathered. Neither movement from nor towards,
Neither ascent nor decline. Except for the point, the still point,
There would be no dance, and there is only the dance.

(T.S. Eliot (1944: 15), 'Burnt Norton', *Four Quartets*, Faber & Faber)

Whereas the point of departure for Bausch and Newson, for example, was to begin an exchange with theatre and its strategies for representation, for Jérôme Bel this 'dialogue' has been more explicitly with the philosophical and ethical propositions of both performance theory and French post-structuralist thinking. In a public lecture, for example, entitled 'The Last Performance' (1998), Bel explicitly claims inspiration in his work from Gilles Deleuze's *Difference and Repetition* (1994), playing particularly with the (im)possibilities of repetition. For Bel (and others) this kind of (re)alignment has moved dance theatre not so much *away* from theatrical pre-occupations as simultaneously towards the landscapes of live or performance art. In this 'performance-dance' the only foundation is the *non*-foundational proposition that demands the porosity of boundaries between art forms, and a default position which embraces both the visceral delights and philosophical opportunities of cross-arts practices.

It is important to acknowledge, however, that much of this performance-dance work is also in conversation with dance histories, rather than in denial or rejection of those pasts. Indeed, in some respects what has been labelled as the 'conceptual' or 'minimalist' (Lepecki 2004: 121) qualities of these practices is a direct and conscious re-engagement with dance choreographies associated, for example, with the Judson Church movement and the Grand Union in 1960s New York (ibid.). Within significantly different philosophical frameworks and trajectories, these contemporary choreographers might well feel comfortable with many aspects of Yvonne Rainer's *No to Spectacle* manifesto.

Jérôme Bel's theatre of physical presence

The uniqueness of Jérôme Bel is that he finds his inspiration in semioticians such as Ferdinand Saussure or Roland Barthes, rather than in the traditions of dance which he knows very well: the result is not dance, but a theatre of physical presence, in which Bel abruptly offers his actors the audience, and lets their bodies or the objects linked to them tell their own story.

Peter Anthonissen De Morgan, 1997: http://dance4.co.uk/nottdancesite04/Artists/Jérôme Bel

---

In much of Bel's work we can detect a preoccupation with critiquing the extent to which more traditional choreographic methodologies, and the relationships between choreographer and dancer that flow from this baseline, are complicit in reinforcing ideological power structures of subjugation and oppression. Like many of his contemporaries and, it has to be said, his avant garde forebears too, Bel is concerned to wrestle with – and challenge – dominant forms of representation. In *The Last Performance*, Bel has four performers constantly changing and exchanging identities, characters and names: a looping, circular play between themselves, tennis hero André Agassi, Shakespeare's Hamlet and dancer Susanne Link. Here, Bel seems to be asking us: What are bodies and how can they be represented in performance? In recognition of the impossibility of assigning stability to identity, Bel proposes a celebration of ambiguity. In this respect, he is probing some fundamental questions about acting (and performing) as a dominant form of artistic representation. As André Lepecki states, 'the question of presence, visibility, representation and subjectivity are brought to the fore, and then examined, probed, exhausted' (2006: 47). Bel himself expresses his relationship to dance, and methods of generating work, like this:

Dance as dance doesn't interest me; I'm interested in it more as language. So my work is sort of discursive. Sometimes – and this may help people to understand – I describe it as a theatre of dance . . .

I spend a lot of time studying philosophy, sociology and psychoanalysis, and on the basis of current thinking in the social sciences and humanities, I try to apply my methods of expression to examine what performance is, specifically what live performance is. There are people on a stage under lights, and opposite them are other people sitting in the dark—it's the simplest of equations. That's the equation I'm examining. You can't really call it inspiration; it's more of a reflection.

(Jérôme Bel, 2005, National Arts Centre of Canada, interview.www. artsalive.ca/en/dan/ mediatheque/ interviews/ transcripts/ jerome_bel.asp)

In *The Show Must Go On* (2000) Bel returns again to matters of representation, and this time particularly around theatre/dance histories, asking questions about acting as possible representation of the 'natural', and the intersection of this paradigm with avant garde formations which mark attempts to depart and escape from 'character'. In this piece, a disc jockey plays 19 well-known pop-songs as 20 or so dancers/performers try to execute the movements and emotions exactly as conveyed by the lyrics. There is no attempt to interpret or comment on the music and accompanying songs. In its unfolding *The Show* shifts from occasional dances, quoted as if to raise them slightly from the minimal movement vocabulary which frames and surrounds them, to small gestures that physicalise the words of a song, to looks and gazes between each other and towards the audience. Throughout, the performers' actions are physical tasks to be undertaken without comment or embroidery, appearing devoid of any investment in meaning, or significance, beyond that inscribed by the lyrics of the song. Here we see a demystification of acting and the processes of theatre, or, as Philip Auslander suggests in the context of the Wooster Group, a trading in of 'illusionism for a more profound ambiguity' (1997: 42).

In writing about *The Show* Tim Etchells suggests that Bel's performance-dance is better described as 'conceptual time-based sculpture' (2004b: 198), once again placing Bel's work more in conversation with the traditions of live art than with theatre itself. For Etchells, such stillness and slowness paradoxically provide a rich canvas upon which the audience can compose their own fantasies, imaginings, narratives and thoughts. Etchells puts it like this:

Bel's dancers are present before us in their perfections and their defects, in their ticks, in their stupid ideas and enthusiasms, and in their cover ups. . . . The gift of *The Show*, in common with so much of Bel's work, is that it gives me the space and the time to look, the space and the time to be bored, the space and the time in which to find an interest. The uniformity of the line, the coolness of the performers as they approach their task, the slowness of change in the piece and its simplicity of movement, all hide (or rather occasion) an amazing wealth of vivid detail.

(Ibid.)

Gerald Siegmund suggests something similar is going on, but articulates the point in a different way, proposing a framework for the kind of performative bodies we are witnessing and responding to:

(Siegmund 2003: 87)

> By avoiding both the bodies of the avant-garde and the bodies of bourgeois theatre, Bel opens up an area of negotiation with the audience. His eloquent linguistic bodies appear to be truthful not because they act naturally or do not act at all (everything is on the contrary perfectly staged and rehearsed), but because they are untheatrical bodies.

Finally, before leaving the work of Jérôme Bel we want to look at an apparently very different piece from *The Show*, but one which allows us to engage with a central premise of this book, namely that by altering or playing with the lens through which we look at performance, a piece of theatre, for example, may be reframed to represent something very different from its original purpose or reception.

SCENE 3

In 2004, Bel collaborated with the Paris Opera Ballet to work with classical dancer Véronique Doisneau to make a piece entitled *Véronique Doisneau*. Doisneau, 41 years old and shortly to retire, had been a middle-rank dancer, a 'sujet': sometimes soloist, but more often foot soldier within the corps-de-ballet; certainly, a dancer who rarely danced the major roles of repertoire. At the beginning of the piece Doisneau enters the stage. She is carrying a bottle of Vittel water, a tutu and some pointe shoes. She has a wireless head microphone attached to her face, and begins to speak to the audience. She has a husband and two children. She makes 3500 euros a month. She explains her place in the strict hierarchy of dancers within the ballet. With great honesty, she tells us that this situation is because she was both too fragile (a back operation at 20) and just not gifted enough to rise higher. Doisneau goes on to talk about her childhood love for dance and classical ballet, an infatuation which sustained her through a long but uneventful career.

She speaks of the choreographers whom she has most admired, and even those she has disliked, citing Maurice Béjart and Roland Petit by name. She took particular pleasure in working with Rudolph Nureyev, and then reprises her role as one of the shades soloists in Nureyev's *La Bayadère*. Doisneau dances this to the accompaniment of her own humming. She goes on to perform the opening dance of *Giselle* with Prince Albert. But this she does alone, again humming the music and telling us when she is to be lifted. As she finishes the four-minute excerpt, Doisneau is breathing heavily. We can hear her efforts to breathe through the microphone close to her chin. The illusion of grace and effortlessness which classical ballet strives to create for its audience is now suffused and interrupted by her attempts to regain breath.

She then takes off her pointe shoes to demonstrate Merce Cunningham's technique of working in silence. Finally, Doisneau introduces us to the experience of the corps dancer in the second-act adagio – the 'Lac de Cygnes' – from *Swan Lake*. She explains how difficult it is to stay motionless for long periods as the backdrop to the principals' *pas de deux*. Gesturing to a technician, Bruno, to switch on the recorded music she starts dancing, but soon hits a still pose which she holds, with minor adjustments, for nearly 10 minutes. She has moved – danced – for about 30 seconds within this whole period. The sound-track is from a recording of an existing ballet performance. So when Doisneau makes her single-legged steps across the stage we hear all the rest of the swans makes her single-legged steps across the stage we hear all the rest of the swans thumping on the floorboards, as one-legged as she. At the end she is engulfed by applause from this (absent) audience, apparently enthralled by a scene performed we know not where or when.

Véronique Doisneau's performance of *Véronique Doisneau* ends by her demonstrating three different ways of taking applause. She leaves the stage only to return once more – and finally – to accept more acclaim and approbation. This time she is with Bel himself who is dressed in T-shirt, jeans and casual jacket.

Véronique Doisneau, more explicitly than some of Bel's other work, interrogates dance histories and forms, and, in this case, in a generous and tender manner attends to ballet as cultural production through the personal history of one dancer near the end of her career. The piece evidently presents a significant number of those qualities we identified earlier in this chapter which are often present in contemporary dance-theatre and performance-dance.

In *Véronique Doisneau* Bel takes the conventions of classical ballet and the cultural economy of the career of one middle-ranked dancer and gently exposes many elements of her experience to his audience. We learn a little about her personal life, what she earns and of her passion for ballet, an ardour which allows her to become a more or less willing accomplice to the physically punitive regimes of ballet training and performing. In both a literal and figurative sense Bel is giving voice to Doisneau. Together with watching and being complicit in the exquisite skill she demonstrates while reprising certain roles and experiences, Doisneau speaks her life as a dancer. Of those qualities identified earlier in the chapter we find:

- an exploration – gently, but assertively in her consent to collaborate with Bel – of the cultural politics and ethics of dance practices and histories
- a playful shifting across the boundaries of the real – tiredness, out of breath, the bottle of Vittel, for example – into the fictions and constructions of ballet
- the fragility of virtuosity
- a shifting between a performance mode which demonstrates the formal requirements and skills of dancing particular roles, and a presentation of her own physical presence
- an opportunity to witness the tensions and interrelations between the highly codified movements and associated conventions of classical and modern ballet and Doisneau's daily and personal physical actions and gestures
- through a quiet play between Doisneau as dancer-performer and author-creator of the material we are invited to share in the experience.

The context of *Véronique Doisneau* is critical in our reception of it. The piece was planned by Bel to follow the annual spectacle of the Paris Opera and Ballet's 'grand défile'. This major event in the French ballet calendar is homage to the extraordinary conventions and rituals of ballet as dance form. The 'grand défile' sees the entire school and company progress down the stage to Berlioz's 'March from the Trojans', in a tightly choreographed and reverential homage to the sacraments of ballet. Here, it seems, classical ballet meets Hollywood and Busby Berkeley. Usually the 'défile' is followed by a short ballet and the set programme for the season, but on this occasion *Véronique Doisneau* is presented as a question mark to everything that ballet seems to represent. This juxtaposition gives Véronique Doisneau and *Véronique Doisneau* a startling political impact as well as an affecting poignancy as the audience are forced to compare these two realities.

In writing about contemporary performance-dance, André Lepecki identifies a number of questions which he feels Bel's practice addresses, and three in particular seem appropriate to *Véronique Doisneau*:

(Lepecki 2006: 46)

- What mechanisms allow the dancer to become the choreographer's representative?
- What is the strange power at the core of the choreographic that subjects the dancer to rigorously follow predetermined steps even in the choreographer's absence?
- How does choreography's alliance to the imperative to move fuel, reproduce and entrap subjectivity in the general economy of the representational?

Finally, returning to the point made at the beginning of this section, Bel's *Véronique Doisneau* is not a 'demonstration' by a ballet dancer, simply reprising, showing and reflecting upon roles she has performed and loved. It is far more than this and in some respects is not *about* ballet at all. Through and with Véronique Doisneau Bel has created a performance which is a warm meditation upon the issues of physical virtuosity, and its relation to daily corporeal behaviour. It is about ageing, about audience expectations and interactions, about site and context as generators of meaning in any performance, about dance practices and histories, about wounds both physical and emotional, and the painful disciplining of a dancer to the rules and imperatives of her art form.

Physicalising narrative

As we have argued in chapters 2 and 3 it is impossible for any theatre piece *not* to convey meaning – intended or otherwise – through the bodies of the actors. As spectators we construct meaning through all the senses even in a conventional play with its apparent reliance on the script and its spoken articulation. Within the conventions of realism and naturalism the rhythm of an actor's walk, the manner of smoking a cigarette, the texture of an embrace or kiss, the performance of moving a chair or object, and the relationship between mouth and eyes in the creation of a smile, all make a highly significant contribution to the audience's understanding of both the particularities of character and the overall narrative of the piece. Of course, for the actor and director with an attuned sensibility to the physical possibilities for conveying meaning, the task is a complex one necessitating considerable corporeal skill, dramaturgical intelligence, embodied imagination and an eye for detail.

In what follows, we focus on examples of theatre from the last three decades where physical and visual performance languages are privileged to articulate, refine and drive the narrative of the piece in question. Here we are considering particular tropes of performance making which contain a number of the following elements:

- heightened and stylised gestural and vocal languages of performance
- a resistance to the dramatic protocols of realism, and – often – in their place a predilection for the conventions of melodrama, clown and the grotesque
- an explicit and celebratory sense of ensemble in both the process of making and performance
- an expectation that performers will share in collective authorship of the work alongside, for example, director, writer and scenographer
- a readiness to draw upon strategies and methodologies of devising in the generation of material and rehearsal process
- actors/performers possessing skill and disposition to transform their bodies – often drawing upon mime techniques – into physical objects and other human and non-human forms
- forms of representation which are more likely to draw upon archetypes rather than finely wrought psychological characterisation
- a willingness to explore the telling of stories in a non-linear manner where an audience is given scope for interpretation, and expected to work at the construction of meanings.

Clearly, harnessing performers' physical skills and expressivity in the task of telling a story is not the exclusive monopoly of artists who work within the theatrical codes identified above. The dance-theatres of Pina Bausch or Lloyd Newson, scrutinised in the previous section, where movement skills are exploited in the service of carrying political and other meanings, would also fit within this framework. Likewise, within that territory where theatre practices meet performance and live art, the work of the Wooster Group, Forced Entertainment and Goat Island, for example, could also be seen through this particular lens. Here, of course, these companies are certainly not preoccupied with 'telling stories' in any conventional linear manner and indeed celebrate fragmentation, repetition and disintegration of narrative components in their quest to capture some sense of the complex discontinuities, uprootings and shards of contemporary life and identities.

Théâtre du Soleil and Ariane Mnouchkine, *1789*

Ariane Mnouchkine's work as director of Théâtre du Soleil spans a 40-year period within which there have inevitably been different phases and preoccupations. Here we focus on *1789* (1970), not because it is necessarily more representative of her practice than other productions, but because it is emblematic of a certain kind of highly physical political – and popular – theatre. Before examining selected features of *1789*, it is important to place this production in a wider context, both socially and historically. In a number of ways the forces, dispositions and intentions that impelled *1789* articulated wider structures of feeling of a period which in turn had generated a range of devised physical theatre practices.

The early work of Mnouchkine's Théâtre du Soleil has parallels with, for example, Joseph Chaikin's Living Theatre, the beginnings of John McGrath's 7:84 company in Scotland, the Pip Simmons Group, Charles Marowitz's collaborations with Peter Brook and with his theatre laboratory the Open Space, Nancy Meckler's Freehold Theatre and the work of JoAnne Akalaitis with Mabou Mines. Although we can identify many differences between these companies, what they shared was an attempt to capture and respond vigorously to the social and political unrest of the times in both Europe and North America. All these companies were – in varying configurations – on the political left, but were unwilling to embrace the elements of Brechtian epic theatre uncritically and in their totality. For these artists and their companies, and Mnouchkine in particular, there was a commitment both rhetorically, and to a greater or less extent in practice, to:

- collaborative, and hence potentially democratic, ways of working
- explorations in devising
- theatre as a visual, physical and visceral experience, rather than a purely literary one
- actors as creative authors of work rather than merely technical conduits for the writing and vision of playwright and director
- theatre forms which were at once both 'popular' and political
- popular styles of acting and performing such as masks, clowning and circus skills.

We reiterate these aspirations because, through their various formations in practice, they have generated or contributed to a particular trope or style of physical theatre. Mnouchkine's *1789* is representative of such a modality, and we elaborate on some distinctive elements of this below.

(Kirby 1971: 74)

> In a sense there are two different audiences. One of them, sitting in the stands, can see all the platforms at once and has an overall, simultaneous view of the performance; it is static and distanced from the action. The other, those people within the area defined by the platforms and walkways, becomes a participating audience.
>
> The costumes and acting styles contribute to the atmosphere of a carnival or a travelling show: a festival-circus. . . . The actors are strolling players and *bouffons* from the late 18th century. They use *commedia dell'arte*, *guignol* and operatic styles of acting. Gestures are often amplified, larger than life. There is virtually no 'realistic' acting.

Victoria Nes Kirby's account captures both the singular staging configuration – and hence performer–audience relations – and acting styles of *1789*. Mnouchkine's production was designed as a fairground and constructed around the dimensions of a basketball court, and thus could be performed in almost any small town in France. Five platform stages with linked walkways provided raised spaces for the action, and among these the 'participating audience' (ibid.) would be free to move around, mingle and talk with the actors. Above, in the stands, an apparently more bourgeois audience could watch, looking *down* on the action, and thus spatially and metaphorically shadow the power differentials being enacted below. Here, scenography and spatial arrangements generate particular power relations between bodies. For those in the stands distance and height necessitate a corporeal separation between themselves and both performers and 'lower ranking' spectators below. For the audience at ground level the inescapable and jostling hurly-burly of interaction with each other and the energetic, declamatory action of the actors generates an 'ecstatic collectivity' (Stamm 1982: 18–19) of carnival and popular spectacle. Through this staging Mnouchkine is creating a theatrical arena for an enactment of what Peter Brooks has called 'the "bodiliness" of revolutionary language and representation' (Brooks quoted in Williams 1999: 39). Williams notes that the company's 'theatrical aesthetic at this time owed much to melodrama' (1999: 39) and that Brooks identifies the revolutionary body as 'a melodramatic body seized by meaning' (Brooks 1993: 64–66). He goes on to suggest that the melodramas of the day enacted in:

> a heightened excessive, Manichean, hyperbolic form the national drama being played out in the Convention, in the sections, in the tribunals and on the scaffold. (Ibid.)

The theatrical aesthetic of *1789* exploits the dramatic conventions of melodrama and harnesses them for an alternative telling of the story of the French Revolution. That 'bodiliness of revolutionary language and representation' infuses Mnouchkine's theatrical enactment throughout, but nowhere more so than in a scene where the actors leap on to one of the platforms to re-create a short sequence indebted to Abel Gance's silent film, *Napoleon* (1927). Here, capturing precisely the rhythm, pace and detail of Gance's film, the actors create what is an ecstatic and almost trance-like 'dance' far removed from the apparent truthfulness of realism. By quoting and reproducing the staccato and rapid actions of Gance's cinematic melodrama, this particular scene extends and 'doubles' the theatrical language of melodrama that provides the register for the rest of Mnouchkine's production. Outstretched limbs extend furiously in an inventory of imploring and declamatory movements as the actors rend and tear their clothes in lacerating actions which recite the extreme passions of this revolutionary moment. Harnessing all the physical skills of performing melodrama the scene is played unswervingly at the top end of an emotional register that scores in rapid sequence anguish, longing, despair, excitement, fury, loathing and – above all – hope.

Here, the apparent simplicity of bold melodramatic staging covers a complex layering of meaning. The 'concrete metaphorics of the scene: nobles divesting themselves of their rights, or performing doing so, becomes a kind of operatic, melodramatic striptease – it is literalised, but heightened for *critical* effect' (Williams 2007). In the reality of the times the French nobles didn't really divest themselves of much, but they wanted to be seen to be doing what was required. Thus the 'metaphor and the heightening have critical purchase in Mnouchkine's production, a self-conscious theatricality was the ruse employed by the nobles, and here it is turned against them, their pretence is exposed' (ibid.).

For Mnouchkine melodrama as physical theatre is not a refusal or departure from the truthful, rather another route into authenticity. Acting melodrama is not *overacting*, but an embrace of a theatrical language that tries to represent the extremities of human emotion and sensation through physical and verbal gesture. Melodrama rests on the supposition that extreme circumstances, whether within the personal/domestic arena, or – as in the case of *1789* – on the larger social and political stage, generate intense and tumultuous responses. Hence the scale of emotions within melodrama, and the *size* of their physical and vocal enactment are a proper and congruent answer to the circumstances which have given rise to them. The logic of melodrama necessitates not only extreme emotions, but a 'large' gestural vocabulary to perform them.

Here, Mnouchkine articulates not only the philosophy of her own company, but speaks for an approach to theatre and performance which would be echoed by many physical theatre practitioners:

<table>
<tr><td>(Mnouchkine
quoted in Williams
1999: 172)</td><td>Theatre is not supposed to represent psychology but *passions* – which is something totally different. Theatre's role is to represent the soul's different emotional states, and those of the mind, the world, history. In the Théâtre du Soleil, psychology has negative connotations; 'psychological' acting is a criticism. It means a performance does not reach truth; it is slow, complicated, narcissistic. Contrary to what we believe, psychology does not pull toward the interior, but toward the interior mask.</td></tr>
</table>

Mnouchkine's critique of 'psychological acting' would resonate with many contemporary performers and practitioners of physical theatre. Of course, this is not a refusal of 'psychology' as such, rather a perspective which problematises the relationship between the psychological and the corporeal, and 'inside' and 'outside'. Strongly influenced as she was by her teacher, Jacques Lecoq, Mnouchkine embraces strategies for acting which aim to sharpen and attune all the senses of the body to the challenges of performing. If, like Lecoq, Mnouchkine is at pains to redress the balance of actor preparation away from purely cognitive and psychological approaches towards an exploration of the sensual and the corporeal, it is because she is striving to organise and nurture what she calls the 'muscle of the imagination' (Mnouchkine 2002: 262). Mnouchkine has explicitly acknowledged Lecoq's influence in shaping her work with actors at the Théâtre du Soleil:

<table>
<tr><td>(Mnouchkine in Roy
and Carasso 1999)</td><td>His way of teaching – the very concrete way in which he wanted the body to treat poetry. His down to earth style . . . that showed me a certain truth which is not to imagine that everything takes place in the head . . . the theatre is flesh. It's from the verb made flesh and Lecoq transmits that.</td></tr>
</table>

Complicité: *The Street of Crocodiles*

Complicité, as we noted in Chapter 2, has often been identified as the most accomplished and obvious exemplar of contemporary physical theatres to be framed and driven by the traditions of twentieth-century French mime, particularly, of course, the work of

Jacques Lecoq, at whose school a number of the company's founder members had originally trained. Equally, as we have observed, the 'physical theatres' appellation is one Complicité has neither sought nor claimed, and, moreover, it is erroneously reductive to suggest that the company's practice is uncomplicatedly an expression of the teaching of Lecoq and those other luminaries of the French mime tradition.

As with Mnouchkine's Théâtre du Soleil, Complicité's repertoire of work over 20 years is impossible to categorise beyond a corporeally inventive and playful approach both to performing and to the texts which the company either creates or draws upon. Complicité's practice has moved backwards and forwards between purely devised work, the adaptations of novels or short stories, and the realisation of play texts ranging from Shakespeare through Brecht to Dürenmatt and Ionesco. Across all these different points of departure, however, Complicité has brought the ethos and the creative pragmatics of devising to the task of making theatre. Almost all of the company's work could be examined through the material and lens of physical theatres, but here we will look principally at elements from one production – *The Street of Crocodiles* (1992) – to locate key features of a physical approach to narrative construction and story-telling.

The Street of Crocodiles (hereafter *Crocodiles*) remained in the company's repertoire for eight years, always evolving, transmuting, and never finished, even when it was finally performed in 1999. The production's sense of mutability mirrored aspects of both the substance – instability of matter and form – of Bruno Schulz's short stories, upon which

Figure 3.1 *The Summit* (2006) Ralf Ralf, Jonathan and Barnaby Stone, Cairo Festival of Experimental Theatre. Photo: unknown

Figure 3.2 *The Harry Stork Cabaret* (2006) 'Dog', Théâtre Décalé, Alan Fairbairn and Eline van der Voort.   Photo: Caroline Buyst

Figure 3.3 *Bartleby* (1993) Kevin Alderson and Adrian Preater, Wall Street Productions. Director: Simon Murray.   Photo: Keith Pattison

Figure 3.4 *A Minute Too Late* (2005, revival) Complicité.
Photo: Sarah Ainslie

Figure 3.5 *The Government Inspector* (2003) Théatre de l'Ange Fou. Steven Wasson/Corinne Soum. Photo: Geraint Lewis

Figure 3.6 *In Close Relation* (1998) Louder than Words, directed by Ruth Ben-Tovim and Peader Kirk, Young Vic Studio commission, London.   Photo: Liane Harris

Figure 3.7 *The Hansel Gretel Machine* (1997/8) T.C. Howard, David Glass Ensemble.
Director: David Glass.   Photo: Keith Pattison

Figure 3.8 *Time Flying* (1997) Bouge-de-la. Photo: Richard Heaps

Figure 3.9
DiveUrgence
(1999) Dark
Horse. Director:
Bim Mason.
Photo: Pau Ros

Crocodiles was loosely based, and the dramaturgical approach of Complicité's artistic director, Simon McBurney. *Crocodiles* constructs its own narrative out of three sources:

• themes, details and relationships within Schulz's stories
• Schulz's own life
• the overarching events leading up to and including the Second World War, the rise of Nazism and the Holocaust.

Making little attempt to fuse these elements into a piece of linear story-telling, *Crocodiles* jettisons the sequential rules of conventional narrative structure, instead constructing a developing fabric of loosely linked elements, themes and curious details from the stories within a larger personal and historical frame.

(Théâtre de
Complicité 1999)

> We worked on improvisations in which the actors played out the process of memory which lies at the heart of all his stories. We created the atmosphere of his times and the mechanism of his dreams. We investigated the rhythm of his nightmares and his intense engagement with his beloved and despised solitude.

At the heart of Complicité's work lies the challenge of transformation and, while this is self-evidently the very stuff of acting (although not necessarily *performing*) in any genre of theatre, the range, form and dramaturgical purpose of such transformation within a Complicité production is markedly different from the conventional protocols of realistic representational acting. McBurney regularly invokes the formal patterns of musical composition – rhythm, tempo and phrasing, for example – to help his actors structure material where the normal scaffolding of linear narrative and psychological motivation is absent. In *Crocodiles* transformation operates on a number of levels and forms. Framing and suffusing the whole production there is a rhythmic, spatial and atmospheric transformation which enables the action to be performed in a heightened and often dreamlike way so that we are far removed from the experience of observing actors play Polish characters from the 1930s. Throughout we have a sense of participating in a reverie which fast becomes nightmare, of watching ghosts revisiting their previous lives. Like a dream the narrative moves in and out of 'making sense'; at one moment a scene from a school room, at another a conversation around an adult dinner table about the unstable and mysterious nature of matter. In an interview McBurney articulates his devising and dramaturgical strategy towards dealing with the fragments that are Schulz's stories:

> It became clear that narrative structure would not be the thing that would hold the piece together; it was something closer to a fugue and variations. I constantly had to invent circumstances, games and environments where actors would see what they were doing, but still be happy to spiral off creatively. I developed a whole language of transformation with them, a language which enabled them to control the imaginative leap from one medium to another.

(McBurney in Giannachi and Luckhurst 1999: 74)

At another level the actors exist in a state of perpetual fluidity and readiness for a transition from one performance mode to another. From a heightened, but none the less recognisably realistic portrayal of character, to moments when a performer transmutes into a fly with two dinner forks for antennae, to the animation of chairs held high above the actors' heads to become a forest, to the relative abstraction of two actors locked together rolling slowly and lyrically across the stage as one reads from the pages of a book, to an actor bent double, slowly 'stepping' a pair of heavy boots held by their heels, and to an actor absorbed in searching for some passage in a book as he crosses the space with another performer draped as a scarf over his shoulders.

Schulz's stories provide a perfect proposition for a company like Complicité. With their celebration of mutability, instability, strangeness and mystery these tales offer McBurney and his actors a playground in which to experiment with physical transformations. Here the training with Jacques Lecoq, Monika Pagneux and Philippe Gaulier, experienced by most Complicité actors, provides company members with a common vocabulary that is only partly a lexicon of physical skills, but which has also – and more significantly – engendered a common spirit of play, *complicité* and *disponibilité*. These qualities are explained in some detail in Murray (2003) and Lecoq (2000), but essentially are the driving motors for achieving ensemble and an engaged, alert and vibrant relationship with an audience. Annabel Arden, founder member of Complicité and actor in *Crocodiles,* acknowledges the potent impact which Monika Pagneux has had on the company for over 20 years in nurturing these qualities:

(Arden interviewed in Luckhurst and Veltman 2001: 2)

Performers who work with Monika are 'in play' from the beginning. . . . Monika is able to find a way of releasing full expression of the creative self through the body. She enables the body to become a rich source of different landscapes: your body sings, one moment you are a rock, or a heathland, or a nomad in the desert. The central idea is transformation. No actor needs the perfect body; they need their body to be fully available to them, working at maximum potential with the minimum of effort.

This elastic register of transformative possibilities is presented particularly in a scene in *Crocodiles* where members of the family and friends are seated around a dinner table. There is a sense of ennui but one which is regularly punctured by The Father's strange interjections about matter, life, illness and relationships ('My own brother as a result of a long and incurable illness has gradually been transformed into a bundle of rubber tubing' (Théâtre de Complicité 1999: 33)). The family dinner provides a playful arena that enables Schulz's text to be articulated within the joyful but bizarre physical games of the Complicité actors, a small but powerful case study of how to bring a text to life through physicalisation which is never mere illustration, and a model marriage between the languages of the spoken word and of physical action.

As Adela the maid serves soup, flirting playfully with everyone, inconsequential chatter among the family is punctuated by persistently gnomic utterances from The Father which variously provoke amiable derision, bewilderment and attentive admiration:

(Text taken from Complicité video of *Street of Crocodiles*)

The migration of forms is the essence of life, Joseph.

. . .

Matter can change in an instant. In a wink of an eye we may no longer be whom we think we are.

. . .

Watch, Joseph. We are in a moment of change. Look! Very remarkable, very remarkable.

At this 'moment of change', The Father puts an arm around his son Joseph as they watch the others begin their clucking, crowing and tweeting transformation into birds. The Father moves around the table delighting in this 'migration of forms' as the characters thrust and jerk their heads, necks and elbows: 'here we have a peacock and here [standing behind his wife] we have a broody hen.' Each actor-character is finding their own rhythmic conversion, transparently enjoying the play which the metamorphosis entails. Here, we are confronted with a quality which seems emblematic of all Complicité's work, namely a simultaneous meeting of complete physical commitment to the task with a playful, but rarely ironic, distancing. There is no sense that the actors are trying to sell us the illusion of *becoming* birds; they are, rather, inviting the audience's imagination to engage in the task. In this scene, as in many other instances across Complicité's repertoire, we see both the actor *and* the character evidently enjoying the play of transformation. The fiction and the fabrication are quietly but knowingly signalled as if to say 'this is what we really enjoy doing as theatre makers and performers' at precisely the same moment as the narrative is propelled forward.

The scene finishes in a different mode of transformation as the birds mutate back into human form and the characters pick up books which become an aviary of swooping and diving creatures, their wings fluttering and beating as the actors flap the books from their spines. Again, deliberately, the illusion is temporarily subverted as the book-birds lose flight and are tossed between the characters as they mingle and race around the dinner table. In this moment we are entering into the play of childhood when bodies and objects can be absolutely anything anyone wants them to be. The only rule is the imperative of change and transformation. Stasis and stagnation are never options. The books, too, are not a gratuitous choice to represent birds, but are woven – as object and metaphor – on a recurring basis into the texture of the whole production. The book proposes a tragic symbol for the atrocities of Nazism, and for Schulz's life in the Drohobycz ghetto when, in 1942, he was assigned to work in a library under the authority of the Gestapo to sort and sift books, either to be catalogued or committed to destruction for their 'degenerate' qualities.

In his profile of Simon McBurney, David Williams identifies the recurrent themes in Complicité's work:

> in all of his productions the material components of scenography are encouraged to mutate and recompose, to displace, transform and reinvent themselves temporarily, adopting ephemeral configurations and identities within a theatre language that is itself always migrating, transforming, always on the move. The only constant is change, the protean 'play' of people and things in their becomings: *tout bouge*.

(Williams in Mitter and Shevtsova 2005: 251)

Goat Island Performance Group: *The Sea and the Poison*

> They make us startlingly conscious of the body in space, how difficult it is to run against air, to push oneself forward, to resist gravitational forces, even those which cannot be observed. The flesh is wrought, pressed into contortions, the limits of the body become visually apparent. How hard the floor is when you thud against it, how brittle bones sound against wood, how sweat stings when it gets into your eyes . . . the challenge of endurance. How much can the body take, how many blows, how much stress?

(Becker 1994: 58)

Goat Island Performance Group is a Chicago-based ensemble founded in 1987. In this section we will particularly examine a segment of *The Sea and the Poison* (henceforth *Poison*) which was first performed in 1998. Goat Island sits alongside companies like Forced Entertainment and the Wooster Group in that their work is formally at the edge of what might conventionally be seen as 'theatre', falling readily into categories of performance, live art and – in the case of Goat Island – even dance. Like these other two companies Goat Island's work is emblematic of contemporary theatre practices which, while being deeply preoccupied with matters social, political and ethical, are equally attentive to an interrogation through performance of the very terms and conditions of theatre's existence, and the nature of its relationship with audiences in the modern world. Like many of the companies examined in this book, Goat Island has little interest in claiming 'physical theatre' as the most appropriate marker to identify its working practices. However, through any lens one might wish to select, a Goat Island performance is usually deeply and obsessively corporeal, and one that is constructed upon an elaborate and often very personal vocabulary of movement that frequently makes acute physical demands on the performers.

Over the past 15 years the company has built up a strong and persistent relationship with European audiences and has particularly made and performed its work within Britain, forging productive connections with certain theatre and performance programmes in and around a number of UK universities. Like Forced Entertainment, with which the company may most obviously be compared, Goat Island has an open and generous approach to sharing and exploring its evolving practices with students, other artists and academics. Indeed, the company has played an energetic and quietly provocative role in forums (conferences, symposia, publications, etc.) concerned with examining the shape, purpose and direction of contemporary performance practices.

As a developing response to Goat Island's work, a personal interpolation follows from Simon Murray:

My encounters with Goat Island go back about 15 years through four performance works seen at such diverse UK locations as Stockton on Tees, London's ICA [Institute of Contemporary Arts], Bristol and Dartington College of Arts in Devon. I don't think I 'understand' the Goat's work any more today than I did in about 1990 when I saw 'We Got a Date', but now that matters less, or hardly at all, at least in the sense that frustrated me back in the early nineties. Today, I have more of a feel for what to expect in terms of the frames and vocabularies of performance from a Goat piece, but know also that I will be jerked and troubled into surprise by each new encounter. Of the many responses I have had to the Goat's work two always seem to return: one is around seriousness, and the other is about the quality and texture of their physicality and movement. To take the first. Whenever watching a Goat piece I'm somewhat stunned and overawed by their gravity. There seem to be few smiles, but that's not because they are aggressive or severely didactic. Nor is it because the toil lacks a certain wit or humour. It's more, I think, about a sense of work to be done, to be completed within the time frame we have in front of us. A sense of something quite urgent, to be said, to be worked through, of time running out, but what that 'something' is I have to take on trust, as part of the contract. Something to be both exercised and exorcised. And I'm very engaged by this seriousness and largely through the eyes of the performers and because of an extraordinary single minded commitment to the performance tasks they work through and out in front of us. Sometimes, I am bored, but these days this is less likely to be ennui than an irritation with myself at trying too hard to fathom it all, a certain puritanical resistance to opening up my sensual range, and of allowing the moments to work for me when I'm ready, and when they are too.

And now to the movement and the physicality. It's strange, very intense, but – thankfully – light in both execution and reception. The strangeness is hard to pin down. It's certainly not self-consciously and quirkily odd, rather because the scores seem to engage with difficulty, but not the technical virtuosic overcoming of difficulty as in ballet. In *The Sea and the Poison*, Stephen Bottoms refers to this particular quality as an 'aesthetics of awkwardness' [Bottoms (2004)]. Of course, Goat performers move well and with enviable confidence and skill. The oddness lies perhaps often in the choice of daily actions or gestures made disconcertingly strange through repetition, and the recurring thought: why do they choose to do this? And here, particularly, as a spectator I have a sense of the toll it is taking on them as the sweat rolls and the slight bodies clearly begin to tire. I begin to worry as to how much more Matthew Goulish's spare but wiry body can take. Karen Christopher must be equally fit, strong and resilient but she looks vulnerable, certainly not all sinewy like dancers. Bryan Saner is a big man and looks nothing like how I used to imagine dancers. These dances, these physical scores are far from robotic, but there is often a sense that the performers are trapped in their physical circumstances, and indeed have little choice but to perform them over and over and over again. An odd awareness that the performers have not asked to undertake these arduous physical routines, that this is not what they wish to do as human beings and performers, but since the text of their performance, and the life blood that is within, requires them to do these actions then they surely must. And so impelled, they are executed (as tasks) willingly and without force or resistance, but with detachment and without any sense of bonding between the performers. The work, as all work must, takes its toll. And they tire. And then they stop.

We may note how Matthew Goulish responds to a question about whether 'rigorous athletics' are Goat Island's trademark:

I'm not so sure physicality is a trademark. I think it's a kind of response to dance where you can see the effort but not the pain. But when an audience sees an untrained effort, it's more affecting than seeing a trained or hidden effort. How do we affect the small number of people who see us? I mean everybody goes to movies and gets their senses blown out by high-volume and high-tech stuff. We're just people right there in front of them. How do we compete with the movies? Our physical work is the real answer.

(Goulish in Tsatsos 1991: 67)

And, of course, the physical work in a Goat Island performance is not about spectacle and virtuosity – and is unlikely to be read that way – but initially, at any rate, about challenging conventional ways of relating to audiences, of exploring the visceral and more organic impact of physically based activity on stage. Goat Island director Lin Hixson, when asked why her performers are pushed into such relentless physical activity ('physical torture') says: 'it's one hell of a way of bringing certain political realities home to complacent Americans' (ibid.: 68). And here we receive a sense of Goat Island's ethical and political dispositions, and how the company begins to raise and explore these.

Carol Becker, in an essay entitled 'The Physicality of Ideas' (Becker 1994), sees the company's ethical and political preoccupations as enmeshed in the work, the physical perseverance and the collaborative practices to which all members of Goat Island are committed. 'Eventually', says Becker 'the work takes its stand – whether against war, humiliation, alienation, deception, isolation, anti-Semitism, homophobia or fascism' (ibid.: 61). In *Poison*, Goat Island's process starts by connecting two ideas: dancing and poison. Stimulated initially by Bryan Saner's poisoned finger following an attack by a 'small unidentified creature' somewhere in the Grand Canyon, their research process led them to dancing generated by the experience of poison. To purge the poison from a tarantula bite, victims would apparently dance until the point of collapse so as to rid the body of the spider's venom. St Vitus' dance was triggered by bread poisoned by the Darnel weed found in cornfields and consumed by impoverished Italians in years of famine. The mass consumption of this toxic bread caused epidemics in which the victims 'danced' until their bodies collapsed just prior to death. From these provocations Goat Island began to construct 'impossible dances' from a series of (almost) unperformable movements.

Poison, like all Goat Island's work, in refusing the conventional tools of analysis that we might employ to scrutinise performance, immerses us in the problems of writing on/through/around/about theatre. On the one hand, analysis seems to defile or complicate what is simple in the work, and, on the other, to flatten complexity to a point of facile banality. Perhaps it is better to identify moments, to describe and offer some cautious thoughts. In one sequence towards the middle of the piece, Matthew Goulish, standing motionless, picks up from the table beside him a small canister of dry soil which he empties on to his shaven, balding head. Much of the soil falls to the floor, but a small cone-shaped pile is left, giving him a comical appearance. He remains solemn, engrossed in the task. He picks up a packet of seeds and plants a small number in the soil. Taking a diminutive watering can from the table he moistens the planting, leaving wet, earthy streaks down the sides and back of his head. He picks up a battery from the table, straps it to his waist and holds two connected bulbs in each hand; arms outstretched above his head so that the beams provide the 'sunlight' necessary for growth, he stands immobile as muffled electronic music plays.

Mark Jeffery, who has been seated at the table, places a microphone and stand front-stage and starts a slow, shuffling dance with Karen Christopher. They are holding each other and seem to be supporting each other's weight, heads buried into chests/shoulders. They move slowly around the space in a manner reminiscent of the 1930s American dance marathons where the destitute and unemployed would compete for prize money to be the last couple (literally) upright on the dance floor (*They Shoot Horses, Don't They?*, 1969, Sydney Pollack). As Jeffery and Christopher shuffle on around the marked space, Goulish, still motionless, says forcefully, but without emotion: 'there must be some booze in this dump . . . I'd like a drink.' Bryan Saner clears the table and executes a spiralling and balancing action on its top before falling heavily on to the floor.

He then performs a strange faltering dance carrying the table, his body threaded through the frame and legs. During this sequence the dancers manoeuvre to the microphone and, energising themselves with the excitement of an image, share dialogue as follows:

> KC: I know George wouldn't want me to tell you this, but – right now, at this moment – 32 separate pieces of shrapnel are still embedded in George's body.
>
> MJ: 32! And there he is fighting another kind of war, and fighting to win. Isn't that the great, 'never say die' spirit which makes us the great country we are today.
>
> KC & MJ [together]: *You bet it is*.

Saner removes battery and lights from the still motionless Goulish, and they begin an even slower and more painful 'dance marathon' around the space.

We describe this section of *Poison* in detail, as in some ways it seems to be more obviously supporting a narrative, however fractured, drifting and unravelling, than other parts of the work. It also helps us gain a sense of the political and aesthetic values of Goat Island under Lin Hixson's directorial guidance, and particularly in *Poison* of the plundering and destruction of the planet through political systems which seem inherently to nurture the conditions of catastrophe and atrocity.

> [S]hards of scenic and choreographed interplay appearing as remnants of another system, another world, half lived and half hoped for . . . (working) from many sources, such as personal narrative, documentary footage, found images or observed and copied gestures . . . work that resists the usual hierarchy of formal features consistent with traditional theater practice, or the development of meaning through linear narrative. Instead the performance unfolds as a network of associations.

(Bailes 2001, Goat Island website)

Choreographically, though, the series of events traced above is perhaps less representative of the piece than the lengthy, pounding, repetitive and exhaustive movement sequences that open the work, and are returned to on at least two more occasions. These are somehow extraordinarily emblematic of Goat Island's labour over nearly 20 years. The loud jumping, falling, rolling and spinning, for example, seem to combine mutually incompatible qualities: roughness and delicacy, strength and fragility, stamina and frailty, indifference and passion, courage and vulnerability. In a 'reading companion' to *The Sea and the Poison*, C.J. Mitchell writes:

> Goat Island have spoken about the long, sometimes exhausting, movement sequences which can function to 'introduce' the audience to the time and space of their performances, transforming expectations about and responses to what follows. Hold your breath.

(C.J. Mitchell in Goat Island 1998: 13)

To know *Poison* better you would also have to notice:

- the green, brown and yellow costumes suggesting the institutional uniforms of military and emergency services, connoting battle zones and a time of crisis

- the yellow hazard canister with its pump mechanism and spray gun that Mark Jeffery uses to scatter fine particles of venomous mist over Karen Jeffery, or to paint a thick white line across the floor
- Bryan Saner, T-shirt pulled over head, as a dancing bear
- Mark Jeffery, exhausted and panting after an energetic floor sequence, being forced to drink a large glass of milk by Bryan Saner
- three performers standing in a line a metre apart, one behind the other, waving in unison with right hand, then both hands clasped, shaking and lowering
- the plastic frogs that shower down over Mark Jeffery's sweaty extended back, covering the floor around
- and more.

And to know *Poison* much better, you would have had to be there, not once, but several times. You would have had to feel the stage filling with images, sounds and the odour of sweat. You would have had to be puzzled, probably bored from time to time, and – surprisingly – moved to tears, or near to them. You would not be very sure why. You would have to feel the contamination. You would have to see 'each performer moving props, setting up the next sequence, often on behalf of another performer. Working together, silently colluding' (ibid.: 18). And you would have to hear words spoken like this:

- Dear Mother I am at the foot of a bone bridge . . .
- I never wanted to be a survivor. I wanted to dance Hamlet in a world of frogs.
- We have tried to give the people who came here the chance of forgetting for a brief moment the harsh world outside.
- We have failed, maybe. It is a noble failing. Maybe the stars have not yet been poisoned.
- May I be permitted to share one last thought with you? You don't need to be number one as you amble down life's highway, but don't be last.
- We'll be back at the same time next Monday night, and in the meantime, stay hopeful.

Dario Fo: *Mistero Buffo*

A clown's attempt to climb into a hammock: Dario Fo

It's a question of balance, of equilibrium, and dynamics. So that when you climb up with your knee, you have to give it a good little push. And then wait for it to come back before you put up the second one. Look how it goes up. You shift your weight with your hands. You take a breath. Wait for the swing. Stretch yourself out. And there you go! Stretch out your leg. Wait for the swing. A breath. Change hands. Reverse position. Stretch out. Change hands. Open your legs. One on this side. One on that side. And you're there! It's all in the dynamics.

(Dario Fo, 'Johan Padan a la descoverta de le Americhe', in Joseph Farrell and Antonio Scuderi (eds) (2000: 30), *Dario Fo: Stage, Text and Tradition,* Southern Illinois University Press)

We complete this chapter with a short account of the work of Italian playwright, performer, theatre maker and Nobel Prize winner Dario Fo (1926–). From the practices of Goat Island it may seem an extraordinary leap to connect and consider the politically charged farces and solo performances of Fo. Despite transparent differences in aesthetic, dramaturgy and form there are connections between the Chicago-based company and Fo around political commitment and critique of contemporary capitalism, models of audience interaction, and a refusal to accept the hegemony of theatrical realism. In this brief examination of his work we look exclusively at the relationship between his politics, clown as theatre form and the monumental *Mistero Buffo*, Fo's scabrous and satirical contemporary version of the medieval mystery plays.

In terms of Fo's articulation of physical theatre practices we are taken towards the cultural traditions of popular performance, not of the more recent conventions of music-hall, variety and vaudeville, but to the deeper histories of mystery plays, jesters (*giullari*), *commedia dell'arte*, mime and the rumbustious and visceral physicalities of street theatre, carnival, circus and fairground. Fo's theatre and his working and personal partnership with Franca Rame are completely rooted in and framed by his socialist politics. And for Fo these political convictions not only serve to theorise his theatre, but determine its form, locations and types of relations with audiences. The nature of the 'contract' with spectators is as critical for Fo as the actual content of his work, and indeed the two are completely mutually interdependent. The complicité and rapport that Fo seeks with his audience have an explicitly ideological function in terms of drawing his spectators into a pact with him towards sharing the same political perspectives. However, it also becomes a dramaturgical and formal device through which to propel the narrative of the piece in question. Walter Valeri explains this relationship between Fo and his audience:

> That is to say that the spectator is no longer someone who arrives at the theatre, consumes and goes home. The spectator collaborates with the performer and becomes the force that drives the performance with his/her reactions and suggestions. This process produces a unique aesthetic, which is not based on content and style, but on its profound links with the essential function of the 'theatrical system', rendering it much more effective and powerful than the type of theatre Fo has termed 'literary'.

(Valeri 2000: 28)

For a conceptual framework to drive his practice Fo draws explicitly on the writing and thought of Italian Marxist Antonio Gramsci (1891–1937). Following Gramsci, Fo is preoccupied with the role of culture in Italian society, and his work has always aspired to be a tool to help the Italian working class identify and articulate its own culture, rather than collude in the dominant hegemonic culture of the ruling class. Fo's work offers a cultural intervention into the lives of working-class and peasant peoples so as to assist in claiming and appropriating their own culture while at the same time becoming more powerful in resisting the prevailing establishment ways of explaining the world and of justifying their power. Gramsci and Fo propose a revision to that crude form of Marxism which sees culture as thoughts, views and feelings generated mechanistically by economic experience and power.

As we noted in our account of the work of Ariane Mnouchkine, and particularly in her production of *1789*, there is a 'bodiliness' of revolutionary language and representation (Brooks quoted in Williams 1999: 39). For Fo this 'bodiliness' is less the taut, driven and extended corporeality of Mnouchkine's French revolutionaries, and more the explicit physicality of basic human needs of hunger, thirst, sexuality, desire, digestion and conviviality. Laughter is for Fo a political issue, and potentially a political act, whether reactionary or progressive, and most of his work has been constructed for or out of forms of clowning, buffoonery and farce. As with the traditions of *commedia*, collaborating with an audience to generate laughter has an enormously subversive potential for Fo. The mirth that reveals the king, pope or other member of the ruling class in his underpants has never appealed to those in power. At its best the laughter produced by Fo's performances is an act of solidarity between and among performers and audience, an act of camaraderie, and comic conspiracy in the face of the greed, cruelty and violence of those in power, or those who buttress it, like the Roman Catholic Church.

For Ron Jenkins (academic, Fo collaborator and translator of his writing into English) he is a 'Brechtian clown' who is happy to describe his theatre as 'epic'. Jenkins puts it like this:

(Jenkins 1995: 243)   Fo has developed a modern style of epic performance that speaks to the audience with the immediacy of a newspaper editorial, shifts perspectives with the fluidity of cinematic montage and pulsates with the rhythmic drive of a jazz improvisation.

As 'Brechtian clown' in the numerous short satirical and highly physical sketches which constitute *Mistero Buffo*, Fo is constantly moving from direct audience address and conversation to story-telling and presenting (rather than 'acting') the character in question. *Mistero Buffo* is Fo's great tribute to the Italian theatrical tradition and is an extraordinarily rich and iconoclastic satire. At the beginning of his iconic and popular sketch of Pope Boniface VIII, a corrupt, cruel and greedy monster, Fo takes a towel and begins to rub or dry his head. The audience laugh, and as a good clown, but with a concise political purpose, Fo's conversational monologue to the audience goes like this:

> I have to mop my face, it's normal
> You do the same at home don't you?
> This is my home
> In a while, I'll have a sandwich
> Excuse me
> It's in the Commedia dell' Arte tradition
> At a certain point they take out a towel
> It's in the text . . . between the acts
> They also wash their faces.

Fo then goes on to provide some light historical background to the life of Boniface, but then breaks out of this performative mode once again as he fetches a glass of water from the table. He says:

This glass isn't a prop

I just need a drink

[He drinks as the audience watch quietly]

Feel the silence

Fountains will come out of my ears.

The sketch has, of course, already started, but it is only now that Fo begins to physicalise the narrative of Pope Boniface as he dresses up for a papal procession, stopping occasionally in mid-chant to torture and chastise his altar boys. The sketch, employing mime and skilful physical characterisation, proceeds with Fo punctuating the singing of a Gregorian chant with various demands and outbursts of anger at the altar boys. It is a highly skilful and funny performance, but Fo is working on many levels as the spoken words above indicate. Here, as with any Brechtian direct address, he is making a range of quite complex points to his audience. Fo is at once seducing them to collude in his political project, locating what he is doing in the deep traditions of *commedia*, establishing his own identity alongside the persona of Boniface, making explicit the human condition (sweating and feeling thirsty) and – finally – directing his spectators to a theatrical and atmospheric moment as he invites them to 'feel the silence'. As Jenkins observes, 'using his public as collaborator, Fo structures his monologues with the rhythms of their responses in mind' (Jenkins 1995: 243).

Fo has considered deeply what kind of acting or performing is best suited to his own project, and in his book *The Tricks of the Trade* (Fo and Hood 1991), he analyses and critiques the French philosopher Diderot and his book *The Paradox of the Actor*. To Fo, Diderot exalts the authority of the writer at the expense of the actor, extolling 'the strength a script acquires when it is performed night after night on stage' (Fo and Hood 1991: 14). Instead, Fo praises all the benefits of being an 'author-actor' who 'from the moment he writes the first line, can hear his own voice, and the reaction of the audience' (ibid.: 184). Fo is not interested in approaches to acting which require transformation into character, rather 'in maintaining his/her personality, the actor should develop what Fo refers to as a "poetics", a distinctive and unmistakable, personal imprint' (Valeri 2000: 25).

When watching any of the *Mistero Buffo* sketches the importance that Fo – as a performer – attaches to rhythm is very apparent, and here we may compare Fo's acute sense of rhythmic timing with Jean-Louis Barrault's portrayal of Debureau in Carné's film, *Les Enfant du Paradis* (see Chapter 2). Fo learned his mime and movement skills with Jacques Lecoq in the early 1950s when they both worked in Milan's Piccolo theatre, and before the latter had established his Paris school. Like Lecoq, Fo has attention for the dynamic musicality of a performance and this is particularly evident in his sketch, *The Hunger of Zanni the Clown*, which, argues Ron Jenkins, 'is structured around the rhythms of hunger as experienced by a fourteenth-century peasant' (Jenkins 1995: 244). In such sketches these rhythms are precise and tightly executed, but never delicately hidden from view of the spectator-listener. While orchestrating the rhythm of the character's actions Fo vocalises these through an extraordinary vocal repertoire of sounds – growls, grunts, squeaks, pantings and screechings – which function alongside the physical languages of mime and gesture.

In *Mistero Buffo*, Fo's texts are lightly scored within the overall structure of this epic work, but are continually modified through the audience's reaction to the improvisations upon which each sketch are based. Ironically, for a recipient of the Nobel Prize for Literature, Fo's emphasis on performance over text is closer to an oral than to a literary theatre tradition. This popular story-telling – *teatri di narrazione* – connects him laterally to such diverse figures or companies as Spalding Gray (1941–2004), Mike Alfreds and his work with Shared Experience, some of the earlier work of Théâtre de Complicité, Anna Deavere Smith and numerous stand-up comedians.

In an astute summary of Fo's physical theatre and Brechtian clowning, Bernard Dort writes:

(Dort quoted in Farrell and Scuderi 2000: 23)

Fo is able to play on the timing and the astonishment of metamorphosis . . . His gestures are abruptly suspended. He observes them, comments on them, laughs at them, repeats them or extends them. Through his incomplete gestures, suspended as it were between the past and present, and his words, which call up these gestures, but are never completely resolved by them, Fo not only appeals to the spectators' imaginations; he activates the spectators. He obliges them to *accommodate* him continually, to multiply their perspectives and points of view. He engages them in debate.

Afterwords

We began this chapter with some 'warnings on writing theatre' which essentially counselled on the difficulties of capturing through words what a piece of theatre is or was. The 'how' of writing theatre is as important as the 'what'. We wrote of an almost inexhaustible range of strategies, theoretical positions and authorial perspectives which might aspire to articulate a *sense* of the work in question. And here the word 'sense' is an appropriate one, conveying an approximation, a getting close to but never claiming to be at the centre – and indeed doubting that there is ever a true 'centre' to be found. 'Sense' is also appropriate in that understanding theatre can never be a purely cognitive and intellectual exercise, and indeed is severely diminished when that is the claim or proposition. Rather, the inevitable vocal, visual and physical qualities of theatre demand a response of all the senses if they are to be properly appreciated and 'understood'.

Writing with the body

What is more important is what one puts into his heart and into his body. There are some authors who, as you say, put fine things into the mouth of the actor, but nothing into his heart or his body. . . . The actor's body can only perform when an author gives him material that comes from the heart. . . . actors write with their bodies. It is one of the laws of theatre.

(Ariane Mnouchkine interviewed by Jean Perret in Jacques Lecoq (2006: 131), *Theatre of Movement and Gesture*, Routledge)

CHAPTER 4

Preparation and Training

The creative teacher

Pedagogy as a creative act is the realisation of the need to create a theatrical culture, a dimension of the theatre which performances only partially satisfy and which the imagination translates in terms of vital tension. This is why theatre in the first decades of the century existed primarily through pedagogy (before it became extolled and organised and didactic) and why pedagogy can be seen as a through line in the continuity of the most significant theatrical experiences of the time.

(Fabrizio Cruciani (1991: 26), 'Apprenticeship – Occidental Examples', in E. Barba and N. Savarese,
A Dictionary of Theatre Anthropology: The Secret Art of the Performer, **Routledge)**

Pedagogy as a creative act

To explore contemporary and historical approaches to training for physical theatres is to encounter a diverse range of practices, philosophical positions and cultural contexts. Unsurprisingly, to enquire into regimes of training and preparation for both the making and performing of physical theatres leads us into the same messy territories of tension, hybridity, plurality, semantics and historical legacy as when examining the work itself. In terms of training or preparing the performer, similar questions of classification present themselves. Is it possible, for example, to identify, or indeed imagine, any approach to actor training that does *not* engage with the body and its movement? Of course not.

Here again, the shortcomings of the English language reveal themselves as we are obliged awkwardly to mutter caveats and contingencies about voice production being an embodied and physical activity, and about the complex and symbiotic interactions between mind, body, emotions, movement, musculature, memory, feelings and – even – the 'spirit'.

Alan Read offers us an engaging and inclusive definition of theatre's landscape:

(Read 1993: 10)

> Theatre is an expressive practice that involves an audience through the medium of images at the centre of which is the human body. It is the only arts practice that foregrounds the human body in this way and as such includes performative forms from dance to death rites within its parameters. The presence of the body in the act of theatre presents particular methodological problems and opportunities to theatre analysis.

If, as we believe with Read, the human body is at the centre of 'theatre as an expressive practice', then all preparation for making and performing it is, to a greater or lesser extent, corporeal. This chapter examines a range of practices and propositions about theatre training, and measures these against the tropes and forms of physical theatres already scrutinised in this book. We also focus on regimes of actor training which explicitly articulate preoccupations with a performer's gestural and corporeal expressiveness within the cultural economy of text-based theatre: approaches to training which might unambiguously affirm Alan Read's definition of theatre quoted above.

Enquiries into training for theatre in general, or physical theatres in particular, lead us into contested and often ideological territory. Training is never a neutral or purely technical activity. It presupposes or directs the object-subject of the training regime towards certain kinds of theatre practices or forms rather than others. Explicitly, unconsciously or covertly, models of training are predicated upon complex – and disputed – webs of philosophical thought concerned, for example, with human behaviour, motivation, learning, corporeal construction, power and freedom. The ferocity of some of the 'debates' between certain disciples of Etienne Decroux and Jacques Lecoq in the 1980s and 1990s testify to passionately held beliefs – acts of faith – over the 'true path' for modern mime and physical theatre in that era. Disputes about performer training are never simply that, but have embedded within them far wider sets of questions concerning, for example, the purpose and role of theatre in any particular age, the nature of acting and the poetics of audience-performer relationships and transactions.

The accounts which follow, and especially the case studies, are inflected by almost timeless questions and concerns around the following:

- distinctions between formal and informal modes of training
- tensions – sometimes creative – between the concepts of 'training' and 'preparation'
- the cultural economies of training regimes and their impact on practice

- modes of relationship between teachers and students from collaborative to authoritarian
- the virtue and appropriateness of 'daily' or codified bodies for performance
- relationships with other art forms
- training as research.

Physical preparation for theatre: histories and contexts

Within Western culture, explicitly organised training of actors and theatre makers is almost entirely a twentieth-century phenomenon. Prior to this moment, actors would learn what was expected of them through immersion in the process and performance of theatre, and in some cases through loose forms of 'apprenticeship' with more experienced actors. Historically, within Eastern dance-dramas, training was – and remains – an oral and intensely somatic tradition where skills and practices are – literally – 'handed' down, sometimes from biological father to child, sometimes from a guru who becomes a kind of second parent to the novitiate. Nicola Savarese, however, chooses to differentiate 'training' from 'imitation', suggesting that young Oriental performers 'learn a performance score by imitating a master, and repeat it until they have mastered it perfectly' (Barba and Savarese 1991: 249). Whether this distinction is a useful one is open to question. For our purposes, we prefer to explore the nuances between 'training' and 'preparation', the latter term being increasingly favoured by contemporary practitioners as it suggests a more open-ended, less constraining set of the possibilities for the performer and theatre maker.

An image in Barba and Savarese's *The Secret Art of the Performer* (1991: 30) shows a Balinese dancer sitting behind a small boy of perhaps no more than 4 or 5 years old, physically manipulating his arms to find and learn actions for the dance. As the students grow older they usually stand in front of the master and learn by direct imitation of the actions of the guru. While this form of apprenticeship is transparently and deeply embedded in particular cultural and performance traditions, it would be naïve to suggest that contemporary Western training practices are any less rooted in or informed by a web of cultural and economic assumptions ranging from beliefs about how bodies 'work', to the contemporary commercial imperatives of the theatre industry.

In the West the growth of systematically organised regimes of training and preparation down the twentieth century mirror and are a direct consequence of the professionalisation of theatre and the performing arts. Richard Schechner (in Barba and Savarese 1991: 248), when responding to the question of the purpose of theatre training within an intercultural framework, identifies five functions:

- interpretation of a dramatic text
- transmission of a performance text

- transmission of secrets
- self-expression
- group formation.

For our purposes we will be focusing mainly on the second, fourth and fifth of these functions, while the physical expression, or interpretation, of a dramatic text is clearly also within our sights. Although the 'transmission of secrets' seems a strange formulation within a Western context, if we translate this to mean the development of skills and dispositions within a group dedicated to working *against the grain* of established theatrical conventions we can begin to recognise an interpretation appropriate for the circumstances of this book.

With the rise of the autonomous theatre director, and other divisions of labour within the economies of theatre making, we can observe the emergence of time and space, deliberately set aside from the process of devising or rehearsing theatre, to prepare and train young actors. The issue of the separation of training from actual theatre making is a tension which recurs in many different guises as we begin to look closely at different practices and the philosophies and goals which underpin them. Moreover, if we also conceptualise training, less as the deliberate and systematic acquisition of new skills, and more as the slow, daily extension and modification of existing dispositions and abilities, then it becomes inseparable from the generative experience of members of an ensemble working productively together over a long period of time. Here, training becomes reconfigured into a quotidian questioning, thickening and enriching process, rather than an activity which one 'contracts' to undertake with a particular teacher over a discrete period of time.

Another feature which reveals itself by scanning the development of Western theatre training down the twentieth century is the interconnectedness of apparently disparate approaches and practices. While such a claim is not to suggest that there exists some kind of bland consensus between the key innovators in actor/theatre training, it is to remind ourselves of the truism that no figure – however pioneering – creates in a cultural and intellectual vacuum. Thus, down the century there are complex webs of embellishment, critique, extension and refusal between the training methodologies on offer. To a greater or lesser extent, each innovator of performer training is in conversation – sometimes explicitly and antagonistically – with both historical figures (and models of training) *and* his/her contemporaries. For example, Meyerhold's relentlessly innovative pedagogies have to be understood and contextualised by his early experiences alongside Stanislavsky at the Moscow Arts Theatre, while Jacques Lecoq – at times quite explicitly – contrasts his more open-ended approach to mime and movement training with what he regarded as the closed and aesthetically restrictive approach of his contemporary, Etienne Decroux. One way of helping to understand and locate the pedagogies of Meyerhold and Lecoq is to see them as a dialogue with Stanislavsky and Decroux respectively.

A rich dialogue of intertextuality

Copeau, Grotowski and Barba have used Meyerhold's exercises and Decroux's mime, while Decroux studied with Copeau, Meyerhold and Michael Chekhov with Stanislavsky, and Copeau and Grotowski evolved exercises from Dalcroze's eurhythmics. Copeau declared an affinity with his readings of Meyerhold; Grotowski and Barba drew on Delsarte's work, but only in training and not directly in performance; Mnouchkine began by using Stanislavsky's methods, also read Copeau and trained with Lecoq; Lecoq knew Decroux's work but declared it too mechanistic and too rigid to be integrated into theatre. The links are many more: indeed, such a rich dialogue of intertextuality is excitingly pervasive, though very difficult to chart.

(Lea Logie (1995: 232), 'Developing a Physical Vocabulary for the Contemporary Performer', *NTQ* 43)

Training as cultural production: models of provision

In the West, the twentieth century is marked by at least four schematically different but overlapping modes of delivering theatre training. While these models have emerged chronologically and sequentially, the boundaries between them have become increasingly blurred. Today they co-exist with each other in varying degrees of mutuality and suspicion:

- the director or professional theatre practitioner as teacher and trainer. Within this relationship we can particularly identify the emergence of terms and practices such as 'laboratory' and 'atelier'
- the emergence of professional academies whose purpose is largely to train actors, but also to prepare for other roles in the theatre-making process (e.g. designers, technicians, choreographers)
- the highly significant role of the modern university as a conceiver and conveyor of a range of degree programmes which prepare students for the performing arts, and the economies which sustain and constrain them
- the growth of the short workshop as a training opportunity for practitioners of all experiences and ages.

The director and actor as professional trainer

Throughout the twentieth and into the twenty-first century professional directors and actors have been centrally involved in the training and preparation of performers and theatre makers. This is no less true today than it was around the time when, for example, Meyerhold and Copeau were establishing innovative training practices for young actors in the Soviet Union and France. What is significantly different, however, are the structures and contexts in which such training is conceived and undertaken. Moreover, the question of 'who is to be trained?' receives a very different answer in 2007 from that it would have done in 1926. Clearly, too, the cultural circumstances and possibilities between these key figures of early twentieth-century theatre were also significantly diverse. Meyerhold, working in the revolutionary Soviet Union of 1917, faced a very different set of conditions and challenges from either Copeau at the Vieux-Colombier in France during the same period, or Michael Chekhov at the Dartington Hall Estate in 1930s England. All, however, share the experience of both directing and teaching theatre, each task informing the other, and of regarding teaching not as the transmission of existing skills, but as a vehicle for experimentation and risk in a quest to re-invent the practices and goals of theatre in relation to the world it then inhabited.

Although Stanislavsky, Meyerhold, Copeau and Chekhov ran separate classes for actors in their own companies and for others, teaching and directing often became almost indistinguishable activities. As each of these men was reacting passionately to the established theatrical conventions of his time and particular context, and hence pioneering new approaches to acting or theatre making, rehearsal processes were pedagogic in far more than just the loose sense of the term. Central to the work of Meyerhold, Copeau and Chekhov, and to the later thinking of Stanislavsky, was a preoccupation with both refining and redefining the actor's physical presence and its subsequent articulation and transmission in performance. In different ways, these innovators all challenged the Cartesian notion of a controlling mind disciplining and training an unruly body, and in turn posited a psychophysical continuum upon which all human actions and endeavours might be understood.

The framework in which Meyerhold and Copeau prepared young actors was within the relatively closed world of their own companies. In 1913, Copeau started his own company which became known as the Théâtre du Vieux-Colombier with 10 actors. Mark Evans notes that:

(Evans 2006: 10)

> Though a formal training programme was not an option at this early stage, Copeau decided that he none the less needed to take his young actors 'outside the theatre into contact with nature and with life!' (Copeau, 1967: 452). . . . This period of training, rehearsal, discussion and preparation was a nourishing experience for all concerned – bonding the group of actors into an ensemble and helping to establish a company ethos, shared aims and ambitions.

For Copeau, therefore, during this period, training and preparation were integrated into the process of rehearsal and forming an ensemble. For Meyerhold in Moscow a few years later, this blend of experimental workshop, rehearsal, technical training (bio-mechanics) and the development of ensemble skills and dispositions was similar in form – if not in content – to Copeau. Both models remain an aspiration – although largely unrealisable – for certain directors today (Pitches 2003: 38), and we can recognise contemporary parallels in how Peter Brook, Eugenio Barba, Lev Dodin and Joan Littlewood have run their companies. What anchors these examples clearly within the frame of physical theatres is that this *immersion* in training practices, this *crucible* of intense and protected experimentation, inevitably directs and focuses attention towards the enhanced articulation of performers' bodies in the direction of innovative forms of 'new' theatre.

In the last decades of the twentieth and into the twenty-first century we can still find a periodic re-emergence of this immersive crucible, but within significantly changed cultural circumstances and expectations. In addition to the examples identified above (Brook, Barba, Dodin and Littlewood) directors such as Simon McBurney, Alain Platel, David Glass, Tim Etchells and Lin Hixson will all have worked with their performers in ways that integrate training, preparation, creative composition and rehearsal within the framework of the 'laboratory'. Today, however, a critical difference between these contemporary figures and their early twentieth-century counterparts is that the former are as likely to spend as much time directing their teaching energies outside the context of their companies, and instead running classes and workshops for (other) actors, university students, community groups and school pupils.

Professional theatre schools and the modern university

In the nineteenth century a small number of performing arts conservatoires were opened in a few major European cities, although the earliest record of a specialist European drama school – Le Conservatoire National d'Art Dramatique in Paris – dates back to 1786. However, in the West the rise of institutions devoted specifically to the training of actors and theatre makers is almost exclusively a twentieth-century phenomenon. In London the Royal Academy of Dramatic Art (RADA) and the Central School of Speech and Drama (CSSD) were founded in 1904 and 1906 respectively. Today, there are 22 member institutions of the UK's Conference of Drama Schools, an organisation connecting and representing the leading establishments within the field.

Most of the capital cities of Europe have a small number of private fee-paying theatre schools – alongside those integrated into the structure and funding system of the state higher education system – which offer courses that claim to engage with the physical or movement training of actors, or more specifically with the generation of physical theatres. Sometimes, these include mime as the main preoccupation of the curriculum. In Paris, Jacques Lecoq's International School of Theatre reached its fiftieth anniversary in 2006 and continues to flourish despite the death of its founder in 1999. Until the late 1980s Etienne Decroux, and later his son Maximilian, ran a small school in corporeal mime from the cellar of the family house in Boulogne Billancourt, a suburb of Paris. In London, the quarterly journal, *Total Theatre*, lists at least six permanent schools of mime and physical theatre, and many more companies or organisations offering similarly tagged workshops on a regular basis. A number of these specialist schools in London and other European cities explicitly explain and legitimise their teaching by invoking the influence of key figures such as Lecoq or Decroux in their pedagogy and purpose.

In the USA there are over 300 departments in either public or private universities offering a variety of courses which are largely rooted in the assumptions and techniques of method acting and text-driven theatre. Those that offer acting programmes sometimes identify specific modules on movement training, and occasionally these will further specify mime and physical theatre as particular inflections of such courses. Tom Leabhart at Pomona College in California edits the international *Mime Journal* from this base and teaches courses on Decroux's technique. Cal Arts offers an approach to theatre making which challenges the dominant tenets of mainstream theatre, emphasising particularly the visual and physical dimensions of theatre making.

Over the past 15 years the influence of Tadashi Suzuki's training system in the USA, derived in part from traditional Japanese forms of noh and kabuki, and seeking to generate what he calls 'animal energy' in performers, has been considerable on actor training programmes willing to push beyond the confines of Stanislavsky and method acting. Historically associated with Suzuki, and equally influential in similar university contexts, has been the work of Anne Bogart who heads the acting programme at Columbia University in New York. Bogart's system of actor preparation (*Viewpoints*) has focused particularly on the generation of ensemble and the creation of new approaches to movement training. We explore Bogart's work in more detail later in this chapter.

Outside the structures of American universities, as in the UK and other European countries, many self-proclaimed mime and physical theatre companies participate in a cultural economy of offering regular workshops and courses alongside their own performances. These vary between systematic and repeated programmes run on a habitual basis, and sometimes enshrined by the term 'school', and others offered more as an adjunct to the company's schedule of performance work. Many of these companies invoke the teaching of either Jacques Lecoq or Etienne Decroux, but increasingly claim to be experimenting pedagogically with the conventions and histories of live/performance art and dance practices. Artslynx, an agency promoting and facilitating theatre resources, identifies over 50 companies or groups across the USA and Canada working in the territories of physical theatre and offering forms of training, the most prominent of which include: American Mime Theatre, Celebration Barn Theatre, Dell'Arte International School of Physical Theatre, Iron Pig Theatre Company, Liminal Performance Group, the Pacific Performance Project, Sprung Theatre Company, TooBa and the Margolis Brown Performance Company. Tom Leabhart, perhaps the leading exponent through his writing and teaching of Decroux-based mime in the USA, also runs courses in Europe, South America and parts of Asia.

Over the last two decades, however, the relentless expansion of higher education in Europe and North America has reconfigured the post-school experience of theatre and performance training. In Britain, although the 'independent' drama/theatre academies still exist, they are now largely integrated into the regulatory structures of the higher education sector. In universities, while the study of drama as a largely literary endeavour continues, especially in the older institutions, many higher education establishments in the Western world now offer a bewildering variety of under- and post-graduate courses rooted in the practices of actual theatre making and performing. These programmes range across a number of axes from the paradigm of 'Performance Studies' through to professional acting degrees, from purely devised theatre practices to generic performing arts courses, from mime and physical theatre to the British realist tradition, from applied theatre practices to routes specialising only in live or performance art.

During the 1980s, from New York and Richard Schechner, the conceptual paradigm of 'Performance Studies' began to influence and reframe contemporary academic thinking in relation to the territorial boundaries of theatre, dance, live art, anthropology, psychology and sociology. At a similar intersection, the discourses of feminism and women's studies propose that 'performativity' and the 'performative' might add new dimensions to both our practice and our thinking about performance and theatre. Judith Butler, leading cultural and feminist theorist, writes about 'acting gender':

> The act that one does, the act that is performed is in a sense an act that has been going on before one arrived on the scene. Hence, gender is an act which has been rehearsed, much as a script survives the particular actors who make use of it, but which requires individual actors who make use of it in order to be actualised and reproduced as reality once again.

(Butler 1990: 277)

Arguably, the massive expansion of higher education opportunities in theatre and the performing arts provides at least a partial answer to the question of why the last two decades have marked such a significant increase in physical and visual theatres. For a variety of reasons, many university programmes in theatre and associated performing arts practices have challenged the apparent hegemony of the play text and the spoken word as the dominant paradigm for generating and performing theatre. In their place, a loose and eclectic matrix of embodied and visual practices have expanded and confronted conventional views about what theatre is, and how it can engage differently with spectators. At the centre of many of these practices has been a preoccupation – often framed and sometimes driven by theoretical discourses – with the performer's body in all its expressive and communicative possibilities. A number of university theatre departments have been highly influential in nurturing performance practices which lie squarely within the frame of physical theatres. Of course, there is much more to be said about this route into contemporary physical theatres, and to assert its importance as an explanatory trend is to say nothing about how effectively such university departments are preparing young theatre makers to compose and perform work that is sharp, articulate, compositionally mature and genuinely innovative.

Elevating ephemera through research

Here we hit another conundrum in the art/academia relationship. . . . Post-modern theories promote the death-of-the-author/birth-of-the-reader POV on live performance, opening up the formally narrow definition of text to the totality of *mise en scène* and the all-seeingness of reception theory. Theatre is liberated from its previous domination by its durable by-products: the literature of published play texts. While this suggests a wide-open embrace of post-Artaudian illiteracy, paradoxically theatre academia is now striving to archive and analyse – and thereby elevate – the ephemera of it all with deeply probing written research. . . . While academic research is gradually building itself up as a respectable field of enquiry all of its own – distinct from its roots in literary studies – the tendency of the work itself is to move away from the word-driven and towards the interdisciplinary in that slippery-sliding search for asserting performance as an authentic product of its makers.

(Anna Furse (2002: 70), 'Strategies, Concepts and Working Decisions', in Maria Delgado and Caridad Svitch (eds), *Theatre in Crisis?*, Manchester University Press)

Figure 4.1 Kenneth Davidson (1994) *Moving into Performance* Workshop-Symposium, Manchester, England.   Photo: Simon Murray

Figure 4.2
Dugald Ferguson
(2005) Theatre
student,
Dartington
College of Arts,
Devon, England.
Photo: Kate Mount

Figure 4.3 Theatre movement class at Dartington (1995) Dartington College of Arts, Devon, England.   Photo: Kate Mount

Figure 4.4 *Tea Without Mother* (2005) Lynette Oakey and Mark Stephens, National Student Drama Festival, Scarborough, England.   Photo: Allan Titmuss

The rise and rise of the workshop as training opportunity

Alongside the rapid expansion of university courses in theatre and the performing arts since the 1970s there has been a parallel – though slightly later – growth in opportunities for professional and aspiring actors and theatre makers to take a bewildering variety of short workshops to enhance their existing skills, and to explore new and sometimes exotic possibilities in related arts practices. The growth of the workshop – typically between one and five days, though occasionally extended through the form of residential summer schools, for example – has been a feature of the last two decades, and has had a symbiotic relationship with the actual development of physical and visual theatre practices, and the promotional rhetoric that enveloped them.

A range of interrelated, though not necessarily complementary, reasons may be identified for this striking expansion in workshop opportunities from the mid-1980s:

- a widening culture of acceptance that professional training could and should be a continuous and recurring career-long experience, and not merely a one-off event after leaving school or university;
- demands from a growing constituency of young physical theatre makers and performers for training opportunities which were not being provided by professional drama schools;
- an awareness that a diet of Stanislavskian and 'method' approaches was a partial and limited preparation for the demands of contemporary theatre;
- in the spirit of widening access to and participation in the performing arts, an increasing requirement by funding bodies that recipients of grants should develop an educational wing to their practice. A more instrumental imperative also acknowledged that workshops accompanying performances were a productive marketing device for theatres and arts centres;
- recognition among certain practitioners and companies that through offering the short course or workshop they could find breathing space to review and develop their own practice outside the relentless cycle of rehearsal, production, touring and grant applications;
- a genuine democratising impulse by certain theatre makers to share their knowledge, skills and compositional strategies through structures of education and learning;
- a developing sense of internationalism, partly facilitated by increasing mobility of artists – and students – due to enhanced travel opportunities afforded by low-cost air travel;
- market and income-generating opportunities both for companies/practitioners and arts organisations both to *create* and *satisfy* the demand from actors and theatre makers for new and continuing short training opportunities that could be easily accommodated around their working commitments.

The structure for delivering workshops varied between companies and the contexts in which they operated. Here different cultural economies jostled and overlapped with each other. In the 1980s and 1990s UK-based companies such as Forced Entertainment, Théâtre de Complicité, the David Glass Ensemble or the Right Size might choose, or be obliged, to offer workshops while on tour for school and community groups, be invited to university theatre/drama departments to work with undergraduates, and organise their own courses for young or more experienced professional theatre makers. These latter activities afforded such companies an opportunity not only to experiment with ideas as work in progress, but to use these occasions as informal and sometimes covert auditioning processes.

For host organisations, whether theatres, arts centres, galleries or university departments, the ability to embellish – for a variety of motives – their own programmes by offering workshops to a range of differing publics became highly significant. For theatres and art centres this facility became central to the institution's overall marketing strategy, and for university theatre departments, an ability to bring in noteworthy companies and artists to run workshops with both under- and post-graduates – at best – enriched the curriculum and exposed students to particular skills and performance-making strategies not provided by the established staff.

The **MIME CENTRE BERLIN** concentrates on questioning the basis of movement in theatre. This aim is connected with a certain phenomenon of separation, still persistent in German thought: theatre is text, and dance is movement. Challenging this point of view creates a scope of work with greater dimensions: from the question of the basis of movement in 'text' theatre, to the role of theatricality in dance. To this end, our work is about the physical and psychical presence of an actor, and about movement as the ground and connection of several different ways of creating theatre.

(From the Berlin Mime Centre website: www.mimecentrum.de)

It is impossible to overestimate the importance that an increasingly varied and extensive range of workshop opportunities has had for the developing culture of physical theatres in Europe and North America from the 1980s. Generative in these developments were a number of organisations with various functions, but among which were the organisation of training events and workshops, and an advocacy role in raising the profile and support for visual and physical theatre practices. In this context we now look at three such organisations: Mime Action Group (MAG), the International Workshop Festival (IWF) and the Centre for Performance Research (CPR). In Germany, the Berlin Mime Centre and the Amsterdam-based European Mime Federation also served similar purposes. Although based in Britain, MAG, IWF and the CPR are resolutely international in aspiration, profile and practice.

For MAG, later to become the Total Theatre Network, facilitating, coordinating and publicising training for emerging physical theatre practitioners was central to its overall activity and purpose. The argument that a more extensively trained workforce of physical theatre artists would produce richer, more sophisticated and articulate work had a persuasive logic, and one that was readily engaged in by funding bodies, notably the Arts Council and Regional Arts Boards. MAG, in addition to publishing the single most important vehicle – *Total Theatre* – for advertising and promoting the disparate range of workshops being offered in London and beyond, also organised throughout the 1990s a number of ambitious seminars, symposia and conferences which were both *about* training for mime and physical theatre, and the activity itself. These addressed issues of access, awareness, organisation and strategy on the one hand, and more substantive matters such as writing, directing, collaborative practices and creativity on the other.

The most sophisticated of all these events was a workshop symposium entitled *Moving into Performance* (September 1994, Manchester) organised jointly with Manchester Metropolitan University and the European Mime Federation. This linked five days of exchange workshops for professional practitioners to a two-day international symposium. Highly ambitious in its scope, *Moving into Performance* brought physical theatre and other types of performance practitioner together with academics and arts administrators to exchange and learn from each other's practices and methods. The structure of the event reflected and articulated an emerging perspective among some practitioners which proposed that sharing and exchanging practices – searching for the rules of 'translation' – was potentially a more productive way of satisfying the training needs of physical theatre artists at this cultural moment than offering them opportunities to learn technical or compositional skills from a 'master' or highly esteemed teacher-practitioner of theatre and movement.

Moving into Performance provides an interesting case study of the assumptions, aspirations, rhetorics and pretensions of a loosely connected constituency of artists, theatre makers, academics and administrators coming together under the banner of the grandly (sub)titled *European Mime and Physical Theatre Workshop Symposium*. The conjunctions and disjunctions between the resolutely disciplined disciples of Etienne Decroux, a larger but more anarchic band of practitioners ascribing allegiance to Jacques Lecoq and Philippe Gaulier, a disparate collection of artists whose dispositions lay more with live or performance art than contemporary French mime, and a small but articulate grouping whose practices spoke the legacy of the iconic 1980s Impact Theatre Company, all made for an edgy and heady mix, a blend that was perhaps at its most productive during the workshop elements of the event, but one which was less plural and inclusive than many participants cared to acknowledge. This point was made trenchantly by roving rapporteur and cultural provocateur for the *Workshop Symposium*, Enrique Pardo, who during an evening debate under the masthead of 'Burning Questions', asked:

> Why is the Odin not around? Is this a Decroux, Lecoq and Gaulier club? If so what is the underlying performance philosophy bias?

(Pardo quoted in *Moving into Performance Report*, Mime Action Group 1995: 24)

Pardo might justifiably also have asked: Where was the dance tradition of German *tanztheater*, Pina Bausch and Lloyd Newson?

Moving into Performance, for all its flaws, remains an event of some cultural significance and moment within theatre historiography. It provides today, with all the wisdom of hindsight, a fascinating barometer for the state and shape of the physical theatre movement or constituency around that time, when the claims and the rhetoric for the innovatory qualities of these forms were at their height. It offered a snapshot of a number of tentative but potentially productive alliances and exchanges, and revealed the dominance – in the UK at least – of the Lecoq–Gaulier paradigm for physical performance practices. Moreover, it traced perhaps the high watermark of a self-confident cultural moment when it might have been assumed – if never actually claimed – that *physical theatres* were on the verge of attaining theatrical hegemony, or a take-over of the citadel that was text-based theatre. The blend of brashness and naivety that such a position represented is, of course, easy to scorn 12 years after the event, but at the time – and in the thick of it – the qualities of excitement and self-belief were palpable, energising and not without charm.

Apart from MAG, the leading – and arguably most significant – player in developing and defining the culture of the workshop has been the International Workshop Festival (IWF), an innovative and energetic organisation started by Nigel Jamison in 1988. Jamison had been director of Trickster, a physical theatre company established in the early 1980s, and in 1994 moved to Australia, handing over artistic leadership of the enterprise to Dick McCaw (see *PT:R*, 'Claire Heggen Goes Fishing', p. 9). The IWF has evolved over nearly two decades, but has basically brokered workshop encounters between theatre and performance practitioners from across the world. In an essay for *Total Theatre* in 1999 which charted the development of the IWF, McCaw identified the philosophy and purpose of the organisation:

(McCaw 1999: 14)

> Firstly, to encourage the creation of new work through providing a place for the exchange of new ideas and practices. And secondly, to sustain artists through the lifelong development of their careers. Add to this the central belief in the value of international and interdisciplinary exchange and you have all the shaping forces behind any IWF programme.

Beyond the organisation of workshops the IWF has facilitated lecture-demonstrations, seminars and discussions between performance practitioners of all ages and experiences from across the world. From 1998, through a project entitled *A Body of Knowledge*, the IWF has also made a commitment to documentation, and to this end produced a video and DVD archive of hundreds of hours of workshops and conversations between practitioners. Until 1994 when McCaw took over, festival programmes had no theme or title, but simply brought interesting and often legendary figures of theatre pedagogy to London to offer workshops in an eclectic mix of forms, histories and practices. From the mid-1990s, McCaw attempted to inject some sense of coherence into the programme by theming each festival, and thus began to present a more systematic and thoughtful approach to what was offered and experienced.

The Performer's Energy project (1995) explored ideas of energy between the performing and the martial arts. In 1996, the theme was movement, and investigated the differences between how actors and dancers use and understand movement. The 1997 festival consisted of a Voice/Dance/Movement project in London, and one in Belfast entitled *With the Whole Voice*. In 1998 the festival explored rhythm particularly through the work of early twentieth-century experiments by figures such as Jacques-Dalcroze, Laban and Appia.

The IWF has been a central part of the landscape of experimental, visual and physical theatre practices since its launch in 1988. Shaped by the emerging culture of body-based theatres, it has been equally significant in moulding those practices through its resolute internationalism and through the form and structure of the learning process itself.

We conclude this section below with a reflection on some conflicting views and voices on the consequences of the workshop culture for the quality of practice itself. However, before we examine these issues we shall briefly consider the work of a third organisation that has made a highly significant mark on the practices of physical and visual theatres.

The Centre for Performance Research (CPR) was established in Cardiff in 1988, by Richard Gough and Judie Christie. It was born out of the Cardiff Laboratory Theatre which in turn had been founded by Mike Pearson (see *PT:R*, p. 142), Sian Thomas and Richard Gough in 1974. The CPR's website describes its work and purpose thus:

> a pioneering and multi-faceted theatre organisation located and rooted in Wales, working nationally and internationally. CPR produces innovative performance work: arranges workshops, conferences, lectures and master classes (for the professional, the amateur and the curious); curates and produces festivals, expositions and exchanges with theatre companies from around the world; publishes and distributes theatre books, as well as the journal *Performance Research*, and houses a resource centre and library that specializes in world theatre and performance and maintains an archive on contemporary Welsh performance.

(http://www.thecpr.org.uk/about/index.php)

The CPR shares qualities, aspirations and histories with both MAG and the IWF, and significantly they have comparable longevity. All have been preoccupied with performance and training practices outwith the mainstream of text-based and play-generated theatre; all have placed the body and its performative possibilities at the centre of the theatrical nexus; implicitly or explicitly, all have celebrated both the internationalism and hybridity of contemporary theatre practices; and all have placed pedagogy and learning as a critical dimension of their purpose and function. The CPR, in addition, has its own very particular history in being born out of Grotowskian physical theatre practices embraced by the Cardiff Laboratory Theatre in the 1970s, and in defining its identity as being resolutely and simultaneously in Wales *and* the world. The CPR's positive engagement with the project of Welsh nationhood, while at the same time embracing both the politics and pragmatics of internationalism, has given this unique organisation a very particular quality and stamp of its own.

In addition to these characteristics, the CPR has always sought and enjoyed a productive relationship with theatre academics and their university departments. Now a significant limb of the Department of Theatre, Film and Television Studies within the University of Wales at Aberystwyth, the CPR has actively engaged in the more theoretical, discursive and research-based dimensions of contemporary performance practices, as well as offering a wide and challenging range of practical courses and workshops for professional practitioners and students from the UK and across the world. Through its joint editorship of the journal *Performance Research*, other publishing ventures and being strongly influenced by the discourses of performance studies, the CPR continues to make an influential contribution to the theoretical, pedagogical and performative practices of contemporary world theatre. Like MAG and the IWF, the CPR has played a major role in articulating, communicating and debating the substance and contours of physical and visual theatres over the past three decades.

The phrase 'workshop culture' has been used both descriptively and pejoratively over the past two decades, on the one hand to identify a pragmatic development in the organisation and delivery of training pedagogies, but, on the other, to express disquiet over what has been perceived to be a number of negative consequences for the quality, integrity and coherence of the theatre practices shaped by these training experiences. The debate was initially framed by Rivka Rubin, a former dancer and experimental theatre practitioner, who had set up her own workshop training organisation, Physical State International, in Manchester in 1987. In an essay for *Total Theatre* in 1995, Rubin articulated her concerns about the low levels of skill she was encountering from participants in the workshops and classes she was teaching:

(Rubin 1995: 11)

> Today the poor level of technical and interpretative abilities of many of the 'professionally trained' participants in Britain is shocking many workshop leaders. . . . Many formal training courses today are covering too many subjects too superficially. In depth training and profound understanding of one area as an initial base has become almost extinct.

Rubin's frustrations were directed as much towards the claims she felt university theatre departments were making on behalf of their own curriculum, and the graduates they produced, as to workshops as such. She noted, too, that for many workshop leaders and the organisations that employed them, the activity had become a conveyor belt 'taught mainly by flavour of the moment artists and some master makers, but rarely master teachers' (ibid.). Rubin was not alone in expressing these concerns, and was pointing usefully to the impact that certain models of cultural production may have on the quality of actual practices – and the practitioners who embody them. For Rubin, the proliferation of short workshops raised awkward questions about skills levels; superficiality, both in terms of understanding and the embodiment of practice; weaknesses in compositional knowledge and strategies; and – not least – the cultural politics embedded in the workshop transactions she witnessed.

Rubin's essay in *Total Theatre* was 'answered' by Dick McCaw in a subsequent issue of the same journal the following year. Essentially, McCaw argued that Rubin was naïve to lay the shortcomings and ills of contemporary performance work at the door of the workshop phenomenon and organisations (like his own IWF) which facilitated such activities. For McCaw:

> A workshop is simply a space in which professionals can meet to exchange and explore ideas and skills, and to experiment freely without the pressure of the rehearsal schedule. The same workshop can answer a variety of professional needs: a means of reviving flagging morale and energy, a way through a creative block, or a new insight into the creative process.

(McCaw 1996: 19)

The exchange between Rubin and McCaw continues to be rehearsed and echoed in a variety of different contexts. Clearly, participants engage with a workshop with different motivations and goals, and it is hard to generalise about the cultural and performative impact on particular individuals. None the less, if one perspective on the proliferation of workshops is that this abundance is largely a product of a continuing commodification of the arts marketplace – a commodification that has little concern for deepening the quality of the work being ultimately produced – then Rubin's anxieties are not misplaced. This is a lens through which one might also deduce that arts policy makers and funders are content to see the mechanisms of the market offer a variety of short-term (workshop) opportunities which can be labelled and claimed as 'training'. Here, it might be argued, an obligation to think through (and pay for) more substantial, strategic and in-depth possibilities is removed from the agenda. However, it is overly reductive to single out the workshop training experience as the main source of a range of performative and compositional weaknesses in British and European contemporary physical theatre practice.

Contemporary training: principles and practices

No emotions, no reason:
From an interview with neurologist Antonio Damasio

We experience the world so differently with our body and our mind. Our body is tangible and finite, whereas our mind seems transitory and unable to be bound by time or place. It is logical that we should think that the two are completely different, but the obvious is not always true. After all, when you are walking on the surface of the earth, you cannot imagine you are moving on a sphere and that in addition this sphere is spinning on its axis at dizzying speed. A similar thing applies to the way we think intuitively about the mind and the body. When in neurology we look scientifically at the facts, mind and body turn out not to be so different after all. And that's where Spinoza comes in. He said that our mind is a very specific bodily process. Since then, biology and neurology have shown that the processes at work are microscopically small, but are nevertheless material and physical.

(Damasio interview recorded on *Les Ballets C de la B* website: www.lesballetscdela.be)

Different times generate and demand different conditions, frameworks and possibilities for modes of actor training. In this section we consider a number of late twentieth-century figures whose practices as directors and/or teachers have marked them as having particular preoccupations with the corporeal dimensions of theatre making and performing. Indeed some of these figures are regularly and explicitly linked to the varying practices of the physical theatre canon. Of those practitioners below who continue to direct theatre, all have regarded training as an integral part of their work as theatre makers. Like a number of their early twentieth-century counterparts, many of these figures regularly elide approaches to training with the actual process of making theatre. Sometimes training is separate and differentiated, but often integral to devising, rehearsal and to the search for achieving ensemble.

In the short accounts that follow we are seeking to identify the main principles behind the training and preparatory activities which these figures espouse, practice and continually revise. Here we will identify a range of common assumptions alongside discontinuities, differences and sometimes radically divergent views on the role, for example, of codified movement, and the forms of theatre which these training regimes are designed to serve. All these figures would contest the wisdom and efficacy of separating the psychological from the physical in training and preparation, although most are inclined to explore embodied practices as generative of emotional and psychological states and dispositions. Here the body is more likely to be the starting point of a training exercise than analysis of text, motivation and character psychology. Once again we are let down by language which obliges us to articulate an uneasy and false binary between body and mind, the physical and the emotional, and movement and psychology.

In addition to an implicit rejection of the Cartesian separation of mind and body, we suggest that there are at least five additional areas which might engender some degree of common cause between these theatrical innovators:

1   *Continuous training*. Although this begs the question how each defines and practises training, there is a common assumption that early training at university, or in the professional conservatoire or academy, should not be a once-and-for-all experience. Training in its broadest sense is unending and integral to the process of making theatre that is never 'finished' or complete, but is always mutable and capable of being pushed further.

2   *Working against the grain*. All these figures identified above would claim to be working outside the frame of the established traditions and conventions of theatre and dance. Consequently, there can be no pre-existing models of training which will satisfactorily and comprehensively equip performers for the practices they are aspiring to create – practices for which there is no formula and where rules are to be invented, only to be broken again in a continuous loop of experimentation and development.

3   *Technique is never enough*. Although the practitioners identified represent diverse practices in relation to their performers acquiring a codified grammar of *extra-daily* techniques that will form the dramaturgical and compositional framework for their

creative work, none of these artists regard technical skill as an end in itself. Many of those whose practice requires the acquisition of movement codes and grammars – such as Etienne Decroux – would argue that it is, none the less, the underlying principles, or what Jacques Lecoq called the 'driving motors' (Murray 2003: 46) *beneath* the technique that are in fact crucial for creative work.

4   *Preparing for ensemble*. All these figures regard their various approaches to training as a means towards forging a common spirit between every member of the group or company. For Lecoq this is complicité, for Dodin it is a 'common language', and for Brook it is the 'invisible network'. We return to examining these notions in more detail below, but for now it is important to stress that for each of these practitioners the quest for ensemble is crucial to both the creative compositional process and the perception/reception of the performance itself. Ensemble is both the subject and object of the making process. It cannot be achieved through drilling, but can only be engendered through a complex learning process which encourages corporeal attentiveness and sensitivity.

5   *The creative actor*. The training practices of all these innovative pedagogues – but with varying degrees of emphasis – place the actor in a position of compositional creativity, rather than merely as the conduit for either the writer's script or the director's interpretation. All regard the actor as part of the shared authorial process of making the work in question. Strategies towards this ambition vary enormously, and none of these figures relinquish all directorial authority to their actors. None the less, all certainly articulate a rhetoric which gives actors permission to share in the generation of the performance text rather than simply being its 'technical' executants.

In the profiles which follow we focus on the varying ways in which these figures create circumstances that explore and exploit the *aliveness* and the engagement of the actor in relation to both fellow performers and spectators. All these director-teachers have a shared preoccupation with enabling their actors to develop a scale of physical attentiveness and sensitivity to themselves, to each other and to their audience beyond the often blunted awareness and stale interactions of daily life. These qualities are never reducible to technical skills, but neither are they 'God-given' or genetically determined marks of genius, lying outside human agency and invention. They are dispositions and inflections which can be acquired partly through structured exercise, but more importantly through a slow and repeated immersion in the process of play, reflection, experiment and human interaction. Above all, these are dispositions which lie in the body-mind, rather than in either motor actions, or in a state of mental empathy.

Lev Dodin and the Maly Theatre of St Petersburg

Dodin is director of the Maly Theatre, widely acknowledged as one of the world's most creative and physically inventive ensemble companies. Unlike many of his Western counterparts, Dodin has had the luxury of extensive rehearsal and research periods for each new production and a commitment to a continuous programme of training which is critical to his overall working process. Dodin's training regime is partly designed to equip his actors with high levels of physical and vocal skill, and to this end – in addition to voice and music classes – members of the ensemble undertake a daily ballet class which he believes provides them with a fundamental repertoire of physical resources such as stamina, strength, coordination and equilibrium. These are extended by personal tuition in, for example, acrobatics and circus skills when they are necessary for the demands of a particular production.

However, accomplishment in this range of physical, vocal and musical skills is not by itself what makes the Maly such an astonishing company. Dodin is equally preoccupied with subtler and more complex attributes among his actors and these focus upon how to achieve what he terms the 'living life' of particular moments of the unfolding narrative of each production. This 'aliveness' is a sensual, emotional and visceral quality rather than a cerebral or cognitive one. 'Aliveness' is the performative quality which Dodin seeks most to embed in his actors. It is a condition which, claims Maria Shevtsova, 'ensures its regeneration and growth in successive performances where it is fresh every time . . . is fundamental to his whole approach and also undergirds his notion of "authenticity", which he claims he also gleaned from Stanislavsky' (Shevtsova 2004: 38).

Notwithstanding Dodin's insistence on technical skills learned through the disciplines of music and ballet, he does not define training as a repertoire of exercises which yield direct and tangible results. Overall, his methods constantly invite actors to develop physical skills in order to refine and sharpen their sensory imaginations. There is a dialectical loop here in that developing the body's physical sensitivity and articulacy helps to create the conditions for invention and imagination, but also – pragmatically for the actor – the imagination once unleashed has to be expressed physically and translated through actions. Shevtsova quotes Dodin as encapsulating his regime as a:

(Ibid.: 39)

'training of the heart and the nervous system' (Paris, 8 April 1994). This generates an approach that, although not a method in the sense of a set of procedures, is nevertheless methodical. . . . Training the sensory receptivity and responsiveness ('nervous system') *of* each actor and *between* actors allows them to find an appropriate physical expression for whatever internal action transpires ('heart'). The actor's body, in other words, is in a position to articulate the impulses that drive it at *any given instant* of a performance. My italics intend to draw attention to Dodin's concern with the mutability of performance.

Like many director-teachers striving to help their actors acquire this sense of 'aliveness' – or some comparable term – Dodin knows that this elusive quality cannot be taught formally according to a method or system, but can only be cultivated and nurtured through an enormous range of exercises and activities which stimulate the performer's emotions and imagination. 'Aliveness' is almost a by-product of a whole range of other skills and dispositions. It is also a condition of generosity and, as such, crucial for the fostering of an ensemble spirit. Dodin, for example, insists on a number of rituals at the beginning of each day's rehearsal, or immediately prior to a performance. In rehearsal or training each actor is responsible on a daily rota basis for preparing Dodin's table in the studio. Shevtsova describes what lies behind this apparently whimsical ceremony:

> It inculcates discipline but, above all, its purpose is to develop the spirit of fantasy and of what might be called extrapolation, since the arrangement on the table must express in some way, by image, symbolically or through the atmosphere it creates, the work to be done that day.

(Ibid.: 41)

A more elaborate version of the table preparation is what is called the *zachin*. Here a group of students – or Maly performers in professional practice – will prepare a kind of creative prelude to a day in the studio, or before an actual performance. This is a collaborative act and an imaginative one. The *zachin* may contain songs, poems, pieces of prose (found or composed) and short statements, all of which offer a proposition of possibilities for the day of training, or performance, to follow. The *zachin* is an integral part of the training process, and is perhaps better conceived of as the looser process of *preparation*. It fosters creativity, imagination and comradeship and is a physical practice of actions, rather than a statement of aspirations and good intentions.

So, for Dodin the technical skills acquired through voice, ballet and music classes are of little value unless expressed through and permeated by the range of sensibilities we have identified above. This 'training of the heart and the nervous system' (see above) nourishes the imaginations of his actors and fosters a sense of 'aliveness' which makes the Maly Theatre an ensemble of extraordinary power that far exceeds displays of sheer technical virtuosity and spectacle.

Eugenio Barba and the Odin Teatret

Eugenio Barba has written copiously – and been much written about – since founding his own company, the Odin Teatret, in 1964. Along with Grotowski and Decroux, Barba's practice is preoccupied with and constructed around training. Indeed, for Barba, training is central to his dramaturgy and in many senses when watching Odin's work one is witnessing – quite transparently – representations and distillations of the collective and individual training experienced by his actors for over 30 years. Deeply influenced and engaged by traditional Eastern forms of dance and drama, and the training regimes which prepare for them, Barba has been preoccupied with what constitutes 'presence' in the actor. We can detect some similarities between Barba and Dodin here, but – more significantly – a number of distinctions. Like Dodin and Lecoq, for example, Barba has always led his actors through a stripping-away process, a belief that the socialised and inculturated body is not prepared for 'presence', is too corrupted and colonised by habit to achieve that state of corporeal engagement which will fire and charge the spectator.

Barba makes the distinction between *inculturation* and *acculturation*. The former is sometimes misleadingly labelled as 'natural', but is in fact what performers

(Barba and
Savarese 1991:
189)
have absorbed since their birth in the culture and social milieu in which they have grown up. Anthropologists define as inculturation this process of passive sensory-motor absorption of the daily behaviour of a given culture.

Inculturation is far from *natural*, although it may feel so to the subject, but is the product of a complex weave of cultural and temporal factors such as gender, class, education and ethnicity. It is also important to recognise that inculturation is much more than a mental or psychological construct, but is deeply embodied and informs posture, bearing, movement and gesture. Anthropologist Marcel Mauss (*PT:R*, p. 38) calls this 'techniques of the body', while for sociologist Pierre Bourdieu, inculturation provides us with a 'habitus'. For Bourdieu, 'habitus' is the 'taking in' of values, dispositions, attitudes and behaviour patterns which become part of our daily, apparently individual conduct. What is important here – and connects absolutely to corporeal theatre training – is that the 'habitus' is deeply embodied and not merely a mental and cognitive construction:

(Bourdieu in
Danaher *et al.*
2002: 37)
[the] body . . . is open to the world, and therefore exposed to the world, and so capable of being conditioned by the world, shaped by the material and cultural conditions of existence in which it is placed from the beginning.

Acculturation, for Barba, is a secondary 'colonisation' of the body, but a deliberate and planned one. Here actors, mimes or dancers learn – often over many years – an elaborate range of codified behaviours which transform and re-invent the performing body and immediately mark it in such a way that it becomes almost indivisible from the form it is conveying.

Denying 'naturalness'

At the same time, in all cultures, it is possible to observe another path for the performer: the utilisation of specific body techniques which are separate from those used in daily life. Modern and classical ballet dancers, mimes and performers from traditional Oriental theatres have denied their 'naturalness' and have adapted another means of scenic behaviour. They have undergone a process of 'acculturation' imposed from the outside, with ways of standing, walking, stopping, looking and sitting which are different from the daily.

(Eugenio Barba and Nicola Savarese (1991: 190), *A Dictionary of Theatre Anthropology: The Secret Art of the Performer*, Routledge)

After 12 years of intensive training led by Barba himself, Odin actors were invited to undertake their own personal training regimes. This significant change in strategy acknowledged what Barba has described as a loss of faith in 'pure technicity' (ibid.: 244) and a willingness to emphasise each actor's pace and rhythm. The move also registered a shift towards process and the dispositions required for composition. None the less, within and between Odin actors there is a common understanding that presence, or what Barba calls 'scenic bios', is acquired through reaching a state of 'pre-expressivity'. This is a complex – and to many – a controversial position. Essentially, the pre-expressive state is to be found once daily and inculturated habits are erased from the performer's mental and corporeal repertoire. This leaves the body of the individual performer in a state where s/he exists at a basic level of organisation that removes individual difference and idiosyncrasy. It is precisely at this point of pre-expressivity, argues Barba, that the actor's body is rendered scenically alive and so can become a presence which engages the spectator.

While the pre-expressive body is produced through a process of reduction, Barba parts company at this point with someone like Jacques Lecoq in his quest for the *neutral* body. For Barba the pre-expressive body harnesses energy in a particular way which requires very specific attention to the details of corporeal organisation. Pre-expressivity, and hence the achievement of 'scenic bios', possesses three qualities – or dynamics – in particular which Barba articulates in considerable detail throughout his writing:

- alteration in balance
- the law of opposition
- consistent inconsistency.

Barba argues that the play of balance is evident not only in codified forms of performance, but also – deliberately or not – in a wide range of performers possessing this quality of presence. That point of imbalance – between stillness and mobility (falling!) – is an alive and creative moment of readiness. The firmly rooted and corporeally balanced performance state is a condition of stasis and immobility. Here, the performer's energy is directed downward into the earth. For Philippe Gaulier and Jacques Lecoq the moments of *suspension* and of *élan* are similar, but neither would articulate this goal in the same way as Barba.

The principle of opposition is to be found in the different performance traditions Barba has encountered, and is used deliberately or unknowingly by all performers. Essentially, performers are constantly adjusting and playing with principles of counterbalance. We do this instinctively to stay upright, but 'this physical necessity has been refined in art. Many performance practices work with precarious balance as a technique, as it requires the performer to dilate their energy and be "scenically alive"' (Turner 2004: 52).

The third principle of pre-expressivity plays with the paradox of 'consistent inconsistency' and here Barba is referring to the necessary distance (inconsistency) between everyday and performative behaviours, while at the same time looking for a consistency in the form and quality of a performer's internal choices within the territory of theatre. This consistency may often entail a distillation – a reduction or omission – in the component parts of an action so as to condense behaviours to their essential minimum.

Thus for Barba the psycho-physical preparation of the actor is rooted in the study of a wide range of performance practices, particularly from the East, but also drawn from selected principles enunciated by Western innovators such as Stanislavsky,

Meyerhold, (Michael) Chekhov and Decroux. Up to a point Barba embraces the same language of preparation and aspirations for his performers as, for example, Brook, Dodin, Lecoq and McBurney. One of the key differences, however, seems to be between an emphasis on how the *individual* actor acquires 'aliveness' (Barba/'scenic bios'), and on the quality of the relationships and dynamics *between* performers (Brook *et al.*).

Anne Bogart: viewpoints and composition

Scavenging . . .

I am a scavenger. I am not an original thinker and I am not a true creative artist. So the notion of scavenging appeals to me. . . . I read a lot and I take little bits of what I read and I put them together into thoughts and ideas. I juxtapose ideas. I like the satisfaction of putting things together like that.

(Anne Bogart quoted in Shomit Mitter and Maria Shevtsova (eds)
(2005: 221), *Fifty Key Theatre Directors*, Routledge)

Anne Bogart formed the Saratoga International Theatre Institute (SITI) with Japanese theatre director Tadashi Suzuki in 1992, but her work in theatre dates back to the early 1970s. In this short account we dwell exclusively on Bogart's strategies for preparing actors and for composing material, rather than the complex theorisation and practice of Suzuki's training methods. Today, Bogart is an influential figure, not only as a theatre director, but as someone whose innovatory ideas and methods around actor training now represent a challenge to the hitherto largely uncontested dominance of 'the method' and narrowly psychological interpretations of Stanislavsky's system within American universities. The socio-cultural routes into Bogart's practice can be located in the Civil Rights and Vietnam War protest movements, and in the birth of abstract expressionism, minimalism and postmodern dance. Within these the aspiration towards non-hierarchical and democratic forms of organisation, and a disposition to experiment within real-time frameworks, siting work in non-theatre spaces, and an insistence on challenging the traditional boundaries of art forms all provided the base upon which Bogart's subsequent practice as a teacher and theatre director were constructed. The roots of all her ideas on actor training may be traced to these artistic and cultural moments.

In 1979 Bogart began to collaborate with new dance choreographer Mary Overlie, when they both worked at New York University in the Experimental Theater faculty. Overlie had already established her 'Six Viewpoints', a training methodology for dancers, and since then Bogart has continued to adapt and develop these for the purposes of theatre. In addition to the elaborate and comprehensive methods within Viewpoints, Bogart has developed a parallel system entitled Composition, and collaborated intensively with Tadashi Suzuki on a third string of training for her SITI performers, and on numerous courses for professional actors and students. As a theatre maker and director Bogart's practice refuses categorisation within any single theatre genre and has ranged over radical reworkings of (largely) twentieth-century classic play texts, musicals, site-specific work and physical/dance theatre. Like similar directors whose work sits uneasily within the mainstream – Peter Brook, Simon McBurney and Lev Dodin, for example – Bogart has a lexicon of devising, rehearsal and training approaches which she will use across all forms of theatre. Like McBurney, Bogart demands that her actors have a creative – rather than merely interpretative – input into the making of any piece of work, regardless of whether it is devised or realised from a play text.

Bogart's perspective on actor training has been marked throughout her career by considerable scepticism, if not contempt, for method acting's misappropriation of the Stanislavskian legacy: a misuse and misunderstanding of Stanislavsky, she believes, which for over 70 years in America has produced a dominant paradigm for actor training that is shackled by its unswerving commitment to psychology and motivation as the main drivers of successful characterisation. For Bogart, method acting's focus on Stanislavsky's earlier preoccupation with psychology has not only fettered American theatre to the limiting conventions of realism and naturalism, but has also served actors poorly in their attempts to work within these genres. Viewpoints and Composition tackle the *what* and *how* of acting from a perspective which has as its mentors figures from the avant garde traditions of theatre such as Meyerhold, Copeau, Decroux, Lecoq and Grotowski, as well as the world of postmodern dance.

For Bogart and her collaborator Tina Landau, Viewpoints and Composition offer 'a clear-cut procedure and attitude that is non-hierarchical, practical and collaborative in nature' (Bogart and Landau 2005: 15). Viewpoints begins by acknowledging that all performers must respond to the invitation of dealing with time and space, and that at root all approaches to actor training are proposing solutions to this challenge. Bogart and Landau's Viewpoints, building upon the earlier work of Overlie, and within the frame of time/space, engage in detail with: 'shape, spatial relationships, floor pattern, architecture, repetition, gesture, tempo, duration and kinaesthetic response' (Mitter and Shevtsova 2005: 221). Underpinning all the exercises that Bogart has developed to attend to these issues is a reiteration that each performer at every moment in devising, rehearsal and actual performance is confronted with countless choices. Initially, all her training is about *revealing* these choices, making them explicit. With this sense of awareness the actor is then equipped with a range of skills, sensitivities and dispositions which enable him/her to make the best choice in all the circumstances. Moreover, and this is central to the methods of both Bogart and Suzuki, awareness is not primarily a mental or cognitive construction but a corporeal one that employs all the performer's senses in a visceral and somatic relationship with the world. Of course, like other twentieth-century teacher-directors working from task, action, movement and physicality, Bogart does not dismiss psychology, intention and emotion, but is searching for a more productive route into these for the creative actor.

Bogart's Composition was developed as a natural extension of the Viewpoints training, and although for SITI actors the two are integrated in practice, schematically they may be understood apart from each other. Composition is the corollary of Bogart's commitment to the 'creative actor' – the expectation and assumption that whether devising material or searching for ways to animate an existing text, actors will 'propose' solutions and possibilities. Within the protocols of Composition Bogart requires her actors or students to work very quickly and with minimum analysis and discussion. Bogart uses the term 'exquisite pressure' (Bogart and Landau 2005: 137) to suggest the creative potential of working (inevitably) under pressure. She identifies the Composition process as follows:

(Ibid.)

> Participants create short pieces for the stage by putting together raw material into a form that is repeatable, theatrical, communicative and dramatic. The process of creating compositions is by nature collaborative: within a short amount of time, participants arrive at solutions to certain delineated tasks. These solutions arranged and performed as a piece, are what constitute a Composition. The creative process demands cooperation and quick, intuitive decisions.

This strategy would be hardly unfamiliar to many theatre makers habituated to the devising process, and indeed resonates with, for example, Lecoq's **autocours**, Barba's creation of a movement score and the improvisational strategies of Keith Johnstone and Clive Barker. In Viewpoints, Bogart proposes a range of exercises designed to pursue different dimensions of theatre making: story-telling with objects, exploring emotional states, selecting different genres, character work, creating atmosphere and 'worlds', and unpacking a scene for its myriad possibilities. As director, Bogart will then take charge of the process of selecting, editing, changing, extending, linking and recontextualising this material as it builds towards some overall structure. Here, again, she is working in a very similar way to directors such as Simon McBurney, Tim Etchells and Lin Hixson. It is important to note that for Bogart this Composition process is not simply a strategy for devising material, or for finding solutions to resolve a play scene, but equally importantly is a strategy to explore and deepen the qualities needed for a genuine and rich articulation of ensemble.

Jacques Lecoq

Until recently the work of Jacques Lecoq (1921–99) (*PT:R*, p. 187) had only been communicated to the world outside the Paris school through his own occasional workshops and lecture demonstrations (*Tout bouge*), anecdotage, and the imprint of individuals and companies who trained with him. Since Lecoq's death, however, a number of books and essays have begun to explore his complex legacy, and the nature of his pedagogy (Lecoq 2000; Chamberlain and Yarrow 2002; Bradby and Delgado 2002; Murray 2003; Lecoq 2006). Arguably, Lecoq has been the most significant influence on contemporary European and North American physical theatres through his approach to actor prepara-tion and theatre making, and *interpretations* of that pedagogy are conveyed with varying degrees of sensitivity by his many disciples. There are indeed a number of schools and university drama departments across Europe and the USA which explicitly associate themselves with what they sometimes erroneously call the 'Lecoq method'.

While Lecoq is often associated with mime (as art form and training) he was in fact increasingly resistant to this connection since his own practice had little to do with mime as it is commonly performed, articulated and understood. Moreover, although his impact on late twentieth-century physical theatres is undeniable, he never embraced or claimed this term to describe the theatre practices that his school had helped to nurture and generate.

In examining Lecoq's approach to the preparation of the actor we will also associate his pedagogy with figures such as Philippe Gaulier, Monika Pagneux and Simon McBurney. This is not to suggest, however, that these singular characters are simply uncritical imitators of Lecoq's teaching, but, while they have their own distinct pedagogy, they are all deeply associated with approaches to actor training that resonate strongly with Lecoq's project. In terms of an actor's *preparation*, Lecoq's teaching is based in two interrelated states or dispositions: neutrality and play. Both are much invoked, but easily misunderstood or trivialised. The first of two years at Lecoq's Paris school is 'a year of demystification of ready-made ideas' (Lecoq 1973: 41) and within this frame the quest for neutrality is paramount. Lecoq (2000) and Murray (2003) explore this work with the neutral mask in some depth, and acknowledge its history in the teaching of Jacques Copeau. Here, we will briefly consider its main qualities and note similarities and differences with other contemporary figures.

Demystifying all that we know

In the beginning, it is necessary to demystify all that we know in order to put ourselves in a state of non-knowing, a kind of openness and availability for the rediscovery of the elemental. For now, we no longer see what surrounds us.

(Jacques Lecoq quoted in Myra Felner (1985: 148), *Apostles of Silence: The Modern French Mimes*, Associated University Presses)

The neutral mask is primarily a teaching device and rarely used for performance. Lecoq says that 'such fundamental things occur with this mask that it has become the central point of my teaching method' (2000: 36). Although for Lecoq the neutral mask is ultimately a tool towards the articulate physicalisation of character, it is the *process* of working with it that concerns us here. As its name implies this mask removes the expressive biography of the face with all its potential for excess and overuse in the acting process. Consequently, the neutral mask invites the wearer to activate and sensitise the rest of the body, to explore a physical and sensual relationship with the world and its matter. By leading his students incrementally through a range of exercises with the mask, they will be encouraged to find an economy of movement which is uncluttered by extraneous social patterns or habits (see Barba's 'inculturation') and to seek a relationship with matter – human or inanimate – that as far as possible is untainted and uninformed by knowledge, emotion, anticipation or experience.

Lecoq's work with the neutral mask takes us not only to the heart of his pedagogy, but – arguably – also to a range of propositions which are implicit, though often unexpressed, in the physical theatres project, namely an affirmation of knowledge accrued through movement. This is both self-knowledge *and* knowledge of the world in all its material, ideological and conceptual complexity. The neutral mask attempts to return the student to a 'precognitive state, freeing him to gather a new set of sensory impressions in a neutralised state of naiveté' (Felner 1985: 148). This kind of statement arouses considerable apprehension and critique from certain theoretical quarters where notions of precognition and neutrality are seen as romantic and impossibilist formulations that ultimately fail to acknowledge how human beings are constructed culturally and psychologically. Such criticism argues not only that erasure of these inculturated habits and dispositions is impossible because it is based on the myth of an essential and stable identity 'underneath', but that it is also ideologically suspect as it implies an attempt to deny difference between cultural groupings.

The point here, however, is that although Lecoq's use of language may open him up to such criticisms, these practices are essentially heuristic strategies and devices which operate at two reinforcing levels: as imaginative metaphor to facilitate a different way of seeing and being in the world, and as pragmatic teaching instruction to help students open themselves up corporeally and psychologically to a range of possibilities which will help them as actors and theatre makers. None the less, Lecoq's preoccupation with the neutral mask places him – contingently – within the same camp as, for example, Barba, Dodin or Brook who are searching for extra-daily behaviours and actions from their actors. Where, however, Lecoq differs from Barba is in his reluctance – once this state of neutral openness is achieved – then to equip the performer with a whole new set of codified behaviours or techniques upon which to construct his theatre making.

Lecoq's commitment to working with the neutral mask as preparation for the performer has to be placed alongside three linked states or dispositions which he regards as crucial both for the creative individual actor, and for the realisation of a sense of genuine ensemble. Like Philippe Gaulier, Simon McBurney, Tim Etchells and – in a very different time and context – Vsevolod Meyerhold, Lecoq constantly invoked 'play' as a quality he was seeking in his students, not only in their relationship to the spoken text and actual stage objects, but also in the dynamic between themselves and with their audience. However, Lecoq identifies two other linked states which he regards as critical in the realisation of a vibrant and immediate theatre. In French, for there is no immediate translation, *disponibilité* and *complicité* refer respectively to *openness* or *availability*, and to *rapport* or – more piquantly – a spirit of the 'accomplice'. Murray (2003: 70–71) explains these in some detail, but we may summarise the qualities of this trio of possibilities as follows.

PLAY (LE JEU)

- Successful play must attend to 'rhythm, tempo, space and form' (Lecoq 2000: 29).
- 'The motors of play' (ibid.: 98) must be discovered for all styles and genres.

- Without play there can be no creativity.
- Play demands pleasure and lightness.
- Play renders the moment on stage into life.
- 'Play is a state in which meaning is in flux, in which possibility thrives, in which visions multiply' (Etchells 1999: 53).
- The playful actor requires a distance between him/herself and the role.
- The ability to play is an embodied disposition as well as a cognitive one.
- Trying too hard to play kills play.
- Playing is messy, unpredictable, joyous, frightening and sometimes you go too far.

DISPONIBILITÉ AND COMPLICITÉ

- *Disponibilité*: 'a state of discovery, of openness, of freedom to receive' (Lecoq 2000: 38).
- The route to *disponibilité* is through the body and movement.
- Physical and emotional/psychological openness are in symbiosis with each other.
- *Complicité*: a 'form of collusion between celebrants' (Ratcliffe 1994).
- An authentic and profound sense of ensemble cannot be achieved without *complicité* between participants.
- *Complicité* emerges through deep listening, looking, touching, smelling, sensing, thinking, feeling, repetition, pleasure, boredom.
- *Complicité* cannot be drilled and learned through counting.
- *Complicité* requires constant attention to rhythm and tempo.
- Without *complicité* there can be no 'collective imagining' for theatre making.
- *Complicité* recognises – and celebrates – that we are all in the shit together.

Monika Pagneux

Monika Pagneux, one-time teacher with Lecoq at his Paris school, approaches the preparation of actors from a framework that accepts many of the basic propositions inherent in Lecoq's pedagogy. Pagneux has been a most remarkable figure in the landscape of training for and around physical theatres. Like Philippe Gaulier, Pagneux taught at L'École Jacques Lecoq until 1980 when they left to establish their own school together in another part of Paris. Since the late 1980s she has taught her own workshops and master classes across the world and worked closely with companies such as Complicité on movement preparation and choreography.

Pagneux's background is a fitting one to match the hybridity of much physical and experimental theatre practice. She worked with Mary Wigman, has been a circus clown, trained with Moshe Feldenkrais and collaborated with Peter Brook. At the centre of her pedagogy is the work of Feldenkrais, the great Israeli movement teacher, but what makes Pagneux's teaching so singular is her ability to draw upon and meld a range of approaches into the single end of creating the physically articulate and responsive performer. Pagneux is not interested in physical virtuosity for its own sake, but has an extraordinary ability to awaken performers' bodies of any shape or size. Her quest is for the alive, attentive and joyful performing body which marries risk with vulnerability and self-confidence with authenticity. For Pagneux *authenticity* seems less to do with a potentially dubious *truthful* or *essential* body, than about economy of movement, and the fluid responsive organisation of the body's musculature and skeletal structure. Drawing particularly upon the principles of Feldenkrais, Pagneux's work manages at once to function at a meticulous level of detail, and at the same time to operate on a meta and holistic plane which prepares the actor for the generic challenges of performance.

The Feldenkrais experience

Now I am able to lie on the floor and take myself through simple but crucial movements in order to organise myself so that when I come to the show I work with less effort and have more time to enjoy the work. Awareness of balance, your relationship with gravity, skeletal awareness and breathing, give you the space required to find economical movement and freedom in your thinking which in turn allow you to come closer to direct experience of what it is to exist in a theatrical environment.

(Andrew Dawson, performer, director and Feldenkrais teacher (1996), *Total Theatre*, 8(2): 17)

Although Feldenkrais techniques work on and with the body's movement, it is at root a psycho-physical exploration. A central premise is that a change – however minute – in the body's posture or movement will modify other aspects of our corporeality *and* consciousness. E.M. Forster's maxim of 'only connect' might be an appropriate signature for the teaching of Feldenkrais. Hence, for example, a slight realigning or opening of the vertebrae in the lower back may have consequences for posture, breathing, flexibility, walking, other forms of mobility, and – very significantly – shifts in self-image.

Feldenkrais exercises are usually very minimal and their success is not based on muscular strength or physical fitness as such, but upon the body organising itself in a way which allows for the sequence of a movement to travel – without blocks or hindrance – through the body's skeletal structure via the musculature. For Feldenkrais, and Pagneux likewise, much of the work is centred on the spine and its flexibility through both horizontal and vertical planes. Although Feldenkrais exercises often need to be repeated many times, this repetition is not about 'drilling' or building up muscular strength, but out of concern that these minute physical discoveries need to occur organically and sequentially if they are to effect permanent changes in body memory.

One of the features of Feldenkrais exercises is that, despite their 'minimalism' and the need to experience some of them many times, they yield very tangible 'results'. These are not in terms of new *skills* acquired, but in – perhaps – the dropping of the shoulders, the loosening of neck and upper back muscles, a flattening of the spine on to the floor, the release and opening of the hips and pelvic area which together, or singly, will be experienced as a new-found freedom of movement, an expansion of possibilities and awareness of self and others. Pagneux draws upon an extensive repertoire of these exercises, but combines them with a wide range of other activities which reflect both the plurality of her experience in theatre and dance, and her own acute perception of what each individual student needs in order to find this *alive* lightness of presence as a performer.

If there is one principle which encapsulates what Pagneux is looking for and enabling in the students and actors with whom she works it is that of 'attention'. This attention is to oneself, to others and to the material world. In the language of other theatre teachers it might be called 'being present' or 'being in the moment', but it is richer and more complex than this. This quality of attention is non-habitual – it is an extra daily sensibility, but never a narcissistic one. For Pagneux attention is about a finely tuned and deep listening, looking, feeling, sensing and knowing. It combines the paradoxical combinations of letting go and being fully engaged, as well as:

> undertaking the seeming impossibility of being 'near and far' – from the text, 'character', emotion and the full dynamics of movement. It is strategically positioned as a 'platform', a physical 'way in' to maintaining distance and 'slippage' at the site of the performer, and not 'holding too close' the identifications of text, emotion, or even the movement itself. It defies indulgence in projecting itself from 'inside' to 'out' and resists 'personalism' and the 'grabbing' identifications of the ego.

(Laing 2002: 174)

Thus the quality of *attention* seems to possess similar paradoxes to Lecoq's exploration of *play*. Both engage with some of theatre's most fundamental but productive tensions: freedom and discipline, pleasure and seriousness, struggle and lightness, work and relaxation, total commitment and distance. Theatre director and teacher John Wright sums up Pagneux's teaching and manner of relating to her students:

> Unlike many of Feldenkrais' devotees, Monika has never lost sight of the joy in personal discovery that lies at the heart of the work. . . . Aggressive assurance will not be tolerated. She is looking for vulnerability and pleasure at the moment of risk, and the lightness and simplicity of movement that is fully integrated.

(Wright 1994: 11)

Philippe Gaulier

Like Pagneux, Philippe Gaulier's pedagogy is deeply inflected by the experience of working alongside Jacques Lecoq. He has a positive disdain for what he regards as the overblown and pretentious claims of mime and physical theatre ('moi, je déteste le mime') and in this sense, as in many others, he reflects the scepticism of his own teacher and mentor, Jacques Lecoq. For many years Gaulier was one half of a renowned clown double act with Pierre Bylan and his teaching remains anchored in humour, the grotesque and the absurd. He is still, suggests John Wright, 'a clown who has taken to teaching theatre' (Wright 1990: 9). Of course, this is only one truth about Gaulier since, behind a mercilessly incisive, usually hilarious but always provocative teaching style, his work represents a complex and thoughtful set of ideas about the nature of presence, liveness and play within theatre. None the less, like Lecoq, he has had little interest in theorising, writing about and making claims for his work. Not for Gaulier a Brook- or Barba-like propensity for explaining and justifying his practice as teacher and theatre director.

Unlike Lecoq, however, Gaulier has always offered a series of short, usually four- or five-week courses in the various schools he has run. Each reflects areas of the curriculum that constitute the two-year programme at Lecoq's school, but can be taken in and out of sequence, although *Le Jeu* underpins everything else he teaches. Gaulier acknowledges Lecoq as 'the single most important person in my theatrical life. . . . He is the basis of my ideas' (Gaulier quoted by Wright 1990: 9) but Wright astutely goes on to point out that he is:

(Ibid.)

> more concerned with impulse than movement analysis . . . and games that root many of Lecoq's ideas in the imperative of the dramatic moment. Gaulier works with play for the same reasons that Lecoq works with movement, and achieves very similar results.

Across all his courses Gaulier is particularly preoccupied with the instant of performance. What combination of performative qualities will bring that moment to life, regardless of style or genre? Apart from 'play' Gaulier constantly invokes lightness, élan, pleasure, suspension, fixed point and rhythm as qualities that must exist not only *within* the performer, but also *between* them. Gaulier has a number of exercises which entail the apparently banal task of two people standing opposite each other, throwing and catching a tennis ball. From this simple performance structure text may be added: *I give you the ball my little classmate . . . thank you for the ball my little classmate.* (Gaulier is a master of bathos.) The split second the ball leaves the hand, the thrower hits a fixed point and the first line of the text is launched, 'carried' by the ball until it is caught in the hand(s) of the receiver. The throw or the catch is an impulse which yokes text and movement into a marriage of perfect timing. At the moment of the catch the receiver strikes a fixed point and utters the memorable response, *thank you for the ball my little classmate* . . . Actions and text are repeated and, for example, at this juncture Gaulier might introduce the cadences and timbre of melodrama to add dramatic form to the exercise. Here, rhythm and timing will change so as to alter completely the dynamic and 'meaning' of the routine.

Within the simple structural dynamic of this tennis ball game Gaulier is investigating:

- timing
- economy of action and movement
- stillness and eye contact
- the rhythms of particular theatrical genres
- the moment of punctuation in performance where text and action find the perfect relationship

- the pleasure of the play, the pleasure of the game
- theatrical focus: major and minor and the potentially transgressive play between these
- the quality of lightness.

Finally, we will reflect on Gaulier's use of *lightness* and *pleasure* as critical qualities he is searching for in performance. The terms pepper his dialogue with students, and an absence of these qualities is usually central to his withering dismissal of an improvisation he finds wanting. In searching for lightness and pleasure, and more importantly, the generative 'driving motors' behind these, Gaulier and Pagneux are very much at one, although their pedagogical styles are strikingly different. For Gaulier, lightness and pleasure are necessary but not sufficient conditions for creative play. They suggest a corporeal and psychological disposition towards the particular tasks of theatre making which is not *driven* in a single-minded and goal-oriented way. They propose that reflection and intellectual analysis – especially of the more tortured variety – has little place within the actual moment(s) of an improvisation or scene making. They advocate a truly physical sense of elevation and suspension as a pre-condition for play: states which are none the less a consequence of personal confidence and self-affirmation. In a typically gnomic statement Gaulier says that 'the play of the actor takes place in the light. (It is hopeless) to seek refuge in a cave of repentance and remorse' (ibid.: 8). We know what he means . . .

At the heart of Gaulier's teaching lies a paradox, or at least a rather joyful tension, and this is that although there can be few teachers of contemporary theatre who are more direct, fearless and less equivocating than Gaulier in terms of comment, feedback and dismissal ('you are too tense, sit down . . . ', 'you treated your partner like a lavatory brush, a Viennese lavatory brush') (ibid.) he *never* tells students 'how to do it'. Probably the only thing Gaulier shares with Grotowski is a pedagogy based on the *via negativa*, that is to say an approach which rejects prescription and illustration by example in favour of a search for the 'answer' through negation. Through the *via negativa* Gaulier offers no prescriptions and it is up to the student to continue proposing possibilities until the most effective receives some kind of acceptance or affirmation.

Underneath the ruthless candour of Gaulier's teaching 'technique', made bearable for the recipient usually only by virtue of its wit and hilarity, there lies a deep conviction in the power of the oblique – of the lateral – as a strategy (both pragmatic and philosophical) to find that instant of playful aliveness in the moment of performance. Solutions are to be found the less directly, urgently and forcefully you look for them. In other words, although he rarely uses the term, it is intuition which is the driving motor of decision making, and this is an embodied rather than purely cognitive response to the challenge of playing.

In his provocative, poetic and insightful Ph.D. thesis, Australian performer and academic Barry Laing compares Gaulier's preoccupation with lightness to the ideas of Italo Calvino:

(Laing 2002: 170)

Calvino proclaims 'lightness', in literature and in life, as a principle and a virtue. His strategy is the removal of 'weight' – from language, the structure of stories, and the world of literalisms and rationalisations. His method, which he outlines via the Medusa myth, is the application of a precise but *indirect* vision . . . Calvino opposes what he calls this 'lightness of thoughtfulness' to the weight, inertia, noise and opacity of the world. Such lightness and a refusal to look directly, is not a refusal of the world, or our place in it.

Later, in elaborating what he grasps of Gaulier's *lightness*, Laing writes:

(Ibid.: 171)

This is part of his stringent refusal and deprecation of the performer 'knowing too much'. . . . It might be possible to say that Gaulier's assumption could be that the performer's 'self/ego' . . . too often 'identifies' with the task or text, with all of its received associations and traces of normalising assumptions and judgments. These carry 'weight'.

. . .

Gaulier's strategy to defy such mass and 'gravity' is to invoke, provoke and address the task via the *pleasure of the performer*. The pleasure of the *performer* – as distinct from, though not opposed to, the 'character' – contains all the lightness and tactics of game playing.

We conclude by reiterating a sentiment of Gaulier's that is often quoted, but that would receive affirmation from two other key – but very different – figures of contemporary physical and visual theatres, Tim Etchells and Simon McBurney:

(Gaulier quoted by Wright 1990: 9)

I am not interested in truth. Truth is for the Salvation Army. I like to see lies on stage. I would far sooner have dinner with people who lie. They are so funny.

Joan Littlewood and the Theatre Workshop

Joan Littlewood (1914–2002) fits properly but uneasily alongside these other teacher-practitioners. Any awkwardness one might feel about placing Littlewood in this chapter rests on some uncertainty as to whether her practice represents a legacy that still has force today for, although she only died in 2002, her work as active practitioner more or less ceased in the late 1960s. Moreover, like many of the figures profiled here, Littlewood would have been uninterested in, if not disdainful of, being pigeon-holed into practices labelled 'physical theatres'. None the less, any scrutiny of her work, directing, teaching and rehearsal methods reveals a practitioner-teacher who worked seriously and forcefully with actors' bodies, and whose productions were – at their best – highly disciplined examples of theatre which communicated itself primarily through visual and physical languages. Furthermore, Littlewood remains the only British theatre director and teacher to have a drama school dedicated to the continuation of her vision. East 15 was founded in 1961 to continue the approaches and working methods of her Theatre Workshop at Stratford in East London.

Like Lecoq and Gaulier, for example, Littlewood had little interest in claiming a method, or in formulating her practice through theories which offered a concise and timeless statement of her working methods. To have indulged in such activities would have run counter to her persona as an anti-authoritarian socialist who was deeply committed to notions of the collective and ensemble as organising principles, and who favoured a rumbustious anarchic spirit over saintly or worthy self-reflection. She also possessed a stringent intellect and was ready to impose her directorial voice whenever she felt it was necessary. Littlewood fits well into the thematics of this book because she had robust views on the physical training of actors, was deeply preoccupied with creative strategies around ensemble playing, and remained committed throughout her working life to experimentation with form and style. These consistent features of her practice were always framed and contextualised by her socialist politics and a commitment to making theatre which aspired to speak to and of the lives of working-class men and women.

Littlewood's approach to theatre making may be characterised by a number of key features:

- rigorous physical and vocal training
- improvisation and play as creative tools to release the actor, and as a method of generating material
- a reliance on intuition as a dynamic force for the actor's decision making and as a method for driving rehearsals
- ensemble playing as the ultimate goal for all members of her company.

Littlewood drew heavily on the ideas of Rudolph Laban to improve her actor's physical fluidity and articulacy, and in 1948 invited Jean Newlove, Laban's assistant, to join the company to run daily movement classes. By using Laban's analysis of the four main components of movement – space, time, effort and energy – Littlewood hoped to give her actors an embodied confidence and corporeal clarity that would inform their physical characterisation, use of space and handling of materials (props). In a less tangible way, Laban's methods would also develop the actors' sensitivity to rhythm as a driving motor towards achieving ensemble.

For Littlewood, attention to physical training served not only as an actor's generic preparation for the kind of psycho-physical openness needed in a creative rehearsal period, but also in terms of precise and concrete detail so as to extend a performer's range, accuracy and depth in characterisation and gestural choreography. For both these objectives, Littlewood was also influenced by Meyerhold's biomechanics and Jacques-Dalcroze's *Eurhythmics* as methods to enhance the actor's self-awareness and economy of movement. Nadine Holdsworth identifies how Littlewood drew on *Eurhythmics* in her classes and rehearsal sessions:

(Holdsworth 2006: 56)

Littlewood . . . explored how the actor could control and manipulate different rhythms individually and in tandem with other actors. She ran training classes asking participants to complete movement tasks such as walking, skipping and using a pickaxe while responding to rhythmic beats; and incorporated pair work involving couples walking, hopping and running in rhythmic synchronicity. This work encouraged a subtle awareness of how shifting rhythms could alter stage dynamics.

There are a number of other remarkable congruencies between Littlewood's commitment to play and improvisation as the driving motors of a performer's creativity and pedagogies developed later by figures such as Jacques Lecoq and Philippe Gaulier. These connections are 'remarkable' in that there is little evidence that either Lecoq or Gaulier drew explicitly on Littlewood's methods, or that the latter was much aware of Lecoq's early work, either as a choreographer and director, or of the first decades of the Paris school. What these linkages do reveal – and reinforce – are the subtle but sometimes self-consciously explicit and interlocking legacies of Meyerhold, Stanislavsky, Laban and Copeau for a variety of contemporary practices.

Littlewood's use of games and improvisations served a number of purposes, the most important of which were on the one hand 'to develop initiative, excite curiosity, exercise the imagination' (Littlewood 1994: 199) and, on the other, to forge the shape of the production and the acting within it. While games to 'exercise the imagination' are the stock in trade of many contemporary theatre teachers, in 1940s and 1950s Britain they were virtually unheard of. Again, however, we can detect the legacy of, for example, Meyerhold and Copeau. Littlewood's disposition towards ensuring that theatre making should never become too self-referentially worthy allowed her to marry this sense of play with some of Laban's more technical approaches to movement training. Clive Barker, once a member of the Theatre Workshop, makes this point clearly:

(Barker 2000: 119)

The games and exercises became a laboratory through which Littlewood was able to explore such qualities as time, weight, direction and flow – the qualities through which Laban characterised all movements. It was also the process through which the rhythmic patterns of the performance were established. . . . complex interweavings of the individual actor's rhythms into the jazz ensemble.

Like Simon McBurney, Complicité's artistic director, Littlewood was often unwilling to separate 'technical' movement training from strategies for developing an actor's creativity, and from the actual process of composition and rehearsal. One imagines that Littlewood would have subscribed to McBurney's articulation of his rehearsal and creative process:

(McBurney 1992)

The structure is much more of a cross between a sculptor and a football team where I will simply be trying to lead people from a game into an exercise – a physical exercise to build up their strength – into another game, which leads into a scene, and from out of the scene . . . so they hardly know when they are in a scene or not in a scene.

Etienne Decroux

If mime survives, the world will survive

One does not modernise a monument in order to conserve it. One must therefore conserve the body which was strong, skilful, ascetic. What will conserve it? Sport is not one of the beaux arts. One gives oneself to it only to vanquish others. Dance is not a portrait of struggle. Old fashioned pantomime is not an art of the body. Corporeal mime is more than a diversion. If it survives, the world will survive.

(Etienne Decroux, *Paroles sur le mime*, quoted by Tom Leabhart in *Total Theatre*, 9(2), 1997: 17)

The influence of Etienne Decroux (1898–1992) (*PT:R*) on contemporary British physical theatres is, for a variety of reasons, less marked than that of Jacques Lecoq. Together, however, their teaching practices and aspirations for a re-invented, vibrant and corporeal form of theatre encapsulate most of the conflicting philosophies and methodologies around both the training of the actor, and the forms of theatre that this preparation would serve. Although Decroux is a pivotal figure in the histories of 150 years of French theatre and mime, linking Jean-Gaspard Debureau, Jacques Copeau, Charles Dullin, Jean-Louis Barrault, Marcel Marceau and Jacques Lecoq, in terms of models of performer training there is a closer affinity to Grotowski and Barba than to the other key figures who feature in this section. Eugenio Barba, who finds in Decroux strong resonances with his own practice, connects the French teacher to the conventions and discipline of Eastern teaching techniques:

in the same way that a Kabuki actor can ignore the best 'secrets' of Noh, it is symptomatic that Etienne Decroux, perhaps the only European master to have elaborated a system of rules comparable to that of an oriental tradition, seeks to transmit to his students the same rigorous closedness to theatre forms different from his own.

(Barba 1982: 6)

Barba's observation takes us to the heart of Decroux's teaching which is evidently significantly different from, say, Littlewood, Gaulier, Dodin or Lecoq. Decroux's lifelong commitment was to develop and refine a vocabulary and systematic technique for the performer which would establish mime as an autonomous art, formally independent of both dance and theatre. Not for Decroux selective interrogations of different performance histories in order to construct a new theatre order; rather the building from a *point zero* of a new dramatic form – mime – with its own unique grammar and language. Sensitive to mid-twentieth-century aesthetic theory in the visual arts, and deeply influenced by Cubism, Mondrian and Brancusi, Decroux sought a mime grammar that would allow the body to speak 'a vocabulary of set legible movements that would be easily transmissible from master mime to student' (Felner 1985: 58).

Jean-Louis Barrault, the French mime, actor and theatre director, became Decroux's first pupil in 1931 when they embarked on an iconic moment of what in 2007 might have been labelled 'practice as research'. Together, for two years in a studio in Paris' Théâtre de l'Atelier they constructed the revolutionary world of 'Promethean' mime. Tom Leabhart, much later a student of Decroux, describes their process:

(Leabhart 1989: 41)

> for two years they were inseparable: nudists, vegetarians, 'accomplices in search of a new mime' (Barrault 1972: 72).
> . . . Decroux sat and wrote as Barrault improvised – Decroux the analytical codifier, the reasoner; Barrault intuitive, creative and mystical.

This brief account may suggest that Decroux and his practice are of interest only to the archivist and theatre historian. However, his inclusion in this chapter is partly due to the contrast his philosophy and practice pose to the less austere but no less demanding pedagogy of Jacques Lecoq, but also because his legacy continues to have an important impact today on a small but significant body of practices within mime and physical theatres. Apart from a number of contemporary companies whose work has been explicitly and unapologetically constructed upon Decroux's *grammaire* (for example, Théâtre du Mouvement, the Margolis Brown Performance Company, Griftheater, and Théâtre de L'Ange Fou) the essential principles of his teaching have been the dominant force in Desmond Jones' School of Mime and Physical Theatre, and within the training practices of theatre artists such as David Glass. David Glass' early work as a solo artist was deeply shaped by his own corporeal mastery of Decroux's techniques for the control, isolation and punctuation of muscular movements. For Glass, at least in the early stages of his career, working with Decroux's grammar, both on his own performing body and on other professional actors whom he taught or directed, was both a physical discipline and to provide a compositional vocabulary for the making of material. For Glass, Jones and those practitioners whose work is explicitly constructed upon his codification of movement, Decroux provided a set of embodied principles around, for example:

- attention to the spine, its flexibility and well-being
- equilibrium and disequilibrium
- expressive potential of the whole body rather than just face and limbs
- stillness, silence and fixed point
- control and isolation of muscles and muscle groups
- *contrepoids* – 'a tangible muscular compensation for intangible imaginary forces' (Felner 1985: 57)
- *raccourci* – literally a foreshortening, but this is 'evidently not a lessening, shrinking or stylization. It is the condensation of an idea in space and time' (Dorcy 1958: 66).

The critical and significant difference between Decroux and other figures featured in this chapter lies in his single-minded dedication to the construction of an all-embracing and codified language of movement that would both represent the *totality* of the performer's craft and be sufficient for the composition and dramaturgy of the creative process. In this respect Decroux is a remarkable and singular figure in the practices and pedagogies of contemporary physical theatres, but is in many ways out of step with the temper of the times. Of the liberating qualities of a codified technique Decroux wrote:

> My teaching is the breaking apart of the natural and the composition of the ideal. . . . We would like, therefore, for the mime's body to be to the mime as the keyboard is to the pianist . . . technique neither paralyses nor sterilises inspiration, but, on the contrary aids its birth, excites it.

(Decroux [1972] in Leabhart 1989: 57)

Decroux's teaching required enormous reserves of self-discipline and commitment on the part of his students. He envisaged that four years (full time) was the minimum training period for mastery of his techniques. He demanded complete loyalty, less to himself as a master teacher, but more to the codified art form he had researched and meticulously developed over five decades of teaching. A socialist who hid a Russian anarchist in his Paris cellar from the Gestapo during the Second World War, Decroux was part of the early/mid-twentieth-century *Paris Moderne* movement (Rosenberg 1965: 89) which from a total repudiation of naturalism sought a synthesis between art, politics, contemporary science and psychology in order to identify and forge new forms and practices. Corporeal mime was just that form for Decroux. Popularised by his most illustrious pupil, Marcel Marceau, whom he subsequently disavowed, Decroux's codification of movement to create a mime *grammaire* remains authoritative today among only a relatively small band of theatre or mime artists. The key corporeal principles and insights of his research and pedagogy, however, continue to be influential for a significant number of physical theatre practitioners who, while unwilling to embrace the totality of Decroux's project for a *Promethean mime*, find the application of selected aspects of his technical vocabulary a productive preparation for movement theatres.

Afterwords

This chapter has scanned the territory of training and preparation for physical theatres, and approaches to acting particularly predisposed to heightening the corporeal dimensions of performance. We have also focused on the different ways in which these pedagogies have been delivered throughout the twentieth century in the belief that particular organisational models for the preparation of actors have had a significant impact on contemporary forms of physical theatre practice. The short case studies of selected theatre practitioner-teachers, many of whom are (or were) also directors and actors, have illuminated creative tensions and debates between informal and formal modes of training, and between codification of extra daily corporeal techniques, and an embrace of more generic forms of psycho-physical preparation. Varying approaches to training and preparation enshrine, whether consciously or not, different models of the body's construction and behaviour on the one hand, and diverse visions and aspirations for theatre practice on the other. All these key figures, however, ascribe to the belief that learning and preparation are inseparable from the making and performing of physical theatres.

Words on mime

- Everything is allowed in art, provided it is done intentionally. And since man's body is the medium of our art, it must be his body that imitates thought.
- Since we concede to the dancer that the mime lacks lightness, he must concede to us that he, the dancer, lacks weight.
- Dance is an evasion, mime is an invasion.
- Between speaker and mime there is sometimes enmity; between dancer and mime there is always treachery.
- The trunk is more important than the arms and legs.
- The body is a glove whose finger is thought.
- If the marionette is, at least, the image of the ideal actor, we must consequently try to acquire the virtues of the ideal marionette.

(Etienne Decroux, 'Words on Mime', *Mime Journal*, 1985)

CHAPTER 5

Physicality and the Word

Beyond bourgeois drama

Q.   What do you perceive to be the relationship between text and performance physicality?

A.   . . . This thing about text based theatre lacking in visual physicality or dynamic physicality is not really true, once you broaden your focus beyond 20th century bourgeois English drama. What is happening now is a return to a more normal, synthetic art form that theatre has always been.

(Pete Brooks 1993, in conversation with Sarah Dawson, *Total Theatre* 5(2))

Given our insistence that all theatre is physical, it may be fairly asked: 'What is the point of this chapter'? Perhaps, we can answer as follows. It is the physical and visual signs of stance, gesture, angle, movement, juxtaposition and scenography that work *with* the word within the overall *mise-en-scène*. Yet words dominate our theatres (and film/television) for the great majority of practitioners and audience, even when these are described or categorised as 'physical theatre'. Perhaps this dominance helps explain the still uneasy relationship between words, body and scenography in contemporary theatres, with the latter two still in 'Cinderella' role, despite Pete Brooks' optimism.

The following are extracts from reviews of the Royal National Theatre's production of Peter Schaffer's *The Royal Hunt of the Sun* (London, 2006):

(Charles Spencer,
Daily Telegraph,
13 April 2006)

The years have not been kind to *The Royal Hunt of the Sun* . . . [in 1964] its parade of 'total theatre' with exotic music, mime sequences and spectacular stage devices . . . must have seemed fresh and original . . . [these days] attempting to depict a mountain range like the Andes with the help of a few white sheets has become one of the clichés of physical theatre productions . . . the windiness of the writing is often matched by a curiously lumbering production full of empty displays of ritual, dodgy choreography and naff mime sequences . . . in which 20 men pretend to be crossing a wobbly bridge.

(Natasha Tripney,
www.musicomh.
com/theatre)

The techniques of physical theatre are now fairly commonplace, but in a more evolved form than what we see here . . . the massacre scene when it comes, with its strobe lighting, slow-motion mime and use of a billowing red cloth to symbolise bloodshed, feels rather dated.

(Paul Taylor,
The Independent,
14 April 2006)

the men sway and toil between blue-lit sheets to evoke the slog up the mountains . . . in a production that is old-fashioned in stage-craft and style.

The purpose of these quotes is not to make cheap remarks about a particular production but to highlight certain salient points:

- The terms 'physical theatre' and 'total theatre' are used in such ways as to assume a knowledge and recognition in the reader. This matches the assumption, in the use of such staging, that the audience will recognise the devices and techniques with a familiarity that allows them to accept and read the images intended rather than be alienated by these.
- Despite 42 years of training in the use of such techniques, these are being so poorly used in a mainstream, text-based play as to require comment.
- We should now take the techniques of 'physical-total theatre' as a given in our theatres and expect to see these done well as part of the *mise-en-scène*.

However, that such attention is given to these corporeal shortcomings must also alert us to the fact they are still so remarkable as to demand such comment. In other words, 'physical-total-visual theatre', despite its apparent widespread use, is in fact less common than it seems, and when presented still faces the same quality issues of skills and staging, acting and performing as in any theatre, mainstream and otherwise. What Peter Brook characterised as 'deadly theatre' is still an affliction.

The purpose of this chapter then is to look at the physical in theatre which is categorised as 'word-based', to argue that other elements of theatre need to be given equal weight to that ascribed to the word. If this argument for a rebalancing seems like stating the obvious then we would simply point to the overwhelming sense of 'deadly' disappointment (as Brook argues) still experienced in the non-verbal elements of theatre being produced. The dominance given to and taken by the spoken text continues to distort the possibilities of theatre (and drama in other media). We are not seeking to denigrate words, nor arguing that gestures replace them. Words best articulate ideas and meanings with a particularity and focus not available to the non-verbal. But we do wish to reiterate that the word is only one of the constituent sign systems in a dialectic that is the complete performance text, *mise-en-scène*, and experience of theatre as a totality. Our concern is to realise the potential of the multidimensional qualities of theatre rather than the dominant dimension of the word.

This may be regarded as the physical dramaturgy of the play-performance text; perhaps the physical dimension of Brecht's wider notion of gestus – the physical, social and critical attitude of the actor towards character, and of the character towards the action or situation, shown physically. Of course, a particular signifying system may take prominence at any particular point or passage of the performance text; the dialectic is not pure but an always present *agon*, or conflict of the parts in creative tension. It should be noted that the terms used here are ones of convenience and convention. Virtually all plays, even those which cast themselves against the mainstreams of the classical traditions or realism-naturalism – for example, the avant gardes already discussed – are script based; coming from a single author and intended for production in the declared style. But dramaturgically we must distinguish between the play text and the performance text of the *mise-en-scène*. To avoid clumsy repetition, the former will be referred to simply as the 'text' – the common shorthand – and the latter term used where necessary.

Our primary concern is with the performance text as it is on the stage where the physical-visual aspects of the play text are made concrete.

Against a hierarchy of theatre languages

In the essay already cited, Kowzan, in his taxonomy of theatre, defines 13 auditory or visual sign systems. Eight of these are centred on the actor, and five outside. The result of this is to put the speaking actor at the peak of a hierarchy of theatrical sign systems. Not only does Kowzan's taxonomy leave out an equally vital component of theatre – the audience, the fourteenth sign system that defines theatre – but it paradoxically turns on its head the fact that the actor/performer is already a physical-visual presence. As *actant* (see Chapter 2) the actor/performer begins to communicate possible meanings, clues, connotations, before speaking. S/he is a physical-visual function and site of significance before a phonic one. While the *actant* is at the centre of the performance text, this should be seen as the centre; thus Kowzan's sign systems should be grouped around the actor as well as connected to each other to denote the interactive nature of theatre – all elements acting on and with each other.

Again this is not to denigrate words and their speaking, simply to reshape and realign the relationship of the elements of theatre to each other. By opposing word and non-word we simply see another crude dualism which puts intellect above the corporeal, rather than in a healthy and creative dialectical relationship.

By looking at a number of examples of dramatic texts from a variety of styles, forms and eras we hope to illustrate some of the ways in which the physical in theatre may work as part of this dialectic; what we refer to as the 'physical dramaturgy' of any piece. This is to give weight to the proposition that to talk of physical theatre is simply to talk of theatre in its proper sense. Thus issues such as counterpoint, silence and stillness, the audience and the curtain call, realism, and improvisation will be considered as further principles of the physical in relation to theatre. Two further examples from reviews help illustrate these:

(Lyn Gardner, *Guardian*, 14 August 2006)

Hysteria, Edinburgh, 2006

Nervous chatter . . . turns to anxiety that dissolves into hysteria and temporary madness, all watched over calmly by a silent waiter who had seen it all before. . . . The beauty here is not just in the smart script or the precision of the physical work and the way the company meld the two, but in the truthfulness and detail of the observation.

(John Keefe, 1998, *Total Theatre* 10(3))

The Possessed, London, 1998

It is an interactive exchange of aural, musical, physical and visual elements . . . a stunning theatre of human existence and realism . . . there are explosions of energy, of physical images interacting with the words not merely illustrating them, of physical and visual counterpoint . . . An opening fifteen minute monologue is delivered with a centred physical stillness and articulation (not static gesturing) which is counter-pointed by a still, silent, present listening figure.

Agamemnon: the morning watch

We return again to the origins of modern European theatre in the Greek amphitheatre. This is the opening of *Agamemnon*:

(Aeschylus 1953: 35)

l.1   I ask the gods some respite from the weariness of this watchtime measured by years I lie awake elbowed upon the Atreidae's roof dogwise to mark the grand processionals of all the stars of the night . . .

l.8   I wait; to read the meaning in that beacon light, a blaze of fire to carry out of Troy the rumour and outcry of its capture . . .

l.12 Now as this bed stricken with night and drenched with dew I keep . . .

l.21 Oh hail, blaze of the darkness . . . this beacon.

As we saw in Chapter 2, Greek theatre contains its stage directions within the text in such ways that not only is this a theatre of the imagination, but also a theatre of knowledge predicated on the audience (already) knowing the stories and legends being re-presented. The audience know that the action is located in Argos and what happens to the royal family, but here the picture is given detail; we know we are at the palace of the House of Atreus at Argos from the watchman's reference to the 'Atreidae's roof', that it is near dawn (the 'dew'), what he is doing there and so on.

But the acting requirements are also set out; to avoid banal contradiction the actor/watchman must be lying propped on his elbow as he bemoans his task. Directors tend to dislike being 'dictated to' by the text but there must be a minimum compliance with the requirements of that text. To have the actor standing makes a nonsense of the watchman's stated position; to do so means rewriting the words or ignoring them.

The skills of the actor here are to make such an awkward stance interesting, to give the watchman presence as he struggles to comply with his orders. The actor can leap up as the watchman sees the blaze of the beacon at line 21. Thus, Aeschylus gives 20 lines to the actor so as to locate us and to give context to the watchman's physical situation and his state of body and mind. These 20 lines allow us to have empathy and to recognise his situation as embodied, psychological and emotional mimesis.

Mimetic realism has its limits in the original staging. Thus at lines 1343 and 1345 Agamemnon inside the palace cries out: 'Ah, I am struck a deadly blow'. His body is then disclosed to the audience (l.1370) framed in the open doors of the palace. Death is done offstage – **diegetic** space – and then shown as mimetic tableau.

The existing text does not give any written indications as to Clytaemestra's stance or gestures as she appears in the tableau, except to tell us that 'I stand now where I struck him down' (l.1379) and how she struck him three times. Does she mime the murders as she describes them, stand with a still presence reciting the events, gesticulate histrionically in a kind of empty physicality, or gesture in a form of modern realism?

What is the meaning of 'creative staging' in such theatre circumstances and conventions?

(But, as we shall see, when looking at comedy a quite different set of rules then apply. Like the popular traditions already discussed, so comedy has a freedom of staging and expression denied to tragedy and 'serious' drama, albeit still within certain institutional conventions.)

Modern theatre demands a much more explicit and graphic rendering of the murder, often seduced by spectacle which supplants other more significant elements of *mise-en-scène* with the 'wrong' kind of physicality. Perhaps for modern theatre the issue is one of balance between the physical-visual integrity of the author's textual intentions, the appropriate creative skills of the actors/director/designer in making the performance text, and avoiding the hollow physical-visual spectacle that results from an inappropriate or misguided application of these skills. Finding this balance raises crucial questions and tensions about dramaturgy and the integrity of the text.

We suggest that the heart of text-based theatre is the actor's body and voice interpreting and delivering the author's words, and the spectator hearing and interpreting and understanding those words, via the inflections and tones of the speaking body.

It is both a visual (we see the speaker) and a physical (speaking-hearing) phenomenon; a rather strange exchange as the listener has no direct influence on how and what things are spoken. But it is an exchange, nevertheless, as the listener gives attention to what is seen and said, responds to the actor with attention, and with a particular form of participation. It is the balance between the seen and said that the actor must maintain, not slipping into a hierarchy of what is said over what is seen. Unless a person is deprived of one or other (or both) senses, the voice and the eyes together are part of both body and mind, working together in the delivery and the reception of the author's words as part of the larger stage picture.

Difficulties arise when verbal, visual and physical languages are separated, or placed in a false hierarchy. That deadening effect when words being spoken are delivered by a static actor who locates his/her physical and visual focus merely on the speaking face. (See discussion on neutral mask in chapters 2 and 4.)

The acts of speaking and hearing are fundamentally physiological; the product of an evolution that allows air pressure, vocal folds and tract, larynx, ear canal and drum to act together to produce vibrations that emerge and are heard as sounds and words. As the body of a child develops, so the production of sounds becomes the construction of words. But this awareness of voice begins pre-birth. The foetus reacts to sounds and voices from 14 weeks' gestation, with a particular recognition of its mother's voice reflected in a change in heart rate. It appears that this sensitivity to sound carries over into the new-born baby with its continuing recognition and response to the mother's voice (and with a marked preference for the mother's voice over the father's).

The eyes are equally physiological in operation; the foetus is sensitive to strong differences of light and dark, the new-born is very quickly responsive to movement, and within four weeks will recognise and respond to the mother's eye contact. As mirror neurons provide the innate physiological basis of empathy, so the foetus and new-born child have instinctive desires, impulses and capacities to communicate vocally and visually. A cry is pitched at the wavelength to which the mother is most sensitive, and eyes attract the parent's warmth with a smile or other facial expression.

As we have suggested, these innate capabilities are the basis for the encultured and socialised formation and development of the child's capabilities and potentials. These are then reflected in the empathetic responses to what we see and what we hear in the processes of mimesis in the theatre.

Tiny gestures of solidarity and exquisite tenderness

Like these women's friendship, the play happens almost entirely in the silences between the 121 words of text. It is like dropping a pebble into a well and hearing a distant splash that reverberates for eternity. At the end, the women clasp hands, a tiny gesture of solidarity and exquisite tenderness. It is such a fruitless defence against a merciless world that it makes you want to weep.

(Lyn Gardner (2006), reviewing Samuel Beckett's 'Come and Go', *Guardian,* 4 April)

Thus returning to the examples from *Agamemnon*, we see two forms of physical mimesis within the conventions of Greek tragedy: a degree of 'everyman' authenticity in the watchman's posture, recognised by sight; and world-weariness in the tones of his voice, recognised aurally, which support the meanings and intentions of the words once heard within a 'realistic' situation. Second, the degree of heightened authenticity in the posed posture and stylised speech patterns of Clytaemestra as she stands over Agamemnon's body in a recognisable but not 'realistic' situation. But in both cases we recognise and empathise with the human reality of two very different bodies in their respective situations.

Realism and the *realistic*

Perhaps we need to accept the complex tensions and dynamics found in the 'realistic' and 'realism' in order to develop this discussion of the physical in text-based theatre. Most fundamentally all drama, in whatever form, genre or medium, is *realistic* in that it is about the human and human life. We will recognise this as such, however far removed from literal resemblance the image may be. In this sense the plays of Aeschylus are as realistic as those of Ibsen or Beckett.

But the term is also used as a kind of shorthand for what we accept as instantly familiar or unfamiliar; in other words, the degree of realism or authenticity or verisimilitude. With the rise of the stage picture as a (photographic-like) reproduction of the human world (a given present, a researched-imagined past, or imagined-projected future) rather than a representation, so realism becomes something to strive for in terms of scenography. Moreover, within the dominant norms it is a mark of the acceptability (or otherwise) of the drama.

Thus 'realistic' and 'realism' are conceptual and ideological constructions as well as empirical states. With the rise and continuing dominance of realism-naturalism, these have become equated with what is the norm for theatre (and film and television); a hierarchy of signifying systems with verbal, psychological, physical and emotional truth at the top of this pyramid. We arrive back at Kowzan's pecking order by another route.

In this hegemony the physical and the visual are given second place as support for such truth, often presented as mimetically familiar at the most superficial and apparently least demanding level. But the realistic and realism when properly used and staged can be as confronting and challenging as the most avant garde text and production, sometimes more so.

The difficulty here lies with the psychological impulse to relate to a piece of work by making it familiar and comfortable; familiarity becomes its own enemy. In this way a disturbing piece of avant garde theatre may be flattened out, a piece of morally challenging family or social drama is turned into the comforting and predictable pleasantries of soap opera.

This same impulse to familiarity manifests itself in other ways; in the rewriting of texts to make them more 'relevant' through the use of modern or colloquial language at the cost of creating period anomalies or contradictions. Or productions can treat all texts as forms of realism with a subsequent flattening to a homogeneous acting/staging style.

To confront this impulse in the actor, the director, the spectator, we have to take Brecht's dictum 'to make the familiar strange and the strange familiar' (estranging) away from its epic context and argue that this should be the task and responsibility of all

Figure 5.1–5.6 *Footfalls* (1976) Billie Whitelaw. Royal Court Theatre, London. Writer/director: Samuel Beckett. Designer: Jocelyn Herbert.   Photos: John Haynes

drama, in any form, style or genre. Thus, rather than an (opposing) distinction between *plaisir* – the comfortable ease of the classic text – and *jouissance* – the frisson of pleasure that comes from the unsettling, the new – it is a tension of pleasure that comes from safe risk.

If a familiar piece only keeps us at ease then it fails to help us rethink our world, the world. But if presented properly, with estrangement, it can jolt us. If a piece fails to make the strange familiar, then it fails to communicate and thus fails in its intention of presenting a radical view from which we can have the pleasure of learning. To achieve this estranging, the physical and visual dimensions must play their part in counterpointing the word.

Space as 'silent character'

We wish to illustrate these issues raised above by looking at a small number of examples from a range of texts, where in some cases familiarity may almost breed contempt. But the text, in fact, requires a performance or staging which allows that familiarity to be made strange by playing with the physical and visual signifiers – the physical dramaturgy already referred to.

Figure 5.7 *Mother Courage* (1949, Berlin) (Bertold Brecht) 'Mother Courage prepares to pull her wagon alone', Helene Weigel.   Copyright: Ruth Berlau Estate/Hilda Hoffmann. Photo: Heiner Hill

(Ibsen 1985: 27)

From Ibsen's *Ghosts*

A spacious garden-room, with a door in the left-hand wall and two doors in the right-hand wall. In the centre of the room is a round table with chairs around it; on the table are books, magazines and newspapers. Downstage left is a window, in front of which is a small sofa with a sewing table by it. Backstage the room opens out into a slightly narrower conservatory, with walls of large panes of glass. In the right-hand wall of the conservatory is a door leading down to the garden. Through the glass wall a gloomy fjord landscape is discernible, veiled by steady rain.

The play text of Henrik Ibsen's *Ghosts* begins with this very detailed description of the room in which the whole action of the play will take place. This is the scenographic mimetic space which should not merely be a photographic reproduction of a middle-class garden-room conservatory, but also stands for the emotionally stunted and physically frustrated state of the characters' lives.

The conventions of nineteenth-century staging would be that the curtain reveals room and characters at the same time, but a staging that arguably reveals Ibsen's greater intentions would allow the room to establish itself gradually in the mind's eye of the spectators as the physical-visual 'character' it surely is, *before* any words are spoken.

Thus Ibsen's ironic joke that we should see Regina watering the plants in the conservatory against a backdrop of steady rain with the *liminal* garden door both shutting out Nature yet being the threshold to it; a rain that must fall for the whole of the first act (as the dialogue keeps telling us), not just for opening 'spot effects'. The audience must become irritated by the sound of the rain so that it is hit by the silence of its cessation at the opening of Act Two. Ibsen wishes us to participate through our senses. The business of watering the plants is no more than that, but it allows us to take in the room.

Its 'spaciousness' will gradually contrast to the closed, stunted quality of the lives of the Alving family. Ibsen also requires a centrally placed table around which the action flows and confrontations occur. This staging instruction is deliberate and carefully calibrated to irritate the characters – and therefore us. Crucially Ibsen has sited the table so that the actors become physical in their characterisation as they navigate the room and around the table. This room therefore becomes as much a 'character' as Pastor Manders or Mrs Alving.

No indication is given as to how long Regina simply has to water the plants, but it must allow the actress time to establish the physical characterisation of the role. This has to convey an attractiveness, sexual aura and psychological strength that both attracts Manders and Oswald, *and* allows her to walk out of the house to follow her own desires. All without words expressed through the articulate body.

The staid quality of the room is again played with by Ibsen in Act One when we see Regina flirting with Manders. The (relatively) overt sexuality projected by Regina as she preens and displays is in ironic contrast to the bourgeois values represented by the room, and to the denial of Nature represented by the conservatory. The scenography outlined by Ibsen is a signifying system in itself and not the mere quiescent setting as so often imposed by his interpreters: an interior that is a corset around an ever-present violence.

It is vital that the room be allowed to establish itself in our consciousness both as a familiar mimetic space and in these symbolic-metaphoric ways, because two pages before the play closes, the room is 'on-stage' by itself. Mrs Alving and Oswald leave for a few seconds, going into the diegetic space of the hallway. We now see the room, on the cusp of dawn, not as a catalyst to new life (cf. the hotel room in *Awakening* by Stramm investigated later), but as the monument to the failure of new life. It will be seen as a *womb-become-tomb* since our original 'look' has now become mediated by the knowledge we have received from the play as it has unfolded in front of us.

Articulate stillness

Referring back to the earlier point about elements of the play being in a creative 'contest' – an *agon* – with each other, in these Ibsen passages we have seen the room itself taking on a prominence within the performance text. In the next example it is the body alone which takes this position.

Anton Chekhov's *Three Sisters* also opens in a specific setting, but although our concern here is with the physicality of the characters it shares the same staging question posed by the opening of *Ghosts*: What is the duration of the action before words, of the image working on us by the physical-visual body alone?

(Chekhov 1983: 1)

> The interior of the Prozorov's house. The drawing-room, with a colonnade beyond which the main reception room can be seen. It is noon, and the day is bright and cheerful. The table in the big room beyond is being laid for lunch. OLGA, who is wearing the dark blue dress laid down for a teacher in a girls' high school, stands correcting exercise books the whole time – walks up and down correcting them. MASHA, in a black dress, her hat in her lap, sits reading a book. IRINA, in white, stands lost in her own thoughts.

Like *Ghosts*, *Three Sisters* locates us in a middle-class house with presumably all the usual accoutrements of such a household. Although Chekhov is less detailed than Ibsen in his textual description, what is specified is the time of day (the clock strikes 12), and that the day is 'bright and cheerful'; again for ironic effect as a counterpoint to the humour of Olga's opening line.

There is some servant business, but here it is in the background as a counterpoint – an important detail as shall be seen. However, the key point about this opening is the choreography of quiet intense movement and – equally – quiet intense stillness. Characters both standing and sitting. We are given no indications of the placing and juxtaposition of the sisters, or what Masha is sitting on. These are decisions of detail which any staging has to settle, but in such a way as to serve Chekhov's purpose – to allow the physical and visual aspects of the *mise-en-scène* to work on the spectator before the words are uttered, and out of which the words will take on a humour of pathos, sadness and loss.

Behind this foregrounded image the table is being quietly prepared for lunch; not with a false bustle and noise which a superficial realism might demand in a staging that does not trust the audience, but as a visual counterpoint to the postures of the sisters. Image and atmosphere are shortly to be broken by the intrusion of the officers. Chekhov is seeking a different realism here – one of atmosphere and spiritual/sexual desolation – which, like Ibsen, depends on trusting the audience with a duration of image and quiet action. How long can the actresses create and hold this image so that it may act on the audience? How long can we watch it?

We may regard this opening passage of the performance text as a piece of 'physical theatre' within the meanings of this term as we are discussing it. No words, with the body of the *actant* being given prominence, given presence as the character, not the performer. As a device it prefigures the use of still, silent counterpoint illustrated in the review of *The Possessed* cited on p. 162.

In terms of physical theatre, this is the skill and technique that differentiates the static body – one that is not moving, is lifeless and lacks presence – and the still body – one that is not moving yet remains dynamic, articulate and with presence intact. With the still body, the image may be sustained as the ground upon which the dialogue may rest and be in counterpoint to so long as the staging and audience can bear it. In this case the body of the character is not only still but also silent, yet remains dynamic.

We cannot have movement without stillness, we cannot have sound or words without silence. Both physical stillness and silence have to sustain a dynamic presence if the words and movement around these are to have any meaning beyond the colloquial. Musician and performance artist John Cage (1912–1992) particularly challenged assumptions about sound and silence through his iconic composition *4' 33"* (1952). For Cage music needed to be liberated from the shackling conventions of the nineteenth century: 'a healthy lawlessness is warranted. Experiment must be carried out by hitting everything' (Cage 2002: 135).

The art of silence

Even in productions with words there are silences during which the actor meditates and develops; long moments during which the text is of no value and in which the actor creates emotion through the way he acts. Does the converse exist?

Have we ever, for even a second, heard a text without the speaker? Never, of course.

The only art unceasingly present on the stage is therefore the art of the actor.

(Etienne Decroux (1985), 'Words on Mime', Mime Journal: 25)

But, to Decroux's dictum, 'to be on stage, you must have something to say' (Dennis 1995:7) we might add the concomitant, 'when on stage always be saying something, be present, with the body'.

In the case of *Three Sisters*, the stillness and silence must have duration enough for the audience to feel and respond to. It is not simply about *recognising* the social and personal situations of the sisters shown through the physically (and hence emotionally and psychologically) articulate body of the actress. Chekhov is creating levels of physical and visual counterpoint through the walking-standing-sitting-working of the characters, and from this sustained physical and visual theatre the opening dialogue emerges with its devastating, morbid humour of sadness:

(Chekhov 1983)

> OLGA. It's exactly a year since Father died. A year ago today – May the fifth – it was on your name-day, Irina.

If these words are uttered within seconds of the image being revealed they lose all the impact that this carefully composed and choreographed picture is crafted and designed to achieve.

Chekhov is playing with the audience's suspension of disbelief that allows us to accept the stage picture for its authenticity, and yet stretches this as the fiction is held beyond the 'normality' of realism in stage time. The longer the duration of the staged stillness-silence the greater the risk that the suspension will be broken. What will hold it is the physical and visual articulacy of the actresses so as to allow a seemingly familiar situation to be made strange; by the skills of the *actant*-character keeping our attention as the domestic circumstances of the play take on their intended dramatic purpose.

For what duration is the audience to be trusted? What is the depth of the risk to be assigned to the audience, allowing the spectator(s) to participate in the making of such an opening? We will return to these issues of participation and risk.

The silent cry

Brecht opens *Mother Courage and her Children* with a banner telling us the date and season, where the action of the episode is set and what that action will be. As in *Agamemnon*, we see the physical state of two soldiers – shivering – carrying out their duties, telling us what these are and what they are thinking about the war.

The play opens with shown information – the banner and the shivering – but goes straight into dialogue; no held images. Then again as with Aeschylus, we are given a stage direction within the dialogue prefiguring the action and image.

(Brecht 1980: 4)

> Recruiter: Hey, here's a cart coming. Two tarts with two young fellows . . .
> *Sound of a jew's-harp. Drawn by two young fellows, a covered cart rolls in.*
> *On it sit Mother Courage and her dumb daughter Kattrin.*

Unlike the opening of *Three Sisters*, this is physicality in text-based theatre harking back to the roots of modern theatre. Word indicates action, the action and word then acting together.

But it is also the action of work; the work of recruiting and the work of war; the work of pulling the wagon and surviving. Not a held image, but one of movement and urgency that does what it needs to establish Fierling's economic and family status at the play's opening. The boys pull the cart, the actors have to use their muscles to be these characters. The strong physical quality here is essential to the dramaturgical structure of the performance text as it sets up the final image of the play – as discussed in Chapter 2 – where we see Courage, now alone, straining to pull the cart as it remains rooted to the spot; her physical effort met by the physical immobility of the wagon. Mediated through 12 episodes of Fierling's foolishness and courage, our estranged empathy is grounded in the opening physical action of the sons.

However, Fierling's courage is shown in a quite different physicality in episode three where she denies her son.

> There comes a moment in *Mother Courage* when the soldiers carry in the dead body of Schweizerkäs (Swiss Cheese). They suspect that he is the son of Courage but are not quite certain. She must be forced to identify him. I saw Helene Weigel act the scene . . . though acting is a paltry word for the marvel of her incarnation. As the body of her son was laid before her, she merely shook her head in mute denial. The soldiers compelled her to look again. Again she gave no sign of recognition, only a dead stare. As the body was carried off, Weigel looked the other way and tore her mouth wide open. The shape of the gesture was that of the screaming horse in Picasso's *Guernica*. The sound that came out was raw and terrible . . . But, in fact, there was no sound. Nothing. The sound was total silence. It was silence which screamed and screamed through the whole theatre so that the audience lowered its head . . . And that scream inside the silence seemed to me to be the same as Cassandra's when she divines the reek of blood in the house of Atreus.

(Steiner 1958: 353–54)

After that, one is almost tempted to finish writing on this subject.

This extended quote, with the dramaturgy of the opening of *Three Sisters*, says what physical theatre is in its 'pure' form: the articulacy of the *actant's* dynamic stillness and silence, whether as character or not. It speaks for itself.

The only stage directions given in the text are that Courage shakes her head twice. As the soldiers carry off the body they speak: 'Chuck him in the pit. Nobody knows him' (Brecht 1980: 42). The 'silent scream' is the invention and improvisation of the actress, just as the actresses playing the sisters and Regina must improvise on stage (this issue of improvisation will be looked at later), as the image is allowed time and space to establish itself, to breathe, to speak.

What is the duration of the scream?

The performance text must play and take risks with the audience's suspension of disbelief to create moments of human empathy and recognition which are not only realistic but which also estrange/distance us to the point of breaking the realism. We see what the other characters do not see. We identify with Courage, with the sisters expressing the profoundest emotions and psychological states through physical articulacy, and which are ours by virtue of common humanity and empathy.

(Physical) text as transformation and imagination

This idea of a physical figure seen by the audience, but not by the other characters, marks our next example, *A Midsummer Night's Dream*.

(Shakespeare
1979: 39)

> (Oberon) But who comes here? I am invisible; and I will overhear their conference
> *Enter Demetrius. Helena following him*

This spoken stage direction is again a moment of simple physicality within the words being spoken. Oberon tells us he is now invisible, but of course only to the characters on stage. To us he becomes again a dynamic, still, silent figure we see observing the lovers. Any responses that we see in him come from his reactions to the tragic-comic dialogue, the lovers' actions, and from any appropriate physical-visual improvisation.

But unlike the sisters, Oberon is not in repose or contemplation. So from the initial silent stillness, he can begin to move 'invisibly', weaving between and around the lovers, perhaps provoking a mild comic quality. Certainly his movement would make the stage space dynamic, in complicity with the audience, in a quite different way to some of the previous examples. A 'simple' statement sets up the physical conditions of invisibility in which no bushes or trees are needed, only the audience's imagination accepting the character's physical state as we watch the *actant* create this.

Again the audience has a dramaturgical role (this is set by the dialogue) within the conventions of the staging as identified by the play text. The audience's seeing of the action is echoed by the lovers' chase in Act Three as they are led – unnoticing and unnoticed – past each other by Puck.

The use of the physical here – Oberon's reactions, the school-yard fighting of the lovers – again takes on a comic quality. A comic style that should neither pander to the audience nor become an upstaging, but remains, in Oberon's case, a counterpoint to the lovers' quarrel, or takes on a darker edge as we hear their threats in the chase. This use of the audience's imagination takes on a more overt quality in the next two examples.

(Brenton 1977: 11,
56, 65)

> *EPSOM DOWNS* (Howard Brenton)
> *The Downs, still.* PRIMROSE *sunbathing* . . . SUPERINDENT BLUE *and* CHARLES
> PEARCE *appear on the skyline, on horseback. The horses are played by naked actors.*
> *The parade ring.* A HORSE *is being led around by a* STABLE LAD
> HORSE. I am a Derby outside chance.
> *The* JOCKEY *comes on, riding the* HORSE.
> JOCKEY. You ride out, over the Downs. To the mile and a half start. Of the Epsom
> Derby Stakes.
> HORSE. Where are you, goat?

When *Epsom Downs* was performed at the Round House in 1977, the actors playing the horses were naked apart from bridles and reins, with the jockey in full riding silks and helmet, Blue in uniform, Pearce in tweeds. The horses high-stepped around the ring and across the Downs, carrying the riders on their shoulders as an adult carries a child.

(Berkoff 1978: 39)

EAST (Steven Berkoff)

The two lads wander up stage to a special spot – MIKE turns LES into a motor bike and jumps on his back using LES's arms as handle-bars. The two clearly create the sound of a motor bike revving up and changing gear during the scene. The strength of the engine and the movement as it careers round the corners should be apparent. Oh for Adventures.

MIKE. I am a Harley Davidson with ape-hangers or maybe I am a chopper made to measure to fit me – a built up Triumph 5000cc. Perhaps I am a Harley Davidson with high rise bars. A Yamaha or a Suzuki 1500cc. Yeah, but who wouldn't mind a Vincent HRD 10,000cc.

Whereas horses and riders used the whole stage area to create the spaces of the Downs, in Steven Berkoff's 1978 production of *East* bike and rider stayed in the spotlight, creating the ride through balance and by swaying and careering their bodies on the spot. They did not move around the stage space.

In both stagings it is the process of transformation that plays with the audiences' imagination; the actor's body becoming something other than human as it steps or sways so that we 'see' the horse or bike. The technique (and words) of the actor tell us what to see and we see it. This is, of course, a form of illustrative mime, already discussed in Chapter 2; not the objective mime characterised by Barrault as 'muscular disturbance imposed by the imagined object' (1951: 27–28), but a form of illusion achieved by the transformation of the body into something else.

It is a representational physicality in which the audience completes the picture being created by the body and words. This is not the stillness or silence of emotional-psychological energy, but the raw energy of the body in motion, hectic or otherwise. We respond to the directness of the image, its place in the structure of the narrative as Derby Day is set out before us, or in Mike describing the visceral, sexual thrills and adventures to be found on the M1 motorway as he 'rides' Les.

We also laugh at it; the laugh that comes from the initial shock of the image, the laugh that emanates from our pleasure in recognising and making the image which feeds the social and political themes of both plays. But we find it comic too, not simply as light, dark, satiric or political humour, but because it is another form of play which we enjoy and recognise. We are reminded of our own childhoods when just by saying 'I am X or Y' we became that in our own imaginations and through those of our friends. Again, we see how physical theatre rests on the deep-rooted human traits and propensities outlined in Chapter 2.

Reaching for comedy and pathos

Here, rather than a discussion of comedy as such (see Bakhtin 1968/1971; Barreca 1988; Fisher 1973; Palmer 1984; Wright 2006) we wish to highlight certain tropes of the comic and the physical in text-based drama. These may be poignant or sad, or use forms of play, but all rest on the audience's suspension of disbelief, and its imagination-anticipation being fed by the images from the stage.

This suspension and imagination takes on a very different role when the physical comedy becomes broader, becomes farcical, but – like tragedy – also plays with the potential disorder of the world.

(King 1946: 42–45)

> *SEE HOW THEY RUN!* (Philip King)
>
> (Miss Skillon is lying in a faint on the floor)
>
> PENELOPE (*to Clive*)   Run, quickly. Run!
>
> CLIVE (*rushing to the window and opening it*) I'm running.
>
> (CLIVE *leaps over Miss Skillon and runs off down L. followed by* LIONEL. *The* BISHOP *enters through window, leaps over Miss Skillon and rushes off after Clive and Lionel.*)
>
> (Dialogue, with Miss Skillon still lying on floor)
>
> IDA (*peeping out of window curtains*) Ow – my goodness!
>
> (IDA *is almost knocked over by* CLIVE, *who dashes in and goes off through the door down L. – leaping over Miss Skillon in best steeplechase manner. He is followed by* LIONEL *who does the same business and exits. The* BISHOP *follows, doing same . . . The* MAN *rushes in through the window . . . leaps over Miss Skillon and exits down L.*)
>
> (dialogue, with Miss Skillon now recovered and going into the cupboard)
>
> (CLIVE *dashes in at the window, followed by a bull terrier. Does a steeplechase leap at the place where Miss Skillon was lying on his previous run through and exits as before.*)

Some of the essentials of certain physical comedy are seen here in Philip King's farce: the chase, clergy and soldiers looking foolish, body on floor, people hiding in cupboards. The physical comedy rests on the set-up, speed, on the gymnastic ability of the four actors to leap in character, on the inherent ridiculousness of the whole situation.

This forces not an extreme suspension of disbelief, but almost putting such a state to one side as we accept the inherent absurdity of what we are watching, knowing it is not 'real' but an exaggeration that nevertheless serves to reveal the absurdity of the world or the fragility of its order; something that is the aim of all serious comedy.

Four pages of dialogue and comic business climax in the leap over the body that is not there. We see an extended set-up where the four men jump over the body seven times. But the eighth time the body has gone but the leap is the same. The state and situation of the character impels him (and the dog!) to leap where he expects the body to still be and so acts accordingly, running and exiting so fast he fails to realise that the body is not there. And as with Oberon's invisibility, the audience know what the character does not and thus have the knowledge to laugh at/with the character, at the situation.

In this comparatively minor piece of comic drama the same physical and psychological impulses and principles are at work as in serious comedy or tragedy. There is a degree of empathy and recognition, blended with the ridiculous, and the same joy of play, mixed with the absurdity of watching grown men, especially a Bishop, behaving as if children in a playground. If all the dialogue was removed, we would still laugh because the underlying physical theatre of comedy would remain, impelled by that recognition and enjoyment of play.

The next example retains elements of farce but also of the pathos and sadness that marks out all great comedy, and which is expressed not only in words but in posture, expression, tone. By taking this from television, we can acknowledge the role that the camera can play in physical acting and performing. From the earliest films of Méliès or Mattershaw, the circus and commedia skills of clowning, juggling and balancing have been used in filmed slapstick to extend the possibilities of the physical. The camera also allows the use of the close-up to accentuate the physical expressiveness of the face or other parts of the body.

FAWLTY TOWERS (John Cleese and Connie Booth)

(Cleese and Booth 1989: 206, 21, 175)

THE PSYCHIATRIST
(Johnson has ordered champagne)
BASIL: It's just coming.
Johnson gives him a very meaningful look and closes the door. In his room, he indicates to the girl, who is sitting on his bed, that someone is hovering about in the corridor. He bolts the door. In the corridor, Manuel runs up with a tray with a champagne bottle in an ice bucket and a glass on it. Basil takes it, puts his other hand on the doorknob. Takes a deep breath and turns the knob and hits the door with his shoulder. As it's bolted he bounces back dropping the tray. Manuel neatly catches the ice bucket with the bottle in it; the tray and glass drop noisily. Johnson's door opens. Basil sees Johnson and slaps Manuel on the head. Manuel drops the ice bucket . . .

A TOUCH OF CLASS
BASIL: What are you doing Sybil . . . entrusts to us a case of valuables in trust.
Sybil places the open case in front of him. He looks into it for a long time. Then he lifts out an ordinary house brick. Disbelievingly, he shakes it close to his ear, lifts out another and sniffs it, then clinks them together. He puts them down and emits a strange growl . . .

COMMUNICATION PROBLEMS
BASIL: That's true. That was a warning, wasn't it. Should have spotted that. Zoom! – what was that? That was your life mate. That was quick, do I get another? Sorry mate, that's your lot.

As this is television, of course the camera shot and framing play a significant part in the dramaturgy here. All three are interior settings, the first in medium-long 2-shot, the second is a medium 3-shot, and the third a medium close-up.

The Psychiatrist follows the same rules of farce as *See How They Run!*. The audience is privy to knowledge which is denied to Basil. We know that *something* will happen but not what exactly. What we see is the slapstick of the bounce off the door, and the wonderful physical dexterity of the actors in their characters as bottle and bucket are caught. The twist, of course, is that, due to Basil's action, Manuel then drops the bucket.

This is physical comedy in the tradition of the *commedia dell'arte* and the 'silent' films of Charlie Chaplin and Buster Keaton. Words play their part in the set-up but it then becomes purely visual-physical theatre. The camera framing allows us to see the full brilliance of the two actor-characters' physical partnership through comic timing and the dexterity with which they manipulate objects.

A Touch of Class is again a piece of 'object theatre' as Basil's view of a better class of world becomes shattered by two bricks. The camera framing allows us to see the dawning realisation on his face as the bricks are handled with bewilderment, disbelief and then rage, with Sybil and Polly providing a silent, almost non-expressive counterpoint as they watch this. The physical comedy takes on a psychological poignancy as Basil's face and actions reveal, without words, the full impact of the 'con', with us laughing not only at his stupidity with the bricks, but also with a degree of sadness as we recognise the scale of his disillusionment.

Communication Problems takes this comedy of poignancy even further as the medium close-up gives us a glimpse of Basil's existential fatalism through words and expression. A quiet, almost serene acceptance of this 'one-life' as he sits momentarily alone, away from the hurly-burly of the hotel. This is a piece of physical acting which is an echo of the life-sadness that opens *Three Sisters,* or Pozzo's lines concerning the transience of life in Beckett's *Waiting for Godot* (1953).

It is Beckett (see *PT:R*, p. 128), perhaps, who brings all these elements of physical text theatre together as total theatre, as total performance texts across his work. The use of camera, stage space and its contained scenography, words which have a physical texture in their expressiveness, and the body of the character locked in the given physical-visual situation: all massively contribute to the dramaturgy. In a canon usually categorised by predominance of the word, Beckett's theatre begins, in fact, from a present, silent but articulate, still but dynamic figure inhabiting a particular space and light. No less demanding for the actor as articulation of the spoken word.

In *Eh Joe* (1965/1984), in nine camera moves – four inches at a time, holding still between each move – we close in on Joe's face as an unseen voice recounts the 'rottenness' and 'losses' of his life. Joe never speaks but as the camera slowly penetrates his face so articulate expression alone reveals the inner man; the face plus our reading of the face as he and we hear the woman's words and tones. Without a body, the woman's voice takes on a physical and thus emotional intensity which matches that of Joe, deprived of his voice. Joe's body and face have to be an expressive, articulate stillness, remaining physically dynamic, not merely static listening. The camera forces an intensity on actor, Joe, us. In a recent London production – July 2006 – the transposition to the stage kept this same intensity of looking and listening by creating a dual image, projecting the enlarged expressions of the stage face simultaneously on to a scrim curtain.

In each and every one of Beckett's plays the physical situation of the characters, expressed visually and with the body, tells us of their existential state which, however strange the circumstances, is recognisable and to be empathised with at an existential human level (see also *PT:R*, p. 213).

Happy Days (1961)
Embedded up to above her waist in exact centre of mound, WINNIE.

(Beckett 1966: 9)

Footfalls (1976)
Curtain. Stage in darkness.
Faint single chime. Pause as echoes die.
Fade up to dim on strip. Rest in darkness.
May discovered (in a strip of light nine steps in length) pacing towards L. turns at L.
paces three more lengths, halts, facing front at R.

(Beckett 1984: 239)

Here we encounter two scenarios in which we see the physical – and thus psychological-emotional – entrapment of these characters before they speak. However strange their location or distorted the circumstances, the figures remain recognisably human and speak physically-visually for the human condition.

In *Krapp's Last Tape* (1958) we first see Krapp sitting at his desk behind his tape machine in a pool of light beyond which is darkness. There then follow some five minutes of movement and stage business before he starts talking, reading from the ledger. A scenario in which the past is relived through the medium of recorded words, and which we watch being experienced again as we listen to Krapp's words and observe his reactions.

In *Quad* (1982) we observe four gowned figures follow a walking pattern of four series of four courses of movement within a square of neutral light to percussive accompaniment: no words are used. We simply watch and read patterns of choreographed movement which speak to us of prisoners/ascetics/meditators or simply the condition of our own everyday lives.

Beckett's plays exemplify the physical-visual-verbal dramaturgical demands of the performance text that must be delivered by the actor and director. We have already seen some of the physical issues facing the actor or performer in Chapter 4. In any of the examples given above the physical dramaturgy could become one of cliché or lazy physicality of movement and gesture. While training is a necessary grounding to avoid such banality, the work also needs to continue on the stage itself beyond what has been rehearsed. Here we are engaging with the imperatives of liveness: the never-ending risk that needs to be present in the physical dimension of all theatres.

Improvising or fixing the text?

We wish to conclude this chapter by looking at two further elements that are present in all theatre but, because they are usually dismissed as unimportant in text-based theatre, may be considered here with some degree of provocation.

Frost and Yarrow categorise and characterise three types (strands) of improvisation emerging from the history of Western theatre practice and conventions:

(Frost and Yarrow
1990: 15)

(a) the *application* of improvisation to the purposes of the traditional play; (b) the use of *pure* improvisation in the creation of an 'alternative' kind of theatrical experience; and (c) the extension of improvisatory principles *beyond* the theatre itself.

It is usually the second of these which gets most critical and theoretical attention, whereby 'improvised' theatre is given or takes upon itself an ideological, aesthetic and political status that the resulting work may or may not justify; the use of italics above for 'pure' is revealing here.

Thus the list of characteristics assigned to 'devising' by Heddon and Milling (2006: 4–5), which may be equally applied to improvisation, become merely a particular rhetoric of particular strands of modern theatre which ignore the finding of many of these aims or practices in so-called 'traditional' theatres. But as exemplified in both of these volumes (PT:I and PT:R), improvising is both a central part of training, a vital part of the traditions of comedy, and a crucial element of rehearsing both text-based and other forms of theatre.

With regard to the duration of the openings of *Ghosts* and *Three Sisters* discussed above, are these best to be found by the diktat of the director, or through the physical improvising of actors in collaboration with the director and the discerned intentions of the author? As we have seen, Brecht gives no stage direction for Fierling's response except that she shakes her head twice; the extraordinary 'silent scream' is of Weigel and Brecht's own physical devising and improvising on the stage.

True or 'pure' improvisation is, like free jazz, contact improvisation dance and the response riff of the stand-up comedian, made in the moment in the performance space without rehearsal or script (but with forms and techniques of preparation); perhaps a 'free theatre' which we can properly call 'improvised theatres' as distinct from improvising-improvisation in theatres. Such a 'free' theatre would be a non-text theatre in that the 'text' disappears as soon as it is created-presented. But as soon as moments, passages, acts are fixed we have a *text*, whether as play text, movement score, performance text made up of Kowzan's 13 sign systems or the text within which we find degrees of physicality and thus a basis for improvisation within the text.

It follows that as soon as a good moment is found or inspired, and then repeated or used again, it is no longer improvised – it has taken on a degree of being 'fixed'. As before in this book, a deliberate schematic definition is being used to illustrate our point about the (mis)use of terms; once something is fixed or repeated it is no longer 'purely' improvised despite the production's claims. It may have come out of improvising or devising, but its status has changed. What is being emphasised here is that all theatre grows out of improvisation and devising to different degrees, in different guises, and for different purposes (Chamberlain in *PT:R*, p. 117). But the real question to be asked of any text or production is whether the *dynamic* of improvising is being taken into the production itself.

Just as we have argued that concepts such as 'gestus' and 'estranging' can be applied beyond epic theatre, so too can the ideas of the practitioner-theorists we have been discussing go beyond their (own) theatres. As seen in a number of extracts in *PT:R*, improvisation is a tool for training and performing.

To be still and silent and yet dynamic-articulate with the body demands that the actor respond to the moment(s) required by the *play text*, yet created on stage in the moment of the *performance text*. It will probably have been rehearsed and thus 'fixed' as a ground for the production to rest on, but the production must still be open to the physical articulacy of angle or stance that comes from the moment itself. Clearly it is inherent in the exploitation of physical action that such moments may be used; the words of the play text themselves cannot be changed, nor tones or nuances which would change the semantic meaning. But moments of physicality can extend such psychological-emotional meaning, playing with the point at which realism may be given or take other resonances beyond simple mimesis.

Fantasia, furbizio, tecnica

As the performance text is 'fixed', but must remain open to improvisation, so with the game plan for a football match. We can now reflect on the quote from the analogous world of football on p. 1 above. The moment reflected on by Zinedine Zidane, the qualities required of football, are also those of the theatre: the same already present liminality of the stage that allows the unfixed, the unrehearsed yet prepared for to happen *in the moment*.

Playing the audience

Many of the same considerations apply to the final principle we wish to look at here – that of participation; a term and idea that has again become associated with a particular set of practices and theatre ideologies, but which ignores the reality that theatre is a spectrum of practices, and not an either-or in its principles.

> Gropius's goal was to destroy the implicit psychological separation of the performer and spectator. . . . In doing so he hoped to encourage the audience to 'shake off its inertia'. The Total Theater was to be a 'mobilisation of all spatial means to rouse the spectator from his intellectual apathy, to assault and overwhelm him, to coerce him into participation in the play'.

(Aronson 1981: 495)

As an attitude towards audiences, this is often a feature of modern theatre; a conde-scending voice that sees the audience as a milch cow for its money, as an anonymous mass to be spoken down to, as a collection of human agents who give up agency at the box office.

While it is the case that a kind of vulgar realism-naturalism is predicated on a 'passive' audience who simply stare at the stage picture through one kind of window or another, this remains banal. Any serious reading of the key writers and practitioner-theorists makes it clear that whatever style of theatre or staging configuration they are working with is itself predicated on the assumption that the audience will be involved intellectually-psychologically-emotionally-physically with the work being presented.

In other words, just as all theatre is physical, so all theatre is participatory; it is the degree and kind that must be distinguished. (For a fuller discussion of response–reception theory see Bennett 1990: 36–91.)

Thus, the final part of Living Theatre's *Prometheus* discussed in Chapter 2 took place on the streets of London with the full participation – physical as well as political, emotional and intellectual – of the audience. We were in large part the final act; we were Boal's 'spect-actors', we were manifesting Artaud's 'sharing of the breath'. But of course we remained spectators who were temporary participants for that evening only. This is not to diminish our commitment or presence but to point out that 'participation' is as much an ideological construct as realism. The spectator remains spectator even when sitting on the actor's lap or joining in her dance – their essential category remains, however much the physical line is broken (see Keefe 1996).

Thus in the summer of 2006, London's South Bank Centre ran its *PLAY orchestra* project in which 56 plastic cubes were set out as an orchestra and wired up as individual instruments, so that by sitting on a cube one 'played' the instrument. The project was described as interactive and participatory as, by sitting on a cube, one activated the instrument. It was wonderful to see children, adults-as-children going from one cube to another, 're-orchestrating' the music as a sound game by means of their physical movement. But of course our participation and interactivity were limited; we could not change the piece of music but simply modify how it was heard – rearranging but not varying the sounds. As a form of play or casual collaboration it was great fun but one which also showed the limits of such proclaimed interactivity and participation; I could not change the game, only some of its ingredients.

We have to ask the hard question: What is it that Gropius would allow in his participation – to change the piece as it is being performed? To allow the spectator to participate as author as well as performer?

While Brecht's theatre breaks the 'fourth wall' he never invites us on to the stage. Yet we are deemed to be politically and socially participating. While Ibsen never breaks this 'wall' he also assumes our political participation by talking about, discussing, showing social issues which we recognise via psychological and emotional and experiential empathy.

They are both grounding their work on assumptions of participation, but of different kinds and by different means – as is the case in all the theatres and practitioners discussed in this book.

It is always an active–reactive participation.

The gorilla's final dance

The audience become part of the strange and intimate half-world in which the performance exists. People drift on and off the stage, in and out of the auditorium like sleepwalkers. Yet, as the slight changes and variations in the piece are gradually revealed, so an alertness and awareness accompanies the tiredness . . . The show can be seen as a twenty-three hour preparation for the closing moments. At 11.53pm the music finally stops. At 11.57pm the gorilla does a final dance, dies and joins the others upstage. At 11.59pm the last minute is counted down. Then 'Stop'. The stage is bare except for a single chair and the resonances of the after images in our minds.

(John Keefe (1999) reviewing 'Who can sing a song to unfrighten me' (Forced Entertainment), *Total Theatre* 11(3))

Theatres are spectrums of practice and principles, and in this sense the act of applauding is a form of physical participation; at the low end of the scale and seemingly almost banal as an act in itself. But of course in the majority of theatre experiences it is the only overtly 'physical act' we make as we put our hands together. (The roots of this idea lie in a conversation with Phelim McDermott, Artistic Director of Improbable Theatre during the writing of this chapter. See *PT:R*, p. 201.)

In their paper, Miller and Page (2004) number four aspects of the act of applauding or giving a standing ovation:

- To send a signal of approval to the stage and actors (and the other theatre makers).
- To conform to the actions of the audience so as not to feel awkward (thus the decision not to applaud or stand becomes quite a big social statement in itself).
- To conform to the influence of the friends or social circle one is with.
- To give in to the influence of the wave of emotion that can sweep an audience as an impulse of the moment (a possibly irrational act of critical approval that may later be revised when the emotional impulse has gone) [parentheses added].

What is noticeably missing here is the physical aspect of applauding; the physical release of how we feel and respond to the piece of theatre by the limited means available, i.e. clapping our hands, standing and cheering. Alternatively there is the possibility of withholding affirmation by booing, stamping or hissing. Tim Etchells recalls the curtain calls at the end of Pina Bausch's *Café Müller* at the Edinburgh Festival where for the performers there seemed a psycho-physical impulsion not to quit the stage and which linked them inextricably to their audience:

> For me, ending performance was always about crossing the line between worlds, or passing on the chance to cross it; refusing to come back. The five or six curtain calls closing Pina Bausch's *Café Müller* . . . were almost pure refusal. Here the gazes of the dancers (Bausch included) were as stern and distant and as lost in private pain as they had been throughout the performance – there was no returning in it, or only a nod to that, as though the image-world could not be quit, its psychic residue too strong.

(Etchells 1999: 59)

The spectator is not passive in the simple or dismissive terms by which this condition is too often discussed. Just as s/he has participated through the psychological-physiological means discussed above, so we wish for some physical release of these feelings and thoughts arising from our mimetic and empathetic engagement.

As an act of physical expression and release at these deeper levels of the complicity and physicality of theatres, it is part of the (missing) fourteenth sign system in Kowzan's taxonomy.

Afterwords

We have devoted a whole chapter to the subject of the physical in relation to the word as a way of reiterating our belief in its centrality to our subject matter. We have stated and argued our belief in the inherently hybrid or total nature of theatre, however messy that might be in practice. As such we cannot exclude the forms of word-based drama that dominate our theatre, film and television.

We have shown, however, that the physical is always and already present, both on and off the stage; even in those theatre forms which pay little attention to this within the spectrum of dramatic and acting style.

<table>
<tr><td>(Brecht 1965: 47, 88, 19)</td><td>

Fragments from *The Messingkauf Dialogues*

If we observe sorrow on the stage and at the same time identify ourselves with it, then this simultaneous observing is a part of our observation. We are sorrowful, but at the same time we are people observing a sorrow – our own – almost as if it were detached from us. . . .

You can't possibly confine criticism to the intellect. Feelings also play a part in the process, and it may be your job to organise criticism by means of feelings. Remember that criticism originates in crisis and reinforces it . . . above all knowledge manifests itself in knowing better ie. in contradiction.

I'm much less concerned with the way in which you represent things . . . than with the actual things you are imitating.

</td></tr>
</table>

What do words do to our bodies?

If text has a role to play in performance, even that which is based primarily in physical performance, the key is not to focus on what the words tell us but how they tell us. What they do to our bodies and what our bodies do to them.

(Tom Wilson (2004), 'Poetry and Motion', *Total Theatre* 16(3–4))

CHAPTER 6

Bodies and Cultures

A dancer's life

It was Balasaraswarti's influence that was the more lasting on Chandralekha . . . because she understood dance to be not a celebration of the gods, but rather a celebration of man and woman – especially women . . . the choreography was often explicit and reminiscent of the erotic sculptures of the Khajuraho temples. 'Celebrations of the human body' is how Chandralekha described her dance productions . . . based on her premise of the indivisibility of sexuality, sensuality and spirituality.

(Obituary of Chandralekha Prabhudas Patel, Raymond Massey, *Guardian*, 9 February 2007)

In his essay 'Assembling our differences: bridging identities-in-motion in intercultural performance' (which prefaces the sister section to this chapter in *PT:R,* p. 239), David Williams invokes the metaphor of bridges and bridging, and quotes performer and theatre maker Anna Deaveare Smith who writes:

The bridge doesn't make them the same, it merely *displays* how two unlikely *aspects* are *related*. These relationships of the *unlikely*, these connections of things that don't fit together are crucial to . . . theatre and culture if theatre and culture plan to help us assemble our obvious differences.

(Smith 1993: xxix, emphasis in original)

Williams pursues the bridging metaphor as an image that fruitfully allows us to explore interrelations, collaborations and co-existences for inventing art with others, and one that affirms 'differences as productive, rather than resisting or rejecting them as a failure of plenitude' (Williams in *PT:R*, p. 239). For Smith, Williams and ourselves bridges connect and allow dialogue and exchange between two or more entities that nevertheless remain separated. For Smith, who sees both herself and her work as a bridge between 'contradictory identities and testimonies' (ibid.: 244), this is a perspective which respects the autonomy of two (or more) subjects while always seeking a creative dialogue – embodied, historical, theoretical, cultural, political – that reiterates and pushes the mutual interdependency of peoples and their cultures.

Flattening differences

In the introduction to this book we explained our decision – partly pragmatic and partly strategic and cultural – not to seek to offer an account of non-Western forms of physical theatres, and their complex interrelationship with European and North American practices. This acknowledged not only a lack of expertise and knowledge beyond our Western 'backyard', but also an awareness of the dangers of tokenism in an already fragile and highly sensitive cultural arena should we try to offer some kind of global mapping of physical theatres. None the less, we decided that one chapter should signal an awareness of the difficult issues that present themselves to any reader when attempting to unravel some of the complexities in understanding physical theatres across and between different cultures.

However, framing the issue – the problem – in such a way is already to mislead and to simplify a set of existing cultural identities and relations which are complex and resist the potentially destructive dualism of 'Western' and 'non-Western'. Before wrestling with the 'intercultural' we must consider some of the difficulties embedded in the 'cultural'. As Richard Schechner has regularly stated (1982, 1985), there is no such thing as a 'pure' culture, unadulterated and uninfluenced by others. To write of 'Western' or 'non-Western' cultures seems at once to propose a homogeneous and undifferentiated monoculturalism on the part of both 'West' and 'East'. And, of course, this is not only 'bad science', but takes us straight to the politics of multi- and interculturalism, and what Edward Said has memorably framed as 'Orientalism' (2003). We are faced, perhaps, with as much difficulty in defining 'cross-' or 'intercultural' as with locating any tidy definition of physical theatre. We will explore how these issues engage with physical theatres later in this chapter, but for now it is important to acknowledge the following points in relation to the charge of monoculturalism identified above.

Throughout this book we have taken pleasure in identifying the mongrel and hybrid nature of all theatre, and within and alongside this, *physical theatres*. Consequently, as we navigate the sites of physical theatres within the complex pathways of multi- and interculturalism we are already acknowledging the messy taxonomies of difference and diversity. To consider the practices of those Western figures already identified in previous chapters – Meyerhold, Artaud, Copeau, Brecht, Brook, Bogart, Lecoq, Grotowski, Barba and Decroux, for example – is to acknowledge the diverse cultural lineages which have informed both their teaching and theatre making. For each of these theatre practitioners we are speaking of influences and dispositions that are already multicultural in their formation, translation and communication. To state this is a matter of fact, rather than a judgement about the quality, effectiveness and cultural politics of their work, or the rhetoric that explains and justifies it. Thus some of the practices we have labelled 'Western' are inflected and formed by teachings, assumptions and understandings which emanate from societies beyond Europe, North America and Australasia. As we have stated, there is nothing 'pure' about culture, and Edward Said puts it like this:

> every domain is linked to every other one, and . . . nothing that goes on in our world has ever been isolated and pure of any outside influence. The disheartening part is that the more the critical study of culture shows us that this is the case, the less influence such a view seems to have.

(Said 2003: xvii)

Similarly, it is both misguided and ultimately pernicious to assume that the theatre practices of 'other' non-Western cultures are reducible to a homogenous equivalence – possibly 'exotic' in their difference, but uniformly exotic none the less. In such a mindset we may detect the assumption that non-Western cultures lack the complexities, pluralities and diversities of their European equivalents, and are thus *flattened* out by Western interpretations and theorising.

The questions which face us here reside in the possibilities for connection, interaction and exchange between different cultural formations and particularly between the practices of physical theatres. Questions, too, about how work is made and received, who is making and who is doing the watching. Questions, moreover, about the hidden and unintended consequences of honourable aspirations to bring cultures together. Questions, finally, about consent, power, context and perception.

Borrowings, takings and muddled thinking

Jay Williams identifies the terms which trace the variety of practices he places under the umbrella of 'cross-cultural negotiations and conversations': 'intercultural, intracultural, extracultural, transcultural, multicultural, transnational, and touristic', and adds that 'they all point to the fluidity of performance in a borderless world' (Zarrilli *et al.* 2006: 485). Here 'intercultural' is defined as 'productions that borrow the . . . vocabularies of one culture and adapt them to another' (ibid.: 486), and 'intracultural' as 'works combining performance modes from different cultural traditions or communities within nation-state boundaries' (ibid.: 491).

These practices may be characterised as a borrowing, taking, sharing or exchanging of one or more sets of theatre sign-systems (see Kowzan 1968) from one culture, or specific material from within such systems, in the making of a play or production text in another culture. However, Jatinder Verma gives a less settled reading of these terms, albeit in an acknowledged British context:

(Verma 1996: 193)

> While the analysis of performance is, at the best of times, an exercise fraught with uncertainties . . . the analysis of multi-cultural productions in contemporary Britain is fairly riddled with imprecision and muddled thinking. 'Cross-cultural', 'inter-cultural', 'intra-cultural', 'integrated', 'culturally-diverse' . . . these are all terms that, in varying ways, are descriptive of 'multi-cultural'.

What this demonstrates is not only the fluidity of the terms themselves, but also the instability of the ground upon which they are constructed. This 'fraught' quality is therefore an inevitable part of their usage. As we shall see, such fluidity, or as we prefer 'hybridity', is simply another and very particular manifestation of the fundamental fusions that constitute theatre. Such hybridity – or 'syncretism' as Jay Williams (Zarrilli *et al.* 2006: 491) terms it – is not a result of globalisation as he claims, but is in the very bones of theatre itself. This is fundamental to Kowzan's categorisation of the sign-systems of theatre, and especially when these are recast in a non-hierarchical manner, as we have argued above. Of course, globalisation creates new conditions, possibilities and contexts for extending – and perhaps re-inventing – the articulation of this hybridity, and with this a range of different ideological traps and tensions.

The point here – and it is made with great scholarship and authority by Said – is that these borrowings and exchanges of material are not conducted and experienced in a zone of political neutrality. Theatre, and indeed any art, is *of* the world and not *in* it (Shevtsova 1989: 180–194) and as a mode of cultural production is formed by 'structures of feeling' (see Raymond Williams in Chapter 1) which give shape and direction to its forms and processes. Jay Williams acknowledges this implicitly by allowing that 'such productions occur within a context of globalisation, with its imbalances of power, and against a backdrop of historical colonialism' (Williams 2006, in Zarrilli *et al.*: 486).

But this arguably rather understates the wider cultural and political dimensions to such actions which may involve the destroying, dissolving, colonising, modifying or taking over of one culture's practices by another. To borrow implies that what has been used will be repaid, given back; that some kind of communal goodwill and reciprocity is at work. At its most benign, relatively speaking, is the sense of such cross-cultural works seeking 'to be transcultural – dealing with universals that are (ostensibly) accessible across cultural boundaries' (ibid.: 486). We will explore later how these 'universals' are sometimes claimed and articulated in physical theatre practices, but for now we remain with *honourable intentions* and their manifest and latent functions.

At one level many of the manifestations of intercultural projects, events and experimentations in theatre have been driven – and justified – by a benign aspiration to build just those bridges articulated by Williams and Smith earlier in this chapter: an exemplary ambition to escape cultural parochialism and to explore – with best intentions – structures of practice which appear to offer not simply the lure of formal innovation, but also a small but utopian pre-figurative model of human collaboration across the potentially poisonous boundaries of race, ethnicity and culture. With many such projects, especially those of the early/mid-twentieth century, but also of the present, there has been a double drive to such experiments. It is not only a curiosity for the 'other' but at the same time often a disdain, contempt and despair at the real or imagined cultural, social and spiritual bankruptcy of the West. Indeed, it is an overwhelming sense of the latter which habitually propels a quest for the former.

It is around these tensions and possibilities that a prolific discourse has developed over the past three decades concerned with analysing the effects and legacies of colonialism, and the intertwined cultural consequences of globalisation. Apart from Said's magisterial *Orientalism* which frames all subsequent writings, there have been countless assessments and counter-critiques of intercultural practices which extend far beyond the reach of theatre studies. Shortly before he died, Said wrote an updated preface for a new edition of *Orientalism*, and in this – perhaps to the surprise of some of his supporters – he argues for reclaiming the humanist project:

> My idea in *Orientalism* is to use humanist critique to open up the fields of struggle, to introduce a longer sequence of thought and analysis to replace the short bursts of polemical, thought-stopping fury that so imprison us in labels and antagonistic debate whose goal is a belligerent collective identity rather than understanding and intellectual exchange. I have called what I try to do 'humanism', a word I continue to use stubbornly despite the scornful dismissal of the term by sophisticated post-modern critics. By humanism I mean first of all attempting to dissolve Blake's mind-forg'd manacles so as to be able to use one's mind historically and rationally for the purpose of reflective understanding and genuine disclosure. Moreover, humanism is sustained by a sense of community with other interpreters and other societies and periods: strictly speaking therefore there is no such thing as an isolated humanist.

(Said 2003: xvii)

Bodies from other cultures

While a diverse range of intercultural practices have been scrutinised by critics within the context of post-colonial theory and Said's Orientalism over the past 30 years, such events have a far deeper history than this. The great 'Expositions' and world trade fairs of the late nineteenth century displayed without apology or much reflection a range of exotic examples of 'cultural' activities from the non-Western world. In 'Dancing around Orientalism', Donnalee Dox (2006: 53) offers a fascinating analysis of belly-dancing and its complex histories of being transported to the West. She argues that its history and popularity in the USA can be traced back to the 1893 World's Fair Midway Plaisance in Chicago where versions of Egyptian, Persian, Moroccan and Tunisian dances were promoted. Dox observes that:

> by the 1920's variations of Middle Eastern social and folk dances, with the addition of veils, had entered the private sphere of Western salons as a form of exotic artistry and self-expression, a vision reinforced by stage performers such as Ruth St Dennis and Maud Allen.

(Ibid.)

However, within the UK by the early nineteenth century we may note the first arrival of Asian magicians on the British stage, but by the end of this century improved trade and travel opportunities between India and Britain had substantially increased this traffic of cultural exchanges. Sarah Dadswell in her historical analysis of Indian magicians and jugglers working in the UK quotes an issue of *The Strand Magazine* in 1889: 'Yes, India's jugglers have been the wonder of India, as well as of that greater India which lies outside its borders and within the British Isles' (Dadswell 2007: 3). Later, Dadswell emphasises that these Indian magic shows of the late nineteenth/early twentieth century were:

(Ibid.: 5)

> characterised by a strong sense of spectacle, of physical feats, and even a sense of the grotesque . . . the physicality of the performance made a lasting impression on spectators and fellow entertainers.

Both of these examples suggest that the astonishment and wonder of perceiving bodies from other cultures performing strangely, erotically, grotesquely and often with enormous skill is central to the experience and ideological complexities of investigating this territory of cross-cultural performance. The challenges and extraordinarily complex tensions entailed in looking at these practices reside absolutely in bodies and physicality: whose bodies are being gazed at, who is doing the gazing (see Chapter 2) and what are the nexuses of power and authority relations that contextualise and determine the cultural *production* of the work? If belly-dancing and Indian magic shows are as much *physical theatres* as the work of Pina Bausch or Complicité then our subject matter lies at the heart of all enquiries into inter- and multiculturalism.

Contemporary moments of cultural exchange today are largely driven and enabled by intricate webs of financial exchange: art as entrepreneurship and business opportunity, and culture as the engine of economic regeneration. The nineteenth-century trade fairs and exhibitions have their equivalence in today's festivals in Edinburgh, Avignon, Toronto, Adelaide or even, perhaps, the London International Festival of Theatre (LIFT). And in all these there is tension between what is at best a generous desire for 'bridging' and solidarity through international exchange, and a dynamic of progress and practice which is a fig-leaf for deeper and less benign realities. And, of course, many multi- or intercultural projects are on the periphery of global commerce, and indeed consciously aspire to escape or subvert the imperatives and expectations that accompany participation in these events. In 2007 there is a considerably sharper awareness on the part of artists of the pitfalls of a naïve and unreflective engagement in such projects than might have been the case two or three decades earlier.

An account by David Fulton (2007) of the third Intercultural Theatre Festival (*Entrecultures*) held at Tortosa in Spain during November 2006 captures a sense of the opportunities and difficulties in such encounters. *Entrecultures* offers a space for dialogue and exchange between artists from different Mediterranean cultures including those such as Lebanon, Syria, Iran and Cyprus already caught up in war, or the threat of it. Although some participants from countries of the Eastern Mediterranean had difficulties obtaining visas, the spirit of the festival was clearly that of a 'bridging' – learning, watching, and listening – between the cultures represented. The utopian ambition of *Entrecultures* is captured by a statement that was read out at the end of the Festival which went as follows:

> Theatre represents life itself because it is a form of creation. Theatre can only call on us to celebrate peace, love, brotherhood, and life, just as peace continues to be a theme for creative people, intellectuals, and artists in their theatrical works, novels, stories, songs and films.
>
> We call on theatre people everywhere to make this stage in Tortosa a doorway opening other windows so that they can continue to express their own diversity while crying out 'no more war. Yes to peace!'

(Fulton 2007: 90)

While it is easy to unpick this statement for a possibly naïve and Panglossian perspective on the role of contemporary theatre, it would be arrogant and ungracious to denigrate the hopes and aspirations which underpin this event. More importantly, perhaps, to dismiss as irrelevant or counter-productive the lived experience of exchange, debate and increased awareness of the contexts and often profound difficulties which theatre practitioners from other cultures actually face when making work would be patronising and demeaning.

In understanding and evaluating these exchanges so much depends on context on the one hand, and the detailed nature of these encounters and what emanates from them in terms of changes in practice on the other. But we must also continue to heed the counsel of those such as Bharucha and Chaudhuri who have argued that interculturalism is not about 'borrowing', with its inbuilt commitment to reciprocity and mutuality, but at best is a deracinated and decontextualised encounter offering a spectacle of exoticism, and at worst is a ruthless form of appropriation and theft; a 'cultural tourism' which ignores social, political and national realities (Bharucha 1990). Moreover, 'colonialism' is not a historical *backdrop* of diminished importance; rather its effects are still with us, whether raw and brutal or more culturally nuanced. The historical roots are tenacious and deep, as evidenced by these two very different examples.

When Bernal published his thesis concerning 'Black Athena' in 1987 he was not only setting out an argument for the origins of Classical Greek culture in Egypt and the Near East (African and Semitic civilisations), but attacking Eurocentric historiographies which sought to deny such 'non-white' roots for reasons of politics and racial prejudice. Bernal is seeking to replace theories on the isolationist origins of culture with a diffusionism that places migration and conquest at the centre of cultural development and identity. It has been argued that Bernal has simply replaced *Eurocentrism* with *Afrocentrism*, that his science is bad, and that he is creating a misbegotten political correctness (see Kristeller 1995; Palter 1993; Pounder 1992). None the less, without entering into this fraught debate, 'Black Athena' serves to illustrate the inescapable political and value-laden dimensions of such inquiries as we set out in the Introduction to this volume. Moreover, given accepted historical analysis that early Greek civilisation constituted the bedrock of European culture, what is valuable in Bernal's investigation is that it raises a series of critical questions:

- What is a culture?
- What are its origins?
- After how long and under what circumstances does that which is borrowed or plundered become absorbed, naturalised and so indigenous?
- What then does 'indigenous' actually mean?

Jeffrey Skidmore explores the same question through music:

(Skidmore 2003)

> This vast collection of wonderful (Baroque) music, which fuses together the culture of three continents, is surprisingly still little-explored in this global age . . . *Los coflades de la estleya* has many Hispanic features but also introduces Cuban and West African rhythmic patterns which eventually developed into the *rhumba* . . . *Convidando esta la noche* also features dance patterns of African origin in the form of the *guararcha*, a dance still popular in Cuba.

This 'musical fusion' comes from missionary influences that followed the invasions of the 'conquistadores' as the cultures of the defeated (when not completely destroyed) are used as stimulants and sources for 'new' ideas to refresh existing artistic forms. At stake here are the ebbs and flows of ideas and practices throughout history, and the issues of power and hegemony which affect these patterns. Often, it is the analyses – subsequent to the events themselves – which frame these as aesthetically apolitical, as intimately engaged with colonial and postcolonial realities, or as part of the economic imperatives of global capitalism.

A note to the reader

By what right can we call the lived experience of others a dream/nightmare? Not because the facts are so oppressive that they can weakly be termed nightmarish; nor because hopes can weakly be called dreams.

In a dream the dreamer wills, acts reacts, speaks, and yet submits to the unfolding of a story which he scarcely influences. The dream happens to him. Afterwards he may ask another to interpret it. But sometimes a dreamer tries to break his dream by deliberately waking himself up.

(John Berger (1975: 7), *A Seventh Man*, Penguin Books)

Meyerhold, Artaud and intercultural theatre

In order to examine in more detail the heterogeneous and plural practices of (physical) theatre making which are emblematic of historical attempts at generating intercultural performance we focus on two key figures of early twentieth-century theatre, Meyerhold and Artaud. These two very different practitioners are rightly regarded as key influences on the development of contemporary physical theatres, and within these, on the role and potential of the performing body.

Although taught by Stanislavsky, and a close friend throughout his life, Meyerhold's working life was a monument against the narrow psychological tendencies of Realism/ Naturalism: 'theatre built on psychological foundations is as certain to collapse as a house built on sand' (Braun 1991: 199). To realise the kind of disciplined physical theatri-cality in the service of a theatre that was at once politically engaged, and a celebration of paradox and complexity, Meyerhold required highly trained actors. Moreover, for his actors to move confidently from genre to genre, such training could not be a short-term affair: 'an actor must study as a violinist does, for seven to nine years. You can't make yourself into an actor in three to four years' (Gladkov 1997: 108). In the quest to create his own modern (physical) theatre Meyerhold looked to inspiration from theatres beyond Russia (then the Soviet Union), both historically and from other cultures. From within the traditions of European popular theatre Meyerhold drew upon the spirit and technical conventions of *commedia dell'arte*, but beyond this he began to investigate, and became receptive to, some of the practices of Eastern dance-dramas.

Braun notes that in his 'Studio Programme for 1916–1917', Meyerhold includes as subjects for discussion 'the conventions of Hindu drama (Kālidāsa)' and 'stage and acting conventions in the Japanese and Chinese theatres (1991: 154) as ingredients towards establishing those elements of the theatrical that he was searching for. In the subsequent syllabus drawn up in 1918 for a new acting school this becomes more precisely inclusive as the study of:

> styles of theatrical presentation . . . and the peculiarities of theatres which develop   (Leach 1993: 51)
> from . . . exotic theatre (Indian, Japanese, Chinese).

As Leach points out, Russia's geographical and cultural heterogeneity and location – proximity on its Eastern borders with India and China – put Meyerhold in a position to see the 'external techniques of Japanese and Chinese theatre', with Kawakami's acting troupe touring in 1902 (ibid.: 55). Leach gives examples from a number of sources of Meyerhold's admiration and inspiration for such techniques:

> the 'negation' . . . was exemplified by Meyerhold in the Japanese theatre's   (Ibid.: 59–60)
> 'hanamichi' or 'flower walk' down which the actor entered while gesturing
> away from the stage . . . he himself found Mei Lan-fang's hands miraculously
> expressive.

But as early as 1909–1910, Meyerhold was writing of medieval Japan as a model for a theatre that would strip away false realism/illusion in favour of an immediacy and imagination. In his notes to his production of Molière's *Don Juan*, Meyerhold tells us that Molière attempted to:

(Braun 1991:
99–100)

shift the action . . . forward to the very edge of the proscenium . . . It was the same in medieval Japan. In the Nō plays . . . the director placed his actors on a stage close enough to the spectator for their dances, movements, gesticulations, grimaces and poses to be clearly visible . . . we know that special stage-assistants, known as 'kurogo' and clad in special black costumes . . . used to prompt the actors in full view of the audience . . . would quickly restore the graceful folds of the actor's train . . . After a battle the 'kurogo' would remove fallen helmets, weapons and cloaks . . . To this day the Japanese preserve the acting style of the days of the creators of Japanese drama.

Meyerhold wanted to find an economy and simplicity of movement in acting, a transparent theatricality; he seems to have followed Craig's injunction not merely to imitate but to use non-Western theatres as part of a means of finding an alternative theatricality to realism-naturalism. Meyerhold must be placed in a certain European context of practices which were rejecting perceived bourgeois theatre in favour of a more overt physical theatricality, a spectacle which would fire the imagination of the audience. For Meyerhold in the particular circumstances of a revolutionary Soviet Union this quest was not merely a refusal of bourgeois theatre, but a search for theatre practices that would be appropriate for the new and ground-breaking human relations of communism.

Meyerhold's innovations rested not only on his rediscovery of earlier European forms of the physical in theatre (for example, *commedia dell'arte*), but the unearthing of non-European practices which were to become part of his repertoire of training techniques and dramaturgies for new and revolutionary forms of theatre. With this brief history of how Meyerhold (re)constructed Soviet theatre we are confronted with questions of how to place his work within the context of contemporary discourses around interculturalism. To what extent did Meyerhold 'borrow' or 'take' without repayment and reciprocity, and in what sense is this way of framing the exchange relevant to the times and social circumstances in which he was operating in the early years of the Soviet Union? Moreover, to what extent is the presence or absence of a colonial context in enabling and framing this transaction critical to our understanding and evaluation of its cultural and ethical legitimacy? From sketchbook accounts such as these it is tempting to opt for a simple reaction that condemns Meyerhold's intercultural 'transplants' as exploitative for their lack of reciprocity and equity. However, we would argue that only a very close reading and contextual interrogation of Meyerhold's transactions, exchanges and ambitions would place us in a position to reach firm conclusions. It is enough at this juncture to pose the questions and to draw Meyerhold's practice into wider (inter)cultural discourses.

The example of Artaud in relation to the politics of interculturalism is better known, partly because of the extreme and passionate nature of his mission for theatre, and partly due to the overtly declamatory style in which he articulated and communicated this vision. Esslin states that in 1922 Artaud saw a troupe of 'Cambodian dancers performing in a replica of the temple of Angkor at the Marseilles Colonial Exhibition' (1976: 120). Nearly ten years later he witnessed a performance by Balinese dancers at the Colonial Exhibition in Paris in 1931. While this experience inspired two essays ('On the Balinese Theatre', 1931, and 'Oriental and Western Theatre', 1935, both in Artaud 1974), Susan Sontag notes that:

> the stimulus could just as well have come from observing the Theatre of a Dahomey
> tribe or the shamanistic ceremonies of the Patagonian Indians. What counts is that the
> other culture be genuinely other; that is, non-Western and non-contemporary.

(Sontag 2004: 91)

The point Sontag is making here is that the influence Artaud derived from the Cambodian and Balinese dancers was not as a consequence of a closely detailed encounter with these two forms, or as a considered artistic judgement about their formal potential for integration into his own practice, but simply because of their (generalised) otherness and his excitement at encountering visceral, sensual and non-psychological forms of theatre. Artaud put it like this:

> The first Balinese Theatre show derived from dance, singing, mime, and music – but
> extraordinarily little from psychological theatre such as we understand it in Europe . . .
> The Balinese produce the idea of pure theatre . . . whose creative ability *does away with*
> *words*.

(Artaud 1974: 38)

Artaud describes the techniques of movement, dance and vocal inflections as a new language based not on words, but signs which emerge through the gestures, postures and cries using the whole of the stage space. For Artaud, Western theatre's rejection of such metaphysical beings as ghosts was part of an increasingly rational psychologising of the supernatural which in turn suggested particular kinds of solution to their staging. The ghost presented in the Balinese way becomes something abstract, a metaphysics as spectacle, and offers Artaud an opportunity of physicalising theatre away from the shallow models of European practice which he increasingly rejects.

> Our theatre has never grasped this gestured metaphysics nor known how to make use
> of music for direct, concrete, dramatic purposes, our purely verbal theatre unaware of
> the sum total of theatre. . . . In Western theatre, words are solely used to express
> psychological conflicts peculiar to man and his position in everyday existence . . . In
> Oriental theatre with its metaphysical tendencies, as compared to Western theatre with
> its psychological tendencies, forms assume their meaning and significance on all
> possible levels.

(Ibid.: 40, 53–54)

Our purpose here is not to denigrate Artaud, but to demonstrate his case as perhaps the quintessential example of the kind of interculturalism that charges critiques from commentators such as Said and Bharucha. Artaud's wholesale dismissal of Western theatres, seductive though it might be at the level of cultural rhetoric, is at best highly selective, and at worst quite simply poor history.

Our book has demonstrated that within these accounts of European theatre which are, of course, only 'Western' in the most general sense, there is a rich and complex history of physically expressive performance practices. These have articulated human existence and its preoccupations as part of a totality of staging and theatricality. Artaud's besottedness with Eastern practices, and his palpable exoticisation of them, speaks as much for an atavistic rejection of Western culture and society as it does for any close reading of these forms. His use of these cultures to construct an ideological and metaphysical alternative to word-based Western 'psychological' theatre represents what Chakravorty characterises as 'the cultural appropriation of the "eternal" Orient as the repository of exotic customs and spiritual mysticism' (2000–2001: 110).

We must reiterate that is not our intention to devalue the extraordinary contributions of both Meyerhold and Artaud to twentieth-century theatres. Self-evidently, they continue to inspire and influence theory, composition and training, and remain central to the practices of physical theatres. But they also stand for a tendency to decontextualise the influences and inspirations that such practitioners themselves take from other forms and practices. We are arguing that this appropriation should always be properly acknowledged as the political dimension and framing of a properly historicised discussion. To do this can only assist in a deeper understanding of such ideas and practices, but without disqualifying them on the grounds of unreciprocated borrowings. What is clear is that such theatrical ideas, stagings and physical practices of the body must be placed in a perspective that acknowledges both the process and spectacle of this 'exotic' other, *and* its consequences for theatre dramaturgy and audience reception. From such uncritical and reverential 'borrowing' it is only a short journey to the global festival circuit which lifts works from their original context and presents them to the gaze of the culturally privileged.

Binglish

This treatise (the *Natya-Shastra*) . . . posits four constituent elements of theatre: *Abhinaya* – Gesture (which includes movement); *Vacikam* – Speech (which includes music); *Aharayam* – Costume (which includes make-up); and *Sattvikam* – the Mind (which includes emotion) . . . At the heart of the *Natya-Shastra* is the theory of *rasa* . . . the closest modern rendering of the word would be 'flavour' [or 'savour'] . . . 'The actor. does not experience *rasa*, nor does the original character, nor even the author, for rasa implies distance. Without this aesthetic distance, there cannot exist literature, only the primary world' (Abhinavagupta).

(Jatinder Verma (1996: 199), 'The Challenge of Binglish: Analysing Multi-cultural Productions',
in P. Campbell (ed.) *Analysing Performance: A Critical Reader,* Manchester University Press)

Contemporary case studies

How do we move from such contextualising matters to global bodies and physical theatres? As we see in the *Natya-Shastra* as cited by Verma, once again there is an emphasis on the interconnectivity of the parts of theatre, and by implication a rejection of any dualisms of body–mind–word. (Of course, this still leaves open the balance between the constituent parts of theatre, or whether one element is deliberately privileged as the dominant language of the piece.)

We look now at two case studies, where we can see how certain embodied practices from other cultures have been transposed into modes of theatre which echo forms we are more familiar with. Both examples could easily be categorised as cross- or intercultural, serving to illustrate both the function and difficulty already seen with such terms.

The Mudrooroo/Müller Project

C A S E   S T U D Y   1

This 'is an exercise in political theatre based on a dual, collaborative perspective – white/European and Aboriginal' (Fischer and Narogin 1993: Preface). It brings together a 'Koori' text by the Native Australian author Mudrooroo Narogin, and Heiner Müller's *The Commission*, presented under the title *The Aboriginal Protesters Confront the Declaration of the Australian Republic on 26 January 2001 with the production of 'The Commission' by Heiner Müller.* It should be noted that the whole play is presented in English. The project and performance is an intertextual play-within-a-play, using different levels of historical events and places. Aboriginal performers present a very particular perspective on the events and issues of colonialism, cultural appropriation and subjugation, and the use of the 'grotesque' in an anarchic, political comedy.

> Slowly the three are dressed entirely in white, with shoes and gloves to match, finally white masks are put on to complete the metamorphosis. It is a vision of Aboriginal performers appropriating for themselves the roles/personae of the white masters/liberators.
>
> (Ibid.: 5)

Mudrooroo is attracted by the project because 'he is interested in a Brechtian type of theatre: that is, a political/sociological rather than a psychological/naturalistic one' (ibid.: 12). The performance is on an open stage, with a set that suggests 'the numerous Aboriginal tent embassies which have been erected at regular intervals during the continuing Aboriginal struggle' (ibid.: 77). But this familiar 'political' signification is disrupted by the appearance of four Djangara, described as like fluttering, giant white moths who 'represent another level of Aboriginal reality/spirituality' (ibid.: 76). These figures take on the performative functions of chorus, irritants to the characters, musical accompanists, dancers. They perform, they create tableaux. They close the performance by dancing **corroboree** with King George.

They never speak, but represent a physical embodiment of spiritual reality: a 'purely' physical performance. But they are also an example of the exoticising effect of a theatre which presents the unfamiliar within a recognisable theatrical frame. In significant respects this is a staging device which anyone familiar with 'Brechtian' political theatre would understand. However, here, that which is recognised is also exoticised by the introduction and use of figures from another culture. This raises difficult questions about, for example, how a white – non-Aboriginal – spectator can look at these figures from Native Australian culture who are being presented as 'other' beings through recognisable devices of physical theatre – movement, costume and sound – without objectifying them as both bizarre and glamorous. Perhaps we are faced with another aspect of the discourses around 'gazing' where we both look at the subject and 'gaze' at it, hence 'exoticising' and objectifying that subject to a greater or lesser extent.

C A S E   S T U D Y   2

Dry Lips Oughta Move to Kapuskasing

The final section of the *Harcourt-Brace Anthology of Drama* (Worthen 2000) is entitled 'World Stages', bringing together ten plays from eight countries, all from the second half of the twentieth century. Tomson Highway's *Dry Lips Oughta Move to Kapuskasing* from 1989 (hereafter *Dry Lips*) is written and played in a mixture of Cree, Ojibway and English. He is a Native Canadian writer and director, aiming to give Native mythologies and narratives a central place in contemporary theatre.

The first setting for *Dry Lips* that we see is a naturalistic one of a living room/kitchen of a Native reserve house; then from behind the couch/sofa the figure of Nanabush appears. Highway describes Nanabush thus,

> The dream world of North American Indian mythology is inhabited by the most fantastic creatures, beings and events. Foremost among these beings is the 'Trickster' . . . Nanabush in Ojibway, this 'Trickster' goes by many names and guises . . . 'he' can assume any guise he chooses. Essentially a comic, clownish sort of character, 'his' role is to teach us about the nature and the meaning of existence on the planet Earth; he straddles the consciousness of man and that of God, the Great Spirit.

> (Worthen 2000: 1377)

Once again we see (an)other figure from a different realm of being – this time an androgynous shape-shifter – erupting into a familiar, realistic setting, who then leaves the living room but remains as a presence throughout the play and entering into the plot in various guises, as a female spirit or principle. Again, we see the physical embodiment of phenomena that, whether considered to be supernatural spirits, phantasmagoria or cultural constructions, are certainly theatrical fabrications. As such they echo much more familiar figures from theatre such as The Ghost (*Hamlet*), the Fairies (*A Midsummer Night's Dream*), or Poseidon and Athene (*The Women of Troy*). Within their own cultural frameworks these are beings accepted for themselves, but now presented within the context of theatre making as rather awkward staging problems to be resolved. From the perspective of this chapter, that resolving has increasingly been one of 'borrowing' or 'taking' from other contemporary cultures, and thus 'exoticising' the spectacle. The danger here is that we use devices from 'other' cultures to make what we feel uncomfortable with acceptable, by turning this discomfort into a spectacle of the exotic.

Wallpaper disasters

We see the disaster which comes to our wallpapers and other crafts by too warm an admiration of Japanese art . . . we must be aware of any sudden influence which would lead to imitation, especially so strange an influence as that to be brought to bear by the East upon the West.

(Edward Gordon Craig, *The Mask 1* (1908) in Earle Ernst (1969), 'The Influence of Japanese Theatrical Style on Western Theatre', *Educational Theatre Journal* 21(2): 130)

Universal bodies

We finish this chapter by examining an issue which often appears to be at the heart of dialogues between physical theatres: the physical in theatre and matters of culture. This connects specific training practices, and assumptions which underpin these practices, with questions about the 'construction' of bodies within and across cultures. It raises issues of sameness and difference, and how these signify and impact in cross- and intercultural encounters. Moreover, these preoccupations invite scrutiny of the potential for trans-cultural encounters and relations. In other words, how and at what point in the generative process of making theatre do bodies evade and transcend the cultures that have nurtured and shaped them?

In Chapter 4, 'Preparation and Training', we examined the pedagogies of a number of influential figures in twentieth-century theatre and performance training. One of the issues which regularly surfaced in these accounts was the quest for the *neutral* or *pre-expressive* body, a body which by implication was stripped of its cultural and social characteristics accumulated through the life of the actor in question, and thereby 'ready' for the myriad challenges of performing. While the task of 'stripping away' the corporeal, emotional and psychological habits of daily life as preparation for the acquisition of vocal and physical skills is common to almost all approaches to actor training, the nature, purpose and philosophical assumptions which underpin such strategies vary considerably between practitioners. As we have seen in Chapter 4, Jacques Lecoq's teaching with the neutral mask to achieve a state of neutrality in his students remains central to the pedagogy of his school several years after his death. For Lecoq, however, this work is less about engendering a state of universal neutrality in his students – 'there is no such thing as absolute and universal neutrality, it is merely a temptation' (Lecoq 2000: 20) – than with the 'demystification of ready-made ideas' (Lecoq 1973: 41). But, crucially it is also an invitation for students to (re) know the world through all their faculties – touch, sight, smell, movement and hearing – as well as through intellectual and cognitive processes. Unlike Eugenio Barba and Jerzy Grotowski, Lecoq does not make claims that neutrality produces a universal and pre-expressive body. For him it is primarily a teaching strategy, 'a tool for analysing the quality of the body's action' (Eldredge and Huston 1995: 127).

For Barba, however, there is a different project at work. As we have seen in Chapter 4, central to Barba's pedagogy is the quest for presence which he defines as the qualities which render the actor 'scenically alive'. To become 'scenically alive' the performer has to find a state of 'pre-expressivity', and this we have investigated in 'Preparation and Training'. Pre-expressivity concerns the energy – or *bios* as Barba calls it – with which any performer, regardless of culture, acting style or theatrical genre, becomes alive and engaging. The techniques of pre-expressivity are therefore pre-cultural and so – argues Barba – escape cultural codings and locations. The point here is that for Barba there is an aspiration to generate theatre which becomes a site of and for cultural exchange, and the state of pre-expressivity is a necessary condition for the success of such a venture. Julia Varley, a long-standing member of Barba's Odin Teatret, articulates the ambition behind the quest for pre-expressivity:

(Varley 1995: 41; emphasis in original)

> What I recognised as familiar and close, as common to my own professional culture, was something that grows beyond theatre and becomes a way of living in this world, of communicating and existing, of standing by one's values and searching for the sense of our craft. These people belong to my *pre-expressive family*.

Towards these and other dimensions of Barba and Odin's work (for example, his creation of the term 'Eurasian theatre'), there has been considerable criticism, notably by Rustom Bharucha. Bharucha, as we have already seen, finds in the pretensions, claims and aspirations of such practices at best an inexcusable naivety, and at worst an exploitative cultural colonialism of West to East.

Attempts to identify and work creatively upon what is common and universal between different cultures has fuelled the practices of many contemporary theatre makers with differing degrees of intensity and ambition. Peter Brook articulates the aspiration as follows:

(Brook 1989: 129)

> Each culture expresses a different portion of the inner atlas; the complete human truth is global, and the theatre is the place in which the jigsaw can be pieced together.

As a plurality of forms and practices, physical theatres have often been at the centre of these attempts to create theatre that transcends boundaries and cultural differences. For obvious reasons the specificities of language have meant that the theatre forms most likely to serve the impulse to transculturalism will be those which are highly visual and which employ and explore vocabularies of movement and physicality. Hence, transcultural directors such as Brook, McBurney, Mnouchkine and Bogart, in searching for what is not reducible to specific cultures, will regularly look to gestural and movement-based theatre languages in the belief that it is in the body that these universal qualities are most likely to reside. Here again, as with all areas of discourse around cultures and their relationships, we are moving across a messy and tortuous terrain in which the parameters between honourable, utopian ambition and opportunistic, politically regressive behaviour are blurred and shifting.

Another axis of difficulty, of course, is the tension between the socially constructed and the biologically given body, and this in turn takes us in to the complexities of identity theory. From doubts around these issues it is a short step to raise questions about the real nature of 'pre-expressivity'. Is it a chimera? What is the essential body beyond tissues, bones, fluids and neurones? Or is it simply a useful code, and, like so many injunctions about theatre practice, merely a metaphor to help interpret and guide our attempts at practice?

Rhetoric, optimism and utopias

Utopias in performance

The force of the utopian text . . . is not to bring into focus the future that is coming to be, but rather to make us conscious precisely of the horizons or outer limits of what can be thought and imagined in our present.

(Fredric Jameson in Jill Dolan (2005: 13), *Utopia in Performance*: *Finding Hope in The Theatre*, University of michigan Press)

In conversation with Andrzej Bonarski, the American theatre director, Joseph Chaikin (1935–2003) said that 'one of the very constant questions is: what can be affirmed?' (Chaikin 1999: 443). In a different time and context Meyerhold insisted that the function of art in a revolutionary context is to inspire. The debate which we traced above, and which has been mapped and rehearsed in hundreds of publications and public events over three decades or more, is a complex series of answers to Chaikin's question, 'what can be affirmed?' It also gives responses to Meyerhold's faith in inspiration.

That the performance practices of hundreds of disparate theatre makers, all committed to what one might loosely call the task of performing utopia, have provoked such mixtures of fury and affirmation indicates that any act of imagining of this kind is an edgy and risky business that constantly teeters on an abyss of political explosion. Hans-Thies Lehmann sums up the difficulty in any practice that attempts to work between cultures:

(Lehmann 2006: 176)

> An underlying ambiguity continues to exist in all intercultural communication as long as cultural forms of expression are always at the same time part of a politically dominant culture or of an oppressed culture, so that it is not 'communication' of equals that occurs between the two cultures.

Thus the issue is very much one of contexts and levels rather than of the rhetoric of aspiration and ambition. Context tells us that the growth of arts festivals across Europe, planned in the spirit of repairing the schisms and wounds caused by the Second World War, must be read differently in times of twenty-first-century globalisation from in the post-war 1950s. A sense of context also requires not only an acute attention to questions of power and (in)equity, but equally a close consideration of the actual – lived and felt – transactions between those individuals and groups engaged in cultural exchange. The refusal of these exchanges to fit neatly into circumscribed ideological agendas, the very unpredictable and disorderly messiness of cultural encounters through the making of (physical) theatres, reveal opportunities for optimism and possibility. David Williams in his essay for *PT:R* puts it like this:

(Williams in *PT:R*, p. 240; emphasis added)

> Too often the detail of the messy and serendipitous histories of exchanges of cultural practices, and the multi-directional complexities of circuits and flows, were overlooked or rewritten in terms of a narrative of appropriative 'one-way traffic'. At the point of *embodied* encounter between performers or forms from different contexts, inevitably this detail is hard to track and map . . . and yet as in all encounters it is central to what can and does animate cultures and identities as 'works in progress'.

Here it is precisely the disorderly, messy, contradictory and multi-directional nature of these embodied encounters which allow them to escape – as 'works in progress' – from what sometimes seems to be a pre-ordained cultural colonialism into more productive, inventive and hopeful exchanges. Later in his essay, Williams eloquently restates his position articulated in Williams (1991) and Pavis (1996) by suggesting that there was a 'critical gap' between what happened during the process of making and performing *The Mahabharata* – 'more complex, multiple and contradictory' (*PT:R*, p. 242) – and what Brook's sometimes naïve and clumsy idealist rhetoric claimed was happening. There are parallels here, perhaps, with Susan Sontag's staging of *Waiting for Godot* in war-ravaged Sarajevo in 1993. Like Brook, but for slightly different reasons, Sontag was accused of both arrogance and naivety in the claims ascribed to her for this project. As with Brook's *Mahabharata*, however, there are different lenses, frames and contexts for regarding Sontag's mission to Sarajevo. Whether *Godot* spoke authentically for the suffering of Sarajevo and the circumstances which gave rise to this genocidal conflict may be debated interminably, and whether Sontag's own utterances were wise or prescient at the time seems less important now than the event itself. The act of performing *Godot* in such circumstances seems to articulate a recognition of both difference and sameness in these extreme circumstances, and what Julie Stone Peters calls a 'multi-vocal political agenda' and 'strategic universalism' (1995: 207).

Brook's *Mahabharata* and Sontag's *Godot* seem an appropriate way to end this chapter: both rich in complexity, both framed and contextualised by highly charged political circumstances, both engaging with embodied displacement, both leaving questions unanswered and both offering the possibility of a 'strange sense of flourishing in the midst of enormity' (Sayers 1990: 146).

The memory of humankind

[Few collections have the scope of the British Museum] to challenge one of the great myths of our time – that civilisations are discrete entities that 'clash', according to . . . Samuel Huntington. Rather the British Museum can illustrate how civilisations are knitted together in a myriad of connections – economic, political, cultural – and are run through by common human preoccupations – birth, death, status, and the sacred . . .

Memory is the precondition of sanity, loss of memory is the loss of identity.

(Madeleine Bunting, *Guardian,* 15 March 2007)

CHAPTER 7

Conclusion by way of Lexicon

Contrary to the practice of good essay writing habitually enjoined by university tutors, we have eschewed the possibility of a worthy conclusion which attempts to summarise and encapsulate our arguments in a sober, linear and unfolding manner. Perhaps, this would have meant rewriting the book, and we have spared you (and ourselves) this. Instead there follows a lexicon, which the *Oxford English Dictionary* variously suggests is a 'complete set of elementary meaningful units in a language', or more prosaically 'a list of words or names'. Daunted by the former, and enjoying the pleasure of list making, we offer an A–Z of thoughts, reflections, interjections and asides around, above and below the subject matter(s) of this book: physical theatres and the physical *in* theatre(s).

Lexicon

Action of the mind and body in gesture, posture, exhibition; violent, cathartic, graceful as one moment is left for the next, but the traces follow.

Art:

(Berger 2005: 3)

> I can't tell you what art does and how it does it, but I know that art has often judged the judges, pleaded revenge to the innocent and shown to the future what the past has suffered, so that it has never been forgotten. I know too that the powerful fear art, whatever its form, when it does this, and that amongst the people such art sometimes runs like a rumour and a legend because it makes sense of what life's brutalities cannot, a sense that unites us, for it is inseparable from a justice at last. Art, when it functions like this, becomes a meeting place of the invisible, the irreducible, the enduring, guts and honour.

Barenboim (Daniel) and Edward Said: a conversation across boundaries, an embodied politics of collaboration.

> Conversations not treatises . . . to share our thoughts amiably and energetically with each other, and with others for whom music, culture and politics today form a unique whole. But what that whole is, I am happy to say, neither of us can fully state.

(Said and Barenboim 2004: xvi)

Bent knees: softening behind the knees, unlocking the legs, a state of readiness for play, a softening for alertness, the opposite of locked shut, closed, fixed, brittle, tight.

Buster Keaton, the stony-faced clown, impassive, doing nothing and everything, physically improvising in the moment.

Circus bodies, trained, muscular, light, erotic, flying, catching, falling, balancing, leaping, diving. Difficult to fake the circus body.

Clown: with the red nose as smallest mask; the fool who makes us sad as we laugh; who disrupts order to invent a new order to disrupt.

Composition: balance – tension – harmony – crisis – filling the space or canvas.

Crisis: a moment of uncertainty, loss: both problem and opportunity.

Dennis Potter:

> In 'Blue Remembered Hills', for example, I used adult actors to play children in order to make them like a magnifying glass, to show what it's like. And because if you look at a child, talk about present tense, that's all they, all a small child lives in. So a wet Tuesday afternoon can actually be years long, and it – childhood – is full to the brim of fear, horror, excitement, joy, boredom, love, anxiety, every . . . you know, loss. Loss.

(Potter 1994: 7)

> **D**own with poisonous slickness, defensive seamlessness and rhetorical authority. We'd rather have the provisional, the vulnerable and the playful. We'd rather have the event that unfolds and unravels. We want intimacy, transformation, negotiation, subversion, provocation, teasing, exchange, exhaustion, confrontation, slipping, sliding, ephemerality and eye contact. Less than this is very likely bullshit.

(Etchells 2004a: 211)

Élan: born out of lightness, pleasure, in and out of the moment, impossible with tight/locked muscles, a state the French have the word for, but other cultures do it differently. An embodiment and physicalisation of generosity. The root/route to presence.

Elbow: search for the articulate elbow.

Ensemble: a gathering showing another way. Not counting, but sensing, noticing, listening, hearing, watching, feeling, smelling, slowing, waiting and listening again – together.

Fool/fooling around: see **C**lown.

Garance (Arletty): lover of Baptiste Debureau (Jean-Louis Barrault), the son of Anselme Debureau (Etienne Decroux): *Les Enfants du Paradis*, Marcel Carné, Paris 1945.

Give and take: see **E**nsemble.

Ham acting: see *cabotinage*, Meyerhold and Forced Entertainment.

Human: at the centre of all theatres.

Humanism: ready to be reclaimed, refined, reconfigured, wrested back (see Edward Said in Chapter 6, 'Bodies and Cultures').

Imbalance: ready to fall, muscle alert, (a)liveness. A critical physical disposition for every moment of performance. A quality of mind–body, body–mind.

Interior monologue:

(Kantor in
Miklaszewski
2005: 28)

> As far as I was concerned, the most important thing in this production was to disclose the multiplicity of all the elements I had selected, so that the spectators, because they are what count all the while, felt the impossibility (which is crucial) of taking in the whole of the performance from a spectator's standpoint.

Intuition: ignored, unexplained, untrustworthy, eluding meaning and intelligibility; not mystical, but a muscle to exercised, strengthened, practised, shared and to be made *expert*; a driving motor for constructing, developing material; a way to join the gaps. A physical skill enabling shifting, moving, unblocking, opening. Often, as good a way as any other.

Journey that does not end, or take us where we intended: often an unknown destination.

Jump cut: the transition from one moment to the next which omits space and time.

Knee: the lower elbow. Search for the articulate knee.

Light: less weight, less dark, but creates shadows within its illumination.

Lightness: sister to élan, child of pleasure, mother of invention, brother to discovery, father to play, lover to foolishness and the oblique.

McBurney, Simon:

(McBurney in
Berger 2005: 77)

> John Berger writes books. I stage events. Both of us address an audience. Or spectators. I am not sure how we work with each other. Most of the time I do not know how to describe how to work with anyone. There is always a gulf. How can I express what I imagine to another. How does one private and solitary imagination be shared with another. How can they be 'put together'? Surely they must do their own separate thing. Where to begin? There are the facts. A project to be completed. A show to put on.

Marlene Dietrich: for Meyerhold and Eisenstein an embodiment of the quintessential 'biomechanic' actor.

(No):

(La Ribot in
Heathfield 2004: 30)

> There is no more representation, only presentation
> There is no more magic, only reality
> There are no more surprises, only variable perceptions
> There are no more statements, only ambiguity
> There is no more stability, only imbalance
> There is no more theatricality, only plasticity.

Olivier, Laurence (Sir/Lord): unknown physical theatre actor (deceased). But thoughts from Kenneth Tynan:

(Tynan 1989:
204–5)

> He holds all the cards . . . (a) complete physical relaxation, (b) powerful physical magnetism, (c) commanding eyes that are visible at the back of the gallery, (d)

commanding voice that is audible without effort at the back of the gallery, (e) superb timing, (f) chutzpah . . . cool nerve and outrageous effrontery combined, and (g) the ability to communicate a sense of danger. . . . Deep in his temperament there runs a vein of rage. . . . One of that select group of performers (great athletes, bullfighters, singers, politicians, ballet dancers and vaudeville comedians are some of the others) whose special gift is to . . . exercise fingertip control over the emotions of a large number of people gathered in one place to witness a single unique event.

Original(ity): an attempt to be avoided at all costs (see *Trying too hard* below). Achieved when least expected and (often) when embracing the cliché.

Platel, Alain (*Les Ballets C de la B*):

On stage I put the beautiful body next to the deformed, the spastic, the desperate body. Because then I feel I put my demons on stage to fight them. I realise how frightening it can be for the actors/dancers . . . I put very different people on stage. In the beginning of the working-process they like this very much. But it is frightening how fast this feeling is changed into a Yugoslavian battlefield where individual racism, sexism and fascism is so obvious. And nobody escapes from it. To recognise and overcome these feelings is one of the hardest steps in the process.

(Platel 1996: 84)

Play:

free movement or capricious actions
A dramatic or theatrical mimetic performance
A game or sport for amusement and competition (Jeu; Ludic)

(Oxford English Dictionary)

Production: work, work, work (making the actions of theatre: the made theatre).

Putting the body back into mind: the mind into body.

Quiet . . . : otherwise you cannot listen. But see/hear John Cage *4'33"* (1952).

Rough theatre, always physical: noisy, bad, embarrassing, passionate, large, vulgar, care-less, refusing deference, hot, sweaty, boisterous, blue and rude.

Sebald, W.G.

In deepest sleep
a Polish mechanic
came & for a
thousand silver dollars made me
a new perfectly
functioning head.

(Sebald and Tripp 2004: 35)

Shit (in the). Source: Philippe Gaulier. That moment of failure when either you leave the floor/stage, or when the body – petrified, numb, wanting to be somewhere/anywhere else – begins a little miracle of (re)invention and again you take the first steps to fly.

Site (specific) theatre:

As you walk keep your eyes peeled for as many (CCTV) cameras as possible.
Potential tactics:

* put on your best clothes and make-up

(Wrights and Sites 2003: 25)

- show off as much as possible
- 'make love' to the cameras
- create routines to perform to anonymous viewers
- knock up placards with messages on them and parade in front of the cameras.

Spectator: always present when theatre is in evidence.

Tools of the trade: the body, the voice, the mind, the passion, the craft, the impulse, the seized moment.

Trying too hard: wanting too much, mistaking process for ends, being out of the moment (knees locked, jaw clenched, eyes tight).

Turn of the body is maybe all it needs.

Unquiet: not listening and so missing the point – maybe.

Unruly: the body to be disciplined? The purpose of training?

Voice: that is seen as well as heard; an extension of the body in space.

Walking: everyday physical theatre, a complex, singular act worth analysing, connecting A to B, and today the politics of walking.

Weight given, weight taken + =: see **E**nsemble.

(Walter Benjamin 1999, quoted in Quick 2006: 150)

What is truly revolutionary is not the propaganda of ideas, which leads here and there to impractical actions and vanishes in a puff of smoke upon the first sober reflection at the theatre exit. What is truly revolutionary is the secret signal of what is to come that speaks from the gesture of the child.

(Johnson 1987: ix)

Without imagination, nothing in the world could be meaningful. Without imagination, we could never make sense of our experience. Without imagination, we could never reason toward knowledge of reality . . . the central role of human imagination in all meaning, understanding and reasoning.

Wonder: at the moment being created in front of us, never the same again.

Xcitement: at the wonder in front of us.

(Perret in Lecoq 2006: 43)

You're disturbing me – I'm working (*at more than 85 years of age he was still working!*). You speak of gestures, now gestures are interesting. But what do you expect me to say about them? You shouldn't be disturbing me while I am working. Lecoq, you speak of Lecoq? Well he, too, is a pioneer. But there's nothing I can say. *Jean Perret's buffeting first encounter over the telephone with Etienne Decroux.*

Zero. Point Zero: elusive. Year Zero (Pol Pot): dangerous.

Zzzzzz: the sound of deadly (physical) theatre.

Glossary

Actant. The actantial model of theatre analysis has become essential in semiotic and dramaturgical research, and is one that does not artificially separate character from action, but reveals the dialectical relationship between them. The *actant* is the embodied relationship between performer/actor and character, and at the same time is the actor's narrative function to (re)present character. It is a conceptual formation which obliges us to understand 'acting' as a doubling of person and the character (or thing) represented.

Agon. In ancient Greece *agon* was the site of contest and competition in arts and sport, and included challenges between choruses and playwrights. In traditional dramatic structures the *agon* characterises the conflict or tension between actor and character, and opposing characters or forces *within* the drama. Thus, it has been argued, it is at the centre of all theatre and its driving forces. Today, however, a whole range of dramaturgies are not based upon the *agon* principle of character, action and conflict.

Autocours is an approach to teaching theatre devising and composition introduced by Jacques Lecoq at his school following the student rebellions of 1968 in Paris and across the world. It remains an indispensable part of the school's pedagogy today, giving time to students to work rapidly through improvisation and devising on a short piece of theatre they will show to their tutors for critique and feedback.

Corroboree is a night-time dance of Australian Aborigines which may be either festive or warlike. It can also be a song or chant for this event.

Denote/connote. *Denote* means to convey the closest most literal meaning of a term, object, setting, etc. A set of furnishings/fittings (e.g. stove, sink, cupboards, freezer) *denotes* that this space is a kitchen where one cooks and – sometimes – eats. If such a setting is lavishly equipped with expensive, state-of-the-art 'white goods' and tasteful, handcrafted furniture then these may also *connote* the wealth and ostentation of a bourgeois family or household. *Connote* means, therefore, to signify *beyond* the fundamental meaning of the object or term.

Diachronic means explaining or understanding an event or phenomenon in relation to historical developments and forces. It is contrasted with *synchronic* which looks for explanations within a particular time frame rather than from historical causes/routes.

Dialectic/dialectical. In classical philosophy dialectical thought is an exchange of propositions (theses) and counter-propositions (antitheses) resulting in a synthesis of opposing assertions, or at least a significant transformation from the original idea. Marxists view *dialectics* as a framework or explanation for historical movement/progress in which contradiction – through the struggle between different classes – plays a vital role in the development of new ideas and social structures.

Diegetic/diegesis refers to the 'pure' (abstracted) narrative of the drama/theatre without it being enacted or presented through mimesis. Spectators are invited to believe and 'take for granted' diegetic action – events, for example, reported but not 'manufactured' or acted out on stage. *Non-diegetic* action reveals its artifice and shows *how* the fiction is produced.

Epic theatre (Brecht) refers to forms of theatre that go beyond classical 'Aristotelian' dramaturgies of character, catharsis and dramatic conflict. *Epic theatre* obliges actors and spectators to 'distance' themselves from the action or narrative so as to offer – to *show* – a critical stance on the characters and stories being told. Epic theatre turns spectators into witnesses by demanding an ethical and political engagement with character, action and story-line.

Gestus. Until Brecht stamped his own particular meaning on the term, *gestus* indicated a *characteristic* way of using one's body. Meyerhold identified 'pose positions' to suggest a character's fundamental gestural and corporeal qualities. Brechtian *gestus* adds a crucial social/political dimension to the word, insisting that a character's physical attitude, tone of voice, facial expression and so on are all determined by social and cultural factors, and that acting must account for these influences. Brecht also takes this further by arguing that a whole play or piece of theatre needs to find its *basic social gestus*. In other words, theatre makers need to identify and realise through scenography and actors' embodiment the social/cultural/political universe of the play.

Hegemonic/hegemony refers to the way that beliefs, ways of seeing and patterns of behaviour become dominant in a society. Particularly developed by the Italian Marxist philosopher/activist, Antonio Gramsci (1891–1937), who saw *hegemony* as the process by which ideas, actions, structures and behaviours come to be accepted by the majority as normal, natural and therefore inevitable and for everyone's 'own good', whereas they are socially/politically/culturally constructed in order to serve the particular interests of the powerful.

Katharsis or catharsis means literally the purification or cleansing of emotions through vicarious experience. For Aristotle, *catharsis* is one of the goals and consequences of classical tragedy, and it has been central to debates about the function of drama/theatre for 2000 years. Brecht, however, challenged the assumptions of *catharsis* by arguing that its existence is due to the spectator's ideological alienation and it is predicated upon the ahistorical and decontextualised nature of dramatic character. Notwithstanding Brecht's influence, many theatre theorists today have a more subtle perspective, viewing *catharsis* in a dialectical relationship between what is felt and a more critical or aesthetic distance from the events of the drama/theatre.

Liminal refers to the space *between* events and objects. It speaks of a disposition within contemporary arts practices to explore and celebrate the – apparently – marginal, incidental and insignificant, and as such represents a political attitude to material and subject matter. *Liminal* spaces invite protagonists to be on the cusp, to enjoy threshold and to explore the nature and feelings of boundaries.

Mimesis/mimetic. *Mimesis* (from the Greek *mimeistkai*) means the imitation or representation of something or someone, usually employing physical or linguistic means, but the term is broad enough to cover the representation of an idea, belief or thought. For Aristotle, in *Poetics,* mimesis is the fundamental mode of all art and not just theatre, although in much contemporary arts discourse/practice there is debate and preoccupation around whether art can exceed or refuse *mimesis*. *Mimetic* means pertaining to or characterised by imitation/*mimesis*: an attempt to represent the real world in arts practices.

Mirror neurons. *Neurons* are a particular network of cells found in the pre-motor area of the brain. These cells are activated when the subject performs a motor skill or action. But when the subject witnesses another subject perform or suffers the same actions, a subset of these neurons are activated also – hence *mirror neurons*. This is a neural mechanism involved not only in action recognition, but also as a mechanism for understanding – coding and decoding – the (action) intention(s) of others.

Mise-en-scène means literally the 'action of putting on the play', and refers to all elements of the staging of a piece of theatre – lighting, design, acting, props and costumes – and their relationship to each other and to spectators.

Polysemic means having several or multiple meanings. As a perspective – or way of seeing – it is indispensable in our approach to understanding physical theatres.

Proprioceptor is a sensory receptor which receives stimuli from within the body, and one that particularly responds to position and movement.

Score. In theatre terms scoring a piece of devised/improvised movement or vocal work requires actors/performers to notate, record and learn the actions or vocal patterns discovered so that they can be repeated and performed with complete accuracy. Directors like Eugenio Barba use *scoring* as part of their compositional strategy and here a *score* created by an actor in rehearsal might be reconfigured (and shared) by altering its size, rhythm and texture.

Somatic means relating to the body and implies an activity or a process which is 'hands-on' and physical, rather than cerebral and intellectual. The term, however, can sometimes unwittingly reinforce a false distinction between 'mind' and 'body'.

Syncretic theatre refers to the 'amalgamation of indigenous performance forms with certain conventions and practices of the Euro-American theatrical tradition to produce new theatrico-aesthetic principles' (Balme in Pavis 1996: 180). We would add that syncretic theatre pays little heed to the context in which these forms were originally conceived and performed, and therefore is often guilty – deliberately or not – of 'cultural colonialism'.

Trope. For the purposes of our usage in this book *trope* refers to a way of identifying regularly repeated and returned to qualities of form, theme, motif, style or structure so that it is possible to propose some fluid typologies that seem to be present among and between different bodies of work. *Trope* is looser than 'category' and more open than 'definition' and we use the term in a manner that acknowledges its schematic and porous nature.

Bibliography

Aeschylus (1953) *Oresteia*, trans Richmond Lattimore, Chicago: University of Chicago Press.

Aggiss, Liz and Cowie, Billy (2006) *Anarchic Dance*, London: Routledge.

Ansorge, Peter (1975) *Disrupting the Spectacle*, London: Isaac Pitman & Sons.

Arden, Annabel (2001) Interview in *On Acting*, ed. Mary Luckhurst and Chloe Veltman, London: Faber.

Aristotle (1967) *The Poetics*, trans I. Bywater, Oxford: Oxford University Press.

Arnheim, Rudolf (1969) *Visual Thinking*, Berkeley: University of California Press.

Aronson, Arnold (1981) 'Theatres of the Future', *Theatre Journal* 33(4), Baltimore, Md.: Johns Hopkins University Press.

Artaud, Antonin (1974) *Collected Works, Vol. 4*, trans Victor Corti, London: Calder & Boyars.

Aston, Elaine and Savona, George (1991) *Theatre as Sign-system*, London: Routledge.

Auslander, Philip (1997) *From Acting to Performance*, London: Routledge.

—— (1999) *Liveness: Performance in a Mediatized Culture*, London and New York: Routledge.

Bablet, Denis and Bablet, Marie-Louis (1982) *Adolphe Appia, 1862–1928, Actor-Space-Light*, London: John Calder.

Bailes, Sara (2001) 'Moving Backward, Forwards Remembering: Goat Island Performance Group', www.goatislandperformance.org.

Bakhtin, Mikhail (1968/1971) *Rabelais and His World*, trans Helene Iswolsky, Cambridge, Mass.: MIT Press.

Barba, Eugenio (1982) 'Theatre Anthropology', *The Drama Review* 26(2): 6, Cambridge, Mass.: MIT Press.

Barba, Eugenio and Savarese, Nicola (1991 and 2005) *A Dictionary of Theatre Anthropology: The Secret Art of the Performer*, London and New York: Routledge.

Barker, Clive (1979) 'The Audiences at the Britannia Theatre, Hoxton', *Theatre Quarterly* 9(34), London: TQ Publications.

—— (2000) 'Joan Littlewood', in *Twentieth Century Actor Training*, ed. Alison Hodge, London: Routledge.

Barrault, Jean-Louis (1951) *Reflections on the Theatre*, London: Theatre Book Club.

—— (1972) *Souvenirs pour Demain*, Paris: Editions du Seuil.

Barreca, Regina (ed.) (1988) *Last Laughs: Perspectives on Women and Comedy*, New York: Gordon & Breach.

Barthes, Roland (1977) *Image, Music, Text*, trans Stephen Heath, New York: Hill & Wang.

Bartlett, Neil (2005) 'Watch'em and Weep', *Guardian*, 10 February.

Becker, Carol (1994) 'The Physicality of Ideas', in *Goat Island Handbook*, Chicago: Goat Island.

Beckett, Samuel (1966) *Happy Days*, London: Faber & Faber.

—— (1984) *Collected Shorter Plays*, London: Faber & Faber.

Bel, Jérôme (2005) National Arts Centre of Canada, interview. Available at www.artsalive.ca/en/dan/ mediatheque/interviews/transcripts/jerome_bel.asp.

Benedetti, Jean (1990) *Stanislavski: A Biography*, New York: Routledge.

Benjamin, Walter (1999) *Selected Writings, Vol. 2, 1927–1934*, ed. M.W. Jennings, H. Eiland and G. Smith, Cambridge, Mass.: Harvard University Press.

Bennett, Susan (1990 and 1997) *Theatre Audiences: A Theory of Production and Reception*, London: Routledge.

Berger, John (1972) *Ways of Seeing*, Harmondsworth: Penguin Books.

—— (1975) *A Seventh Man*, London: Penguin Books.

—— (2005) *Here is Where We Meet: A Season in London* 2005, London: artevents.

Bergsohn, Harold and Partch-Bergsohn, Isa (1997) *European Dance Theatre: An Overview of its Past and Present* (Video), Pennington: Princeton Book Company.

Berkoff, Steven (1978) *East*, London: John Calder.

Bernal, Martin (1991), *Black Athena: Afro-Asiatic Roots of Classical Civilization: The Fabrication of Ancient Greece, 1785–1985, Vol. 1*, New Brunswick: Rutgers University Press.

Bharucha, Rustom (1990) *Theatre and the World: Performance and the Politics of Culture*, London and New York: Routledge.

Bial, Henry (2004) *The Performance Studies Reader*, London and New York: Routledge.

Birringer, Johannes (1991) *Theatre, Theory, Postmodernism*, Bloomington and Indianapolis: Indiana University Press.

Boal, Augusto (1979*) Theatre of the Oppressed*, London: Pluto Press.

Bochner, Arthur P. (2000) 'Criteria Against Ourselves', *Qualitative Inquiry* 6(2), London and Thousand Oaks, Ca.: Sage.

Bogart, Anne and Landau, Tina (2005) *The Viewpoints Book*, New York: Theatre Communications Group.

Bottoms, Stephen (2004) 'Waiting for the World to Come Around', in *Frakcija/Goat Island, Part One: Reflections on the Process*, Zagreb: Centre for Drama Art.

Bradby, David and Delgado, Maria (eds) (2002) *The Paris Jigsaw: Internationalism and the City's Stages,* Manchester and New York: Manchester University Press.

Braun, Edward (1991) *Meyerhold on Theatre*, London: Methuen.

Brecht, Bertolt (1965) *The Messingkauf Dialogues*, trans John Willett, London: Methuen.

—— (1978) *Brecht on Theatre*, ed. John Willett, London: Eyre Methuen.

—— (1980) *Mother Courage and her Children*, trans John Willett, London: Methuen.

—— (1993) *Journals 1934–1955*, ed. John Willett and Ralph Mannheim, London: Methuen.

Brenton, Howard (1977) *Epsom Downs*, London: Eyre Methuen.

Brook, Peter (1965) *The Empty Space*, Harmondsworth: Penguin Books.

—— (1989) *The Shifting Point*, London, Methuen.

—— (1994) 'Interview with Richard Eyre', *Platform Papers 6: Peter Brook*, London: Royal National Theatre.

Brooks, Pete (1993) 'In Conversation with Sarah Dawson', *Total Theatre* 5(2), London: Total Theatre Network.

Brooks, Peter (1993) *Body Work*, Cambridge, Mass.: Harvard University Press.

Bunting, Madeleine (2007) 'The Memory of Humankind', *Guardian*, 15 March.

Butler, Judith (1990) 'Performative Acts and Gender Constitution: An Essay in Phenomenology and Feminist Theory', in *Performing Feminisms: Feminist Critical Theory and Theatre*, ed. Sue-Ellen Case, Baltimore, Md., and London: Johns Hopkins University Press.

Cage, John (1939 and 2002) 'Four Statements on Dance', in *Twentieth Century Performance Reader*, ed. Michael Huxley and Noel Witts, London and New York: Routledge.

Callery, Dymphna (2001) *Through The Body*, London: Nick Hern Books.

Carlson, Marvin (1996) *Performance: A Critical Introduction*, London and New York: Routledge.

Carter, Tina (2001) 'Angelic Upstarts', *Circus Arts News* 6, London: Total Theatre Network.

Cawley, A.C. (1974) *Everyman and Medieval Miracle Plays*, London: Dent.

Centre for Performance Research (CPR) website. Available at http://www.thecpr.org.uk/about/index.php.

Chaikin, Joseph (1999) 'The Search for a Universal Grammar', in *Conversations on Act and Performance*, ed. Bonnie Marranca and Gautam Dasgupta, Baltimore, Md., and London: Johns Hopkins University Press.

Chakravorty, Pallabi (2000–2001) 'From Interculturalism to Historicism: Reflections on Indian Classical Dance', *Dance Research Journal* 32(2), New York: Congress on Research in Dance.

Chamberlain, Franc (1997) 'MAG – The Next Five Years: 1997–2002', Unpublished submission to Mime Action Group/Total Theatre.

—— (2000) 'Michael Chekhov on the Technique of Acting: "Was Don Quixote True to Life?"', in *Twentieth Century Actor Training*, ed. Alison Hodge, London and New York: Routledge.

—— (2004) *Michael Chekhov*, London and New York: Routledge.

Chamberlain, Franc and Yarrow, Ralph (eds) (2002) *Jacques Lecoq and the British Theatre*, London and New York: Routledge.

Chekhov, Anton (1983) *Three Sisters*, trans Michael Frayn, London: Methuen.

Chekhov, Michael (1985) *Lessons for the Professional Actor*, New York: PAJ Books.

—— (2002) *To the Actor*, London and New York: Routledge.

Christie, Judie, Gough, Richard and Watt, Daniel (eds) (2006) *A Performance Cosmology*, Abingdon and New York: Routledge.

Claid, Emilyn (2006) *Yes? No! Maybe . . .*, Abingdon and New York: Routledge.

Cleese, John and Booth, Connie (1989) *The Complete Fawlty Towers*, London: Methuen-Mandarin.

Complicité website. Available at www.complicite.org.

Copeau, Jacques (1967) 'An Essay in Dramatic Renovation: The Theatre of the Vieux-Colombier', trans Richard Hiatt, *Educational Theatre Journal*, Part 4, Baltimore, Md.: Johns Hopkins University Press.

Coult, Tony and Kershaw, Baz (1983) *Engineers of the Imagination*, London: Methuen.

Counsell, C. and Wolf, L. (eds) (2001) *Performance Analysis: An Introductory Coursebook*, London and New York: Routledge.

Craig, Edward Gordan (1980) *On the Art of the Theatre*, London: Heinemann Educational.

Cruciani, Fabrizio (1991 and 2005) 'Apprenticeship – Occidental Examples', in *A Dictionary of Theatre Anthropology: The Secret Art of the Performer*, ed. Eugenio Barba and Nicola Savarese, London and New York: Routledge.

Dadswell, Sarah (2007) 'Jugglers, Fakirs, and *Jaduwallahs*: Indian Magicians and the British Stage', *NTQ* 23(1) (February), Cambridge: Cambridge University Press.

Daldry, Stephen (1992) 'Interview with Giles Croft', *Platform Papers 3: Directors*, London: Royal National Theatre.

Damasio, Antonio (2000) *The Feeling of What Happens*, London: Heinemann.

Danaher, Geoff, Schirato, Tony and Webb, Jen (2002) *Understanding Bourdieu*, London: Sage.

Dasgupta, Gautam and Marranca, Bonnie (1999) *Conversations on Art and Performance*, Baltimore, Md. and London: Johns Hopkins University Press.

Dawson, Andrew (1996) 'State of Ease', *Total Theatre* 8 (2), London: Total Theatre Network.

De Castro, Angela (2000) 'And Why Not', *Circus Arts News* 2, London: Total Theatre Network.

Decroux, Etienne (1972 and 1989) 'Programme Notes for Series of Lectures', in *Modern and Post-Modern Mime,* ed. Tom Leabhart, London: Macmillan.

—— (1985) 'Words on Mime', Claremont: *Mime Journal*.

Deleuze, Gilles (1994) *Difference and Repetition*, New York: Columbia University Press.

Delgado, Maria and Svitch, Caridad (eds) (2002) *Theatre in Crisis?*, Manchester: Manchester University Press.

Dennis, Anne (1995) *The Articulate Body*, New York: Drama Book Publishers.

Derrida, Jacques (1990) *Writing and Difference*, trans Alan Bass, London: Routledge.

Di Benedetto, Stephen (2003) 'Sensing Bodies', *Performance Research* 8(2), London and New York: Routledge.

Dolan, Jill (2005) *Utopia in Performance: Finding Hope at the Theatre*, Ann Arbor, Mich.: University of Michigan Press.

Dorcy, Jean (1958) *A la Rencontre de Mimes et des Mimes*, Neuilly sur Seine: Les Cahiers de Danse et de Culture.

Dox, Donnalee (2006) 'Dancing Around Orientalism', *TDR: The Drama Review* 50(4), Cambridge, Mass.: MIT Press.

Eagleton, Terry (1983) *Literary Theory: An Introduction*, Oxford: Blackwell.

Elam, Keir (1980) *The Semiotics of Theatre and Drama*, London: Methuen.

Eldredge, Sears A. and Huston, Hollis W. (1995 [1978]) 'Actor Training in the Neutral Mask', in *Acting (Re)Considered*, ed. Philip B. Zarilli, London and New York: Routledge.

Eliade, Mircea (1987) *The Sacred and The Profane*, New York: Harcourt Brace.

Eliot, T.S. (1944) 'Burnt Norton', *Four Quartets*, London: Faber & Faber.

Ernst, Earle (1969) 'The Influence of Japanese Theatrical Style on Western Theatre', *Educational Theatre Journal* 21(2), Baltimore, Md.: Johns Hopkins University Press.

Esslin, Martin (1976) *Artaud*, London: Fontana.

Etchells, Tim (1994) 'Diverse Assembly: Some Trends in Recent Performance', in *Contemporary British Theatre*, ed. Theodore Shank, London: Macmillan.

—— (1999) *Certain Fragments: Contemporary Performance and Forced Entertainment*, London: Routledge.

—— (2004a) 'Manifesto on Liveness' in *Live: Art and Performance*, ed. Adrian Heathfield, London: Tate Publishing.

—— (2004b) 'More and More Clever Watching More and More Stupid', in *Live: Art and Performance*, ed. Adrian Heathfield, London: Tate Publishing.

Evans, Mark (2006) *Jacques Copeau*, Abingdon and New York: Routledge.

Farrell, Joseph and Scuderi, Antonio (eds) (2000) *Dario Fo: Stage, Text and Tradition*, Carbondale: Southern Illinois University Press.

Felner, Myra (1985) *Apostles of Silence: The Modern French Mimes*, London and Toronto: Associated University Presses.

Fischer, Gerhard and Narogin, Mudrooroo (1993) *The Mudrooroo/Müller Project*, Kensington, NSW: New South Wales University Press.

Fisher, John (1973) *A Funny Way to be a Hero*, London: Fredrick Müller.

Fo, Dario (2000) 'Johan Padan a la descoverta de le Americhe', in *Dario Fo: Stage, Text and Tradition*, ed. Joseph Farrell and Antonio Scuderi, Carbondale: Southern Illinois University Press.

Fo, Dario and Hood, Stuart (1991) *The Tricks of the Trade*, London: Methuen.

Fortier, Mark (1997) *Theory Theatre: An Introduction*, London and New York: Routledge.

Foster, Hal (1996) *The Return of the Real: The Avant Garde at the End of the Century*, Cambridge, Mass.: MIT Press.

Freedley, George and Reeves, John (1941) *A History of the Theatre*, New York: Crown.

Frost, Anthony and Yarrow, Ralph (1990) *Improvisation in Drama*, Basingstoke: Macmillan.

Fuchs, Elenor (1996) *The Death of Character: Perspectives on Theater after Modernism*, Bloomington and Indianapolis: Indiana University Press.

Fulton, David (2007) 'Mediterranean Dialogues: Spain's Intercultural Theatre Festival', *NTQ* 23(1), Cambridge: Cambridge University Press.

Furse, Anna (2002) 'Strategies, Concepts and Working Decisions', in *Theatre in Crisis?,* ed. Maria Delgado and Caridad Svitch, Manchester: Manchester University Press.

Garvin, Paul (1964) *A Prague School Reader*, Washington, DC: Georgetown University Press.

Geertz, Clifford (1983) 'Blurred Genres: The Refiguration of Social Thought', *Local Knowledge,* New York: Basic Books.

—— (2002) 'The Growth of Culture and the Evolution of Mind', in *The Interpretation of Cultures*, New York: Basic Books.

George, David (1998) 'On Origins: Behind the Rituals', *Performance Research* 3(3), London: Routledge.

Giannachi, Gabriella and Luckhurst, Mary (eds) (1999) *On Directing*, London: Faber.

Gladkov, Aleksandr (1997) *Meyerhold Speaks, Meyerhold Rehearses*, trans Alma Law, London: Harwood Academic.

Glass, David, Ensemble website. Available at www.davidglassensemble.com.

Goat Island (1994) *Goat Island Handbook*, Chicago: Goat Island.

—— (1998) *The Impossible and Poison*, Chicago: Goat Island.

Goldberg, RoseLee (1979) *Performance*, London: Thames & Hudson.

Goorney, Howard (1981) *The Theatre Workshop Story*, London: Eyre Methuen.

Goulish, Matthew (2000) *39 Microlectures*, London and New York: Routledge.

Grene, David and Lattimore, Richmond (1968) *Greek Tragedies Volume 1*, Chicago: Chicago University Press.

Gurr, Andrew (1970) *The Shakespearian Stage 1574–1642*, London: Cambridge University Press.

Haskell, Arnold (1946) *The Making of a Dancer*, London: A&C Black.

Heathfield, Adrian (2004) 'After the Fall: Dance-theatre and Dance-performance', in *Contemporary Theatres in Europe: A Critical Companion*, ed. Joe Kelleher and Nicholas Ridout, Abingdon and New York: Routledge.

Heddon, Deirdre and Milling, Jane (2006) *Devising Performance*, Basingstoke: Palgrave Macmillan.

Holdsworth, Nadine (2006) *Joan Littlewood*, London: Routledge.

Hughes, Robert (1991) *The Shock of the New*, London: Thames & Hudson.

Huxley, Aldous (1932/1955) *Brave New World*, Harmondsworth: Penguin Books.

Iacoboni, Marco, Molnar-Szakacs, Istvan, Gallese, Vittorio, Buccino, Giovanni, Mazziotta, John C. and Rizzolatti, Giacomo (2005) 'Grasping the Intentions of Others with One's Own Mirror Neuron System', *PLOS Biology* 3(3), San Francisco: Public Library of Science.

Ibsen, Henrik (1985) *Ghosts*, trans Michael Meyer, London: Methuen.

Ingarden, Roman (1973) *The Literary Work of Art*, Evanston, In.: Northwestern University Press.

Innes, Christopher (1983) *Edward Gordon Craig*, Cambridge: Cambridge University Press

Jarry, Alfred (1968) *The Ubu Plays*, trans Cyril Connolly and Simon Watson Taylor, London: Eyre Methuen.

Jamison, Nigel (1984) 'The Glory of the Garden – Our Response', *Magazine* 1, London: Mime Action Group.

Jenkins, Ron (1995) 'The Roar of the Clown', in *Acting [Re]Considered*, London and New York: Routledge.

Johnson, Mark (1987) *The Body in the Mind*, Chicago: University of Chicago Press.

Kant, Marion and Karina, Lilian (2003) *Hitler's Dancers*, Oxford and New York: Berghahn Books.

Kaprow, Allan (1994) 'Ages of the Avant-garde', *Performing Arts Journal* 16(1), New York: PAJ Publications.

Katz, Albert (1973) 'Copeau as Regisseur', *Educational Theatre Journal* 25(2), Baltimore, Md.: Johns Hopkins University Press.

Kaye, Nick (1994) *Postmodernism and Performance*, Basingstoke: Palgrave Macmillan.

Kear, Adrian (2005) 'Troublesome Amateurs; Theatre, Ethics and the Labour of Mimesis', *Performance Research* 10(1), Abingdon: Routledge.

Keefe, John (1995) *Moving into Performance Report*, London: Mime Action Group.

—— (1996) 'Activate; The Creative Performance Experience', *Total Theatre* 8(1), London: Total Theatre Network.

—— (2003) *Play Beckett; Beckett's Performance Dramaturgy as Total Theatre*, Conference paper, University of Leeds.

—— (2005) 'Chekhov: The Psychological Gesture and the Fantastic PG; Stage Action or Stage Metaphysics', conference paper, Dartington College of Arts.

Keefe, John and Murray, Simon (eds) (2007) *Physical Theatres: A Critical Reader*, Abingdon and New York: Routledge.

Kelleher, Joe and Ridout, Nicholas (eds) (2004) *Contemporary Theatre in Europe: A Critical Companion*, Abingdon and New York: Routledge.

Kiernander, Adrian (1995), 'The Dance Theatre of Meryl Tankard', *TheatreForum* 6 (Winter/Spring), La Jolla, Calif.: TheatreForum.

King, Philip (1946) *See How they Run! A Farce*, London: Samuel French.

Kirby, E.T. (1972) 'The Delsarte Method: 3 Frontiers of Actor Training', *The Drama Review* 16(1), New York: New York University Press.

Kirby, Victoria Nes (1971) '1789', *The Drama Review* 15(4), Cambridge, Mass.: MIT Press.

Kowzan, Tadeusz (1968) 'The Sign in the Theatre', *Diogenes* 61, London: Sage.

Kristeller, Paul (1995) 'Comment on Black Athena', *Journal of the History of Ideas* 56(1), Philadelphia, Pa.: University of Pennsylvania Press.

Kuhn, Thomas S. (1970) *The Structure of Scientific Revolutions*, Chicago: Chicago University Press.

La Ribot (2004) 'Panoramix' in *Live: Art and Performance*, ed. Adrian Heathfield, London: Tate Publishing.

Laban, Rudolf (2nd edn, 1963) *Modern Educational Dance*, London: Macdonald & Evans.

Laing, Barry (2002) 'Rapture: Excursions in Little Tyrannies and Bigger Lies', Unpublished Ph.D. Thesis, Victoria University, Melbourne.

Leabhart, Tom (1989) *Modern and Post-modern Mime*, London: Macmillan.

Leach, Robert (1993) *Vsevolod Meyerhold*, Cambridge: Cambridge University Press.

—— (2000) 'Meyerhold and Biomechanics', in *Twentieth Century Actor Training*, ed. Alison Hodge, London: Routledge.

Lecoq, Jacques (1973) 'Mime – Movement – Theatre', trans Kate Foley and Julia Devlin, *Yale Theatre* 4(1).

—— (1987) 'Le Théâtre du Geste', Unpublished trans by Gill Kester (2002), Paris: Bordas.

—— (2000) *The Moving Body*, trans David Bradby, London: Methuen.

—— (2006) *Theatre of Movement and Gesture*, ed. David Bradby, Abingdon and New York: Routledge.

Lehmann, Hans-Thies (2006) *Postdramatic Theatre*, trans Karen Jürs-Munby, Abingdon: Routledge.

Lepecki, André (2004) 'Exhausting Dance', in *Live: Art and Performance*, ed. Adrian Heathfield, London: Tate Publishing.

—— (2006) *Exhausting Dance: Performance and the Politics of Movement*, Abingdon and New York: Routledge.

Les Ballets C de la B website. Available at www.lesballetscdela.be.

Littlewood, Joan (1994) *Joan's Book: Joan Littlewood's Peculiar History as She Tells It*, London: Methuen.

—— (1995) *Joan's Story*, London: Minerva.

Logie, Lea (1995) 'Developing a Physical Vocabulary for the Contemporary Performer', *NTQ* 43 (August), Cambridge: Cambridge University Press.

Luckhurst, Mary and Veltman, Chloe (eds) (2001) *On Acting*, London: Faber.

McBurney, Simon (1992) 'Théâtre de Complicité, profiled in rehearsal for *Street of Crocodiles', The Late Show*, September, London: BBC2.

—— (2005) 'We Are Both Story Tellers', in John Berger, *Here is Where We Meet: A Season in London 2005*, London: artevents.

McCaw, Dick (1996) 'A Fraternal Reply to Rivka Rubin', *Total Theatre* 8(2), London: Total Theatre Network.

—— (1999) 'Body Building', *Total Theatre* 11(3), London: Total Theatre Network.

McGrath, John (1981) *A Good Night Out*, London: Eyre Methuen.

McKechnie, Samuel (undated) *Popular Entertainments Through the Ages*, London: Sampson Low, Marston & Co.

Mannoni, Laurent (2000) *The Great Art of Light and Shadow*, trans Richard Crangle, Exeter: Exeter University Press.

Marshall, Lorna and Williams, David (2000) 'Peter Brook: Transparency and the Invisible Network' in *Twentieth Century Actor Training*, ed. Alison Hodge, London and New York: Routledge.

Marshall, Norman (1957) *The Producer and The Play*, London: Macdonald & Co.

Matejka, Ladislav and Titunik, Irwin (1976) *Semiotics of Art: Prague School Contributions*, Cambridge, Mass.: MIT Press.

Max Prior, Dorothy (2006a) 'Old Dogs, New Tricks', *Total Theatre* 18(2), London: Total Theatre Network.

—— (2006b) 'Living Pictures', *Total Theatre* 18(3), London: Total Theatre Network.

Miklaszewski, Krzysztof (2005) *Encounters with Tadeusz Kantor*, London and New York: Routledge.

Miller, John and Page, Scott (2004) 'The Standing Ovation Problem', *Complexity* 9(5), online journal published by Wiley Periodicals. Available at http://www3.interscience.wiley.com/cgi-bin/jhome/ 38804.

Mitter, Shomit and Shevtsova, Maria (eds) (2005) *Fifty Key Theatre Directors,* London and New York: Routledge.

Mnouchkine, Ariane (1989 and 2002) 'Building up the Muscle: An Interview with Josette Féral', in *Re:direction – A Theoretical and Practical Guide*, ed. Rebecca Schneider and Gabrielle Cody, London and New York: Routledge.

Moy, James (1978) 'Train Crash at Crush, 1896: Disaster as Popular Theatre', *Theatre Quarterly* 8(30), London: TQ Publications.

Müller, Heiner (1982) 'The Walls of History', *Semiotext[e]* 4(2): 65, Cambridge, Mass.: MIT Press.

Mulvey, Laura (1975) 'Visual Pleasure and Narrative Cinema', *Screen* 16(3), London: Society for Education in Film and Television; also in Nichols, Bill (1985) *Movies and Methods*, Berkeley: University of California.

Murray, Simon (2003) *Jacques Lecoq*, London and New York: Routledge.

Myerowitz Levine, Molly (1992) 'The Use and Abuse of Black Athena', *American Historical Review* 97(2), Washington, DC: American Historical Association.

Nagler, A.M. (1952) *A Source Book in Theatrical History*, New York: Dover.

Newson, Lloyd (1987) in conversation with Mary Luckhurst on *DV8* website. Available at www.dv8.co.uk.

—— (1998) *DV8 Research Information Pack* (*Dance Makers Portfolio*), London: DV8.

Nicoll, Allardyce (1931) *Masks, Mimes, and Miracles*, New York: Harcourt, Brace & Co.

O'Connor, Alan (1989) *Raymond Willliams on Television, Selected Writings*, London: Routledge.

Oida, Yoshi (2001) 'Foreword' in *The Body Speaks: Performance and Expression*, ed. Lorna Marshall, London: Methuen.

Palmer, D.J. (ed.) (1984) *Comedy: Developments in Criticism*, Basingstoke: Macmillan.

Palter, Robert (1993) 'Black Athena, Afro-centrism, and the History of Science', *History of Science* 31, Cambridge: Science History Publications.

Pardo, Enrique (1995) *Moving into Performance Report*, ed. John Keefe, London: Mime Action Group.

Pavis, Patrice (1982) *Languages of the Stage*, New York: PAJ Publications.

—— (ed.) (1996) *The Intercultural Performance Reader*, London and New York: Routledge.

—— (1998) *Dictionary of the Theatre: Terms, Concepts and Analysis*, Toronto: University of Toronto Press.

Pepys, Samuel (1875–79) *The Diary of Samuel Pepys*, trans Bright Mynors, London: Bickers & Son.

Perret, Jean and Lecoq, Jacques (2006) 'The exposion of mime', in *Theatre of Movement and Gesture*, ed. David Bradby, Abingdon and New York: Routledge.

Peters, Julie Stone (1995) 'Intercultural Performance, Theatre Anthropology, and the Imperialist Critique: Identities, Inheritances and Neo-orthodoxies', in *Imperialism and Theatre: Essays on World Theatre, Drama and Performance*, ed. J. Ellen Gainor, London and New York: Routledge.

Pitches, Jonathan (2003) *Vsevolod Meyerhold*, London and New York: Routledge.

Platel, Alain (1996) 'Body 1995', in *The Connected Body*, ed. Ric Allsopp and Scott deLahunta, Amsterdam: Amsterdam School of Arts.

Pollack, Sydney (1969) *They Shoot Horses, Don't They?* (Film), American Broadcasting Company (ABC).

Potter, Dennis (1994) *Seeing the Blossom: Two Interviews and a Lecture*, London: Faber & Faber.

Pounder, Robert (1992) 'Black Athena 2: History without Rules', *American Historical Review* 97(2), Washington, DC: American Historical Association.

Quick, Andrew (2006) 'The Gift of Play', in *Contemporary Theatres in Europe: A Critical Companion*, ed. Joe Kelleher and Nicholas Ridout, Abingdon and New York: Routledge.

Rainer, Yvonne (1965) *Tulane Drama Review* 10(2): 178, Cambridge, Mass.: MIT Press.

Ratcliffe, Michael (1994) Programme notes for Théâtre de Complicité's *The Three Lives of Lucy Cabrol,* London: Théâtre de Complicité.

Read, Alan (1993) *Theatre and Everyday Life*, London and New York: Routledge.

Ritchie, J.M. and Garten, H.F. (1980) *Seven Expressionist Plays*, London: John Calder.

Roche, Paul (1964) *Aeschylus; Prometheus Bound*, New York: Mentor.

Rorty, Richard (1982) *Consequences of Pragmatism*, Minneapolis: Minnesota University Press.

Rose, Martial (1961) *The Wakefield Mystery Plays*, London: Evans.

Rosenberg, Harold (1965) *The Tradition of the New*, New York: McGraw-Hill.

Roy, Jean-Noël and Carasso, Jean-Gabriel (1999) *Les Deux Voyages de Jacques Lecoq*, Paris: La Septe ARTE – On Line Productions – ANRAT.

Rubin, Rivka (1995) 'The Relevance of the Workshop', *Total Theatre* 7(4), London: Total Theatre Network.

Rudlin, John (1986) *Jacques Copeau*, Cambridge: Cambridge University Press.

—— (1994) *Commedia Dell'Arte*, London and New York: Routledge.

Rudlin, John and Paul, Norman (ed. and trans) (1990) *Jacques Copeau, Texts on Theatre*, London and New York: Routledge.

Said, Edward W. (2003) *Orientalism*, London: Penguin Books.

Said, Edward W. and Barenboim, Daniel (2004) *Parallels and Paradoxes*, London: Bloomsbury.

Saussure, Ferdinand de (1983) *Course in General Linguistics*, trans Roy Harris, London: Duckworth.

Sayers, Sohnya (1990) *Susan Sontag: The Elegiac Modernist*, London and New York: Routledge.

Schechner, Richard (1982) 'Intercultural Performance: An Introduction', *The Drama Review* 26(2): T94.

—— (1985) *Between Theater and Anthropology*, Philadelphia: University of Pennsylvania Press.

—— (2002 and 2006) *Performance Studies: An Introduction*, London and New York: Routledge.

Schneider, Rebecca (1997) *The Explicit Body in Performance*, London and New York: Routledge.

Sebald, W.G. and Tripp, Jan Peter (2004) *Unrecounted*, London: Hamish Hamilton.

Servos, Norbert (1981) *Modern Drama*, 23(4), Toronto: University of Toronto Press.

Shakespeare, William (1979) *A Midsummer Night's Dream*, ed. H.F. Brooks, London: Methuen.

Shattuck, Roger (1968) *The Banquet Years*, New York: Vintage Books.

Shevtsova, Maria (1989) 'The Sociology of the Theatre, Part Two: Theoretical Achievements', *NTQ* 18: 180–94, Cambridge: Cambridge University Press.

—— (2004) *Dodin and the Maly Drama Theatre: Process to Performance*, London and New York: Routledge.

Siegmund, Gerald (2003) 'Strategies of Avoidance', *Performance Research* 8(2): 87, London: Routledge.

Skidmore, Jeffrey (2003) *New World Symphonies, CDA67380* (sleeve notes), London: Hyperion.

Smith, Anna Deaveare (1993) *Fires in the Mirror*, New York: Anchor Books.

Sontag, Susan (2004) 'Approaching Artaud', in *Antonin Artaud: A Critical Reader*, ed. Edward Scheer, London and New York: Routledge.

Stamm, R. (1982) 'On the Carnivalesque', Wedge 1, quoted in Stallybras, P. and White, A. (1986) *The Politics and Poetics of Transgression*, London: Methuen.

Stanislavsky, Konstantin (1989) *Sobranie sochinenii, Vol. 2 (An Actor Works on Himself, Part 1)*, Moscow: Iskusstvo.

States, Bert O. (2002) 'The Actor's Presence', in *Acting (Re)Considered*, ed. Phillip Zarrilli, London and New York: Routledge.

Steiner, George (1958) *The Death of Tragedy*, New York: Alfred A. Knopf.

Studler, Gaylyn (1984) 'Masochism and the Perverse Pleasures of Cinema', *Quarterly Review of Film Studies* 9(4), New York: Redgrave Publishing.

Taplin, Oliver (1985) *Greek Tragedy in Action*, London: Methuen.

Taussig, Michael (1993) *Mimesis and Alterity*, London and New York: Routledge.

Théâtre de Complicité (1994) Programme notes, *The Three Lives of Lucy Cabrol*, London: Théâtre de Complicité.

—— (1999) *The Street of Crocodiles*, London: Methuen.

Total Theatre. Available at www.totaltheatre.org.uk.

Trewin, John (1971) *Peter Brook: A Biography*, London: MacDonald.

Trigger, Bruce (1992) 'Brown Athena: A Postprocessual Goddess?', *Current Anthropology* 33(1), Chicago: University of Chicago Press.

Tsatsos, Irene (1991) 'Talking with Goat Island', *The Drama Review* 35(4), Cambridge, Mass.: MIT Press.

Turner, Jane (2004) *Eugenio Barba*, London and New York: Routledge.

Turner, Victor (1982) *From Ritual to Theatre: The Human Seriousness of Play*, New York: PAJ Publications.

Tynan, Kenneth (1989) *Profiles*, London: Nick Hern Books.

Ubersfeld, Anne (1999) *Reading Theatre*, Toronto: Toronto University Press.

Valeri, Walter (2000) in *Dario Fo: Stage, Text and Tradition*, ed. Joseph Farrell and Antonio Scuderi, Carbondale: Southern Illinois University Press.

Varley, Julia (1995) 'The Pre-expressive Family: Multicultural Experiences in Theatre', in *Incorporated Knowledge*, ed. Tom Leabhart, Claremont: The Mime Journal.

Verma, Jatinder (1996) 'The Challenge of Binglish: Analysing Multi-cultural Productions', in *Analysing Performance: A Critical Reader*, ed. Patrick Campbell, Manchester: Manchester University Press.

Vidal, John (1988) 'Opening Moves: Interview with Jacques Lecoq', *Guardian*, 22 March.

von Kleist, Heinrich (1810/1972) 'On the Marionette Theatre', trans Thomas Neumiller, *The Drama Review* 16(3), New York: New York University Press.

Vuyst, Hildegard de (1998*)* Ballets C de la B website. Available at www.lesballetscdela.be.

Williams, David (ed.) (1991) *Peter Brook and the 'Mahabharata': Critical Perspectives*, London: Routledge.

—— (ed.) (1999) *Collaborative Theatre: The Théâtre du Soleil Sourcebook*, London and New York: Routledge.

—— (2005) 'Simon McBurney' in *Fifty Key Theatre Directors*, ed. Shomit Mitter and Maria Shevtsova, London and New York: Routledge.

—— (2007) Unpublished interview with Simon Murray, Dartington.

Williams, Raymond (1973) *Drama from Ibsen to Brecht*, Harmondsworth: Penguin Books.

—— (1977) *Marxism & Literature*, Oxford: Oxford University Press.

—— (1989) *Resources of Hope: Culture, Democracy and Socialism,* ed. Robin Gale, London: Verso.

Winnicott, David (1974) *Playing and Reality*, Harmondsworth: Penguin Books.

Wittgenstein, Ludwig (1972) *Philosophical Investigations*, trans G.E.M. Anscombe, Oxford: Basil Blackwell & Mott.

Worthen, W.B. (2000) *The Harcourt-Brace Anthology of Drama*, 3rd edition, Orlando, Fla.: Harcourt Inc. (*Dry Lips Oughta Move to Kapuskasing* originally published in 1989, Calgary: Fifth House Publishers).

Wright, John (1990) 'Philippe Gaulier: Genius or Egotist', *Total Theatre*, Winter, London: Mime Action Group.

—— (1994) 'Monika Pagneux', *Total Theatre*, 6(1), London: Total Theatre Network.

—— (2006) *Why Is That So Funny?*, London: Nick Hern Books.

Wrights and Sites (2003) *An Exeter Mis-guide*, Exeter: Wrights and Sites.

Zarrilli, Phillip (ed.) (2002) *Acting (Re)Considered*, London and New York: Routledge.

Zarrilli, Phillip, Fisher Sorgenfrei, Carol, McConachie, Bruce, William, Gary Jay (2006) *Theatre Histories: An Introduction*, Abingdon and New York: Routledge.

Index

Page numbers in **bold** refer to illustrations

7:84 company 94
1789 (Théâtre du Soleil) 93, 94–6, 114
Absurditties (Divas Dance Theatre) 86–7
Abydos-Osiris Passion Play 38
acting 20–2, 38, 55–6, 66–7, 68
actor 17; as actant 35, 38, 45, 51, 68, 161, 171; and aliveness 137, 138–9, 142, 150, 200; and body 55; and intersubjectivity 45
Adaptors 16
aerial dancing 51, 54–5
Aeschylus 3, 34, 35, 162–5, 172
Agamemnon (Aeschylus) 162–5, 172
Aggiss, Liz 29, 77, 84–7
agitprop 37
agon 38, 161, 170
Akalaitis, JoAnne 94
Alfreds, Mike 116
aliveness 137, 138–9, 142, 150, 200
American Mime Theatre 124
Anarchic Dance (Aggiss) 85
Ansorge, Peter 14, 36
Anthonissen de Morgan, Peter 88
Antigone (Sophocles) 14, 36
Appia, Adolphe 55, 66, 67, 133
applause 91, 183
Arden, Annabel 105–6

Aristotle 33, 37, 38, 43, 51
Arnheim, Rudolf 61
Aronson, Arnold 181
art 63, 204
Artaud, Antonin 14, 18, 32, 69, 193, 194–6; sharing breath 70, 182
Arts Lab 14
Artslynx 124
Asian magicians 190
attention 149
audience/spectator 4, 5, 6, 10, 26, 208; and imagination 39, 106, 174–5, 176, 194; participation 69–70, 94–5, 181–4; and perception/reception 31–2
Auslander, Philip 13, 89
Australia, and physical theatre 16
authenticity 21, 95, 138, 148, 164–5, 172
authorship 17, 18, 23, 30, 93
avant-garde 18, 53, 64–8, 64–72; future of 71–2

Balasaraswati 185
Balinese dancers 195
ballet 59, 76, 82, 90–2, 138–9
Barba, Eugenio 4, 9, 122, 139–42, 144, 155, 200

Barenboim, Daniel 205
Barker, Clive 47, 144, 154
Barrault, Jean-Louis 19, 21, 57–8, 115, 156
Barthes, Roland 32, 36, 88
Bartleby (1993) 99
Bartlett, Neil 78, 80
Bausch, Pina 4, 31, 60, 64, 75, 76–81, 93, 183
Becker, Carol 107, 110
Beckett, Samuel 3, 10, 14, 164, 178–9
Béjart, Maurice 90
Bel, Jérome 77, 87–92
belly-dancing 189
Benjamin, Walter 208
Bennett, Susan 6, 22, 32
Berger, John 63, 67, 192, 204
Berkoff, Steven 14, 175
Berlin Mime Centre 130
Bernal, Martin 191–2
Bharucha, Rustom 191, 195, 200
bios 141, 142, 200
Black Athena thesis 191–2
Boal, Augusto 39, 51, 182
body 12, 13, 17, 21–2, 23, 39, 50; attitudes to 52; in avant-garde theatre 64–72; body theory 62, 64, 70; and dance 60–4; as fact 60–1; Feldenkrais techniques 148–9; and feminist theory 29; and intervention 61–2; 'lived body' 61; and mime 53–5; and mind 135; neutral 141; and ritual 38, *see also* masks, and neutrality
Body of Knowledge, A (IWF project) 132
Bogart, Anne 16, 124, 142–4, 201
Booth, Connie 177–8
Bottoms, Stephen 109
Bourdieu, Pierre 140
Bradby, David 53
Braun, Edward 193, 194
Bread and Puppet Theatre 16
Brecht, Bertolt 3, 14, 36, 40–4, 48, 51, 165, 172; audience participation 182; gestus 80, 161; silent scream 173, 180
Brenton, Howard 174–5
bridges/bridging 185–6, 188, 190
Brief History of...(Silence) (Fischer and Spackman) 70–1
Brig, The (Living Theatre) 69–70
Briginshaw, Valerie 86
British Museum 203
Brook, Peter 77, 94, 122, 137, 143, 147, 200, 201, 202–3; deadly theatre 13, 32, 160

Brooks, Pete 81, 159
Brooks, Peter 95
Brown, Carol 29, 85
Bunting, Madeleine 203
Burrows, Jonathan 77
Butler, Judith 29–30, 125
Butoh 16
Bylan, Pierre 149

Café Müller (Bausch) 78–9, 183
Cage, John 171, 207
Cal Arts 124
Callery, Dymphna 7
Callow, Simon 3
Calvino, Italo 151–2
Cambodian dancers 194–5
Canada, and physical theatre 16
Cardiff Laboratory Theatre 133
Carné, Marcel 57, 115
Carter, Tina 52
Celebration Barn Theatre 124
Central School of Speech and Drama (CSSD) 123
Centre for Performance Research (CPR) 130, 133–4
Chaikin, Joseph 94, 201
Chakravorty, Pallabi 196
Chamberlain, Franc 17
Chandralekha Prabhudas Patel 185
Chaplin, Charlie 19, 58, 178
Chaudhuri, Haridas 191
Chekhov, Anton 3, 27, 170–1, 172
Chekhov, Michael 3, 61, 122, 142
Christie, Judie 133
Christopher, Karen 109, 110–11, 112
Churchill, Caryl 31
circus skills 4, 68, 94, 138, 177
Civil Rights movement 142
Claid, Emilyn 59, 85
Cleese, John 177–8
clown/clowning 50–1, 86, 149, 177, 205, *see also* Fo, Dario
Come and Go (Beckett) 164
comedy 175–9, *see also* clown/clowning; laughter
Commedia dell'Arte 18–19, 54, 113, 114, 178, 194
complicité 70, 105, 113, 137, 146, 147
Complicité (theatre) 15, 33, 96–107, 147, *see also* Théâtre de Complicité
Composition 142, 143–4, 205

Conservatoire National d'Art Dramatique, Le 123
Copeau, Jacques 19, 25,Art 54, 55, 56, 58, 121–2, 145
Coronation Plays 37
corporeal fluency 17
Coult, Tony 48
Cowie, Billy 84–7
Craig, Edward Gordon 37, 65, 66–7, 194, 199
Cruciani, Fabrizio 117
Crucifixion, The (Wakefield cycle) 49
cultural materialism 27–8
cultures: bridges/bridging 185–6, 188, 190; interculturalism 185–203
Cunningham, Merce 90

Dada/Dadaists 18, 70
Dadswell, Sarah 190
Dafoe, Willem 21
Damasio, Antonio 45, 135
dance 16, 59–64, 66, 75–92; performance dance 76, 87–92; social 59–60, 64
Daniel, John 64
Dartington College of Arts 61, 85, 108, 127
Dartington Hall Trust 122
David Glass Ensemble, and workshops 130
Davidson, Kenneth 126
Dawson, Andrew 148
De Castro, Angela 51
Dead Dreams of Monochrome Men (Newson) 81, 83
Debureau, Jean-Gaspard 54, 57–8, 115
Decroux, Etienne 19–20, 21, 58, 120, 123–4, 137, 155–7; and masks 56; and silence 171
Deleuze, Gilles 87
Dell'Arte International School of Physical Theatre 16, 124
Dennis, Anne 57
Derrida, Jacques 21
Desmond Jones School of Mime and Physical Theatre 156
devising 17–19, 30, 144, 180
Devising Performance (Heddon and Milling) 16
Di Benedetto, Stephen 61
Diderot, Denis 115
Dietrich, Marlene 206
Difference and Repetition (Deleuze) 87
disponibilité 105, 146, 147
Distinguished Pieces (La Ribot) 70
Divas Dance Theatre 84–7
DiveUrgence (1999) 104
Dodin, Lev 122, 137–9, 143

Doisneau, Véronique 90–2
Dom Juan (Molière) 193–4
Dort, Bernard 116
Dox, Donnalee 189
Dry Lips Oughta Move to Kapuskasing (Highway) 198
Duncan, Isadora 65
DV8 Physical Theatre 14, 31, 77, 81–4

Eagleton, Terry 23, 26
East 15 152–3
East (Berkoff) 175
Ecole Jacques Lecoq, 123, 147, 150
Egypt, and history of theatre 37
Eh Joe (Beckett) 178
Elam, Keir 24, 36
élan 141, 150, 205, *see also* lightness
Eliot, T.S. 87
emotions, and signals to brain 45
empathy 39–44, 47, 48, 61, 164; roots of 44–6, 51
Enfants du Paradis, Les (Carné) 57–8, 115
Enter Achilles (Newson) 81, 82–3
Entrecultures (Intercultural Theatre Festival) 190–1
Epsom Downs (Brenton) 174–5
Erwachen (Stramm) 67
Esslin, Martin 194
estranging 40, 165, 167, 173, 180
Etchells, Tim 13, 50, 75, 123, 144, 152, 205; on Bel 89; on *DV8* 84; ending performance 183; and influence of Bausch 77; influence on Newson 81; on play 146, 147
European Mime Federation 130
Eurythmics 153–4
Evans, Mark 122
eyes 164
Eyre, Richard 34

Fawlty Towers (Cleese and Booth) 177–8
Feldenkrais, Moshe 147, 148–9
Felner, Myra 21, 54
feminism 29–31, 125
Ferguson, Dugald 127
Findley, Karen 31
Fischer, Ernst 71–2
Fo, Dario 112–16
football, qualities required for 7, 181
Footfalls (Beckett) 166–7, 179
Forced Entertainment 4, 50, 80, 93, 107, 108, 130, 182, 205

Foreman, Richard 16
Forster, E.M. 148
Foster, Hal 60
Franko B 64
Freedley, George 37–8
Freehold Theatre 14, 94
Frost, Anthony 179–80
Fuchs, Elenor 13
Fulton, David 190–1
Furse, Anna 125
Futurists 18

Gance, Abel 95
Gardner, Lyn 72, 162, 164
Garten, H.F. 67
Garvin, Paul 36
Gaulier, Philippe 86, 105, 131, 141, 145, 146, 149–52, 208
Gay Sweatshop 31
gazing 190; gaze theory 64; and looking 8, 62–4, 70, 198
Geertz, Clifford 11, 44
Gémier, Firmin 65, 66
George, David 44, 45–6
Gert, Valeska 85
gesture 21, 23–5, 30, 35
gestus 80, 161, 180
Ghosts (Ibsen) 169–70, 180
Glass, David 15, 19, 123, 130, 156
Goat Island Performance Group 4, 12, 16, 93, 107–12
Goldberg, RoseLee 68
Goorney, Howard 37
Gorgias 39
Gough, Richard 133
Goulish, Matthew 13, 77, 109, 110–11
Government Inspector, The (2003) 100
Graham, Martha 21
Gramsci, Antonio 113
Grand Union 88
Gray, Spalding 116
Greece, and history of theatre 38
Gropius, Walter 181, 182
Grotesque Dancer (Divas Dance Theatre) 85
Grotowski, Jerzy 14, 139, 151, 155, 200
Gurr, Andrew 47

habitus 52, 140
Hamlet (Shakespeare) 37, 54, 198
Hansel Gretel Machine, The (1997/8) 102
Happy Days (Beckett) 179

Harry Stork Cabaret, The (2006) 98
Haskell, Arnold 59
Haunted, Daunted and Flaunted (1997) 43
Heathfield, Adrian 79
Heddon, Dierdre 16, 18, 180
Herondas 54
Highway, Tomson 198
Hitler, Adolf 75
Hixson, Lin 109–10, 111, 123, 144
Hocus Pocus Junior, The Anatomy of Legerdemain 50
Hoffman, Reinhild 75
Holdsworth, Nadine 153–4
humanism 189, 206
Hunger of Zanni the Clown, The (Fo) 115
Huntington, Samuel 203
Husserl, Edmund 61
Huxley, Aldous 71–2
hybridity 68, 70, 75, 133, 147, 188
Hyle (hi-le) 61
Hysteria (Edinburgh 2006) 162

I Miss You (2002) 40
Iacoboni, Marco 45
Ibsen, Henrik 27, 169–70, 182
Impact Theatre Company 81, 131
improvisation 10, 69, 73, 83, 116, 144, 153, 154, 179–81
In Close Relation (1998) 101
inculturation, and acculturation 139–40
intercultural performance 185–203; and appropriation 191; and borrowing/sharing sign systems 187–9; contemporary case studies 196–9; and context 202; cultural exchanges 189–92; and optimism 202; and theatrical practices 192–6; and universal bodies 199–201
Intercultural Theatre Festival (*Entrecultures*) 190–1
international festivals 190, 202
International School of Theatre 123
International Workshop Festival (IWF) 130, 132–3
Ionesco, Eugène 14
Iron Pig Theatre Company 124

Jacques-Dalcroze, Emile 133, 153
Jamison, Nigel 14, 36, 132
Japanese theatre 193–4
Jarry, Alfred 65–7, 69–70
Jeffrey, Mark 110–11, 112

Jenkins, Ron 114, 115
Johnson, Mark 208
Johnstone, Keith 144
Joint Stock 31
Jones, Desmond 15
Joos, Kurt 76
Judson Church movement 88

Kant, Marion 85
Kantor, Tadeusz 206
Kaprow, Allan 71
katharsis 39, 44, 51, 70
Kawakami theatrical troupe 193
Keaton, Buster 19, 58, 178, 205
Keefe, John 34, 61, 162
Keersmaeker, Anne Theresa de 81
Kershaw, Baz 14, 48
kinesic analysis 24
King, Philip 176–7
Kirby, E.T. 58
Kirby, Victoria Nes 94
Kontakthof (Bausch) 60, 64
Kowzan, Tadeusz 11, 36, 161, 165, 180, 184, 188
Krapps Last Tape (Beckett) 179
Kuhn, Thomas 7

La Ribot 70, 77, 206
Laban, Rudolf 59, 76, 133, 153, 154
Laing, Barry 149, 151–2
Lanaghan, Helen 19
Landau, Tina 143
Last Performance, The (Bel) 87, 88
laughter 71, 114, 175, 175–8, *see also* clown/clowning;
le Roy, Xavier 77
Leabhart, Tom 54, 56, 123–4, 156
Leach, Robert 193
Lecoq, Jacques 19–20, 53–4, 86, 115, 131; influence on Gaulier 149–50; and neutrality 21, 25, 56, 141, 145–6, 199–200; and play 146–7, 149; preparation and training 9, 96–7, 105, 120, 124, 137, 144–7
Lehmann, Hans-Thies 13, 17, 24–5, 26, 38, 201–2
Lepage, Robert 16
Lepecki, André 88, 92
Les Ballets C de la B 77
Levy, Deborah 86
lightness 147, 150–2, 205, 206, *see also* élan
Liminal Performance Group 124

liminal space 38
Littlewood, Joan 3, 14, 37, 122, 152–4
Living Theatre 16, 68–9, 94, 182
Logie, Lea 121
London International Festival of Theatre (LIFT) 190
London International Mime Festival 19, 70
looking *see* gazing
Luckhurst, Mary 14

Mabou Mines 16, 94
McBurney, Simon 97, 107, 145, 146, 201, 206; and choreography 73, 77; and devising 17, 33, 105, 123, 143, 144, 154
McCaw, Dick 132, 134–5
McDermott, Phelim 183
McGrath, John 46, 94
McKecknie, Samuel 50
Mackrell, Judith 60
MAGazine 15
Mahabharata, The (Brook) 202–3
Maly Theatre, St Petersburg 137–9
Marceau, Marcel 19, 21, 58
Marey, Etienne-Jules 55
Margolis Brown Performance Company 124
Marowitz, Charles 94
Marshall, Norman 56
Marxism 27, 113
masks 38, 54, 56–7; and neutrality 21, 25, 56, 145–6, 199–200
Massey, Raymond 185
Mauss, Marcel 140
Meckler, Nancy 14, 36, 94
Medicinal Plays 37
melodrama 95–6, 150
Messingkauf Dialogues (Brecht) 43, 184
method acting 123, 124, 129, 142, 143
Meyerhold, Vsevolod 14, 146, 201; and intercultural theatre 193–4, 196; and preparation and training 9, 120, 121–2, 142, 146, 154
Midsummer Night's Dream, A (Shakespeare) 54, 174, 198–9
Milgram, Stanley 69
Miller, John 183
Milling, Jane 16, 18, 180
mime 4, 15, 18–20, 36, 53–8, 145, 155–7; French tradition 53, 54; and gestural language 58; illusory/objective 57–8; Promethean 156, 157; subjective 58
Mime Action Group (MAG) 14, 15, 130–1, 132

Mime Corporeal 36
Mime Journal 123–4
mimeisthai 38
mimesis 8, 38–9; and empathy 164–5; and popular theatre 49, 50; roots of 45–6
mimicry 53
Minute Too Late, A (2005) 100
mise-en-scène 7, 48, 66, 125, 159, 161, 170–1
Mistero Buffo (Fo) 113, 114–16
Mitchell, C.J. 111
Mnouchkine, Ariane 93–6, 114, 116, 201
Molière 193–4
Mother Courage and Her Children (Brecht) 168, 172–3
Moving into Performance (workshop symposium) 131–2
Moy, James 47
Mudrooroo Narogin 197–8
Mudrooroo/Müller Project 197–8
Müller, Heiner 25, 197–8
multiculturalism 75, 186–7, 190, *see also* intercultural performance
Mulvey, Laura 62
Murray, Simon 54, 108–9, 145
music, and fusion 192
Muybridge, Eadweard James 55

Nagler, A.M. 54
Napoleon (Gance) 95
narrative, and physical performance 92–116
National Review of Live Art (NRLA) 68
National Socialism 75
naturalness 139–40
Natya-Shastra 196–7
Nazism 75, 107
Neher, Caspar 48
nervous system, development of 44
neutrality 145–6, 199–200, *see also* masks, and neutrality
Never Again (Newson) 81
Newlove, Jean 153
Newsboy (Theatre of Action) 37
Newson, Lloyd 14, 76, 77, 81–4, 93
Nicoll, Allardyce 54
North America, and physical theatre 16
Nureyev, Rudolph 90

Odin Teatret 4, 139–42, 200
Olivier, Lawrence 206
Open Space 94

Open Theatre 16
Orchidee, Die (Divas Dance Theatre) 86
Orientalism 186, 189
Orlan 31
Overlie, Mary 142, 143

Pacific Performance Project 124
Page, Scott 183
Pagneux, Monika 9, 105–6, 145, 147–9
pantomime 19, 54, 57–8, 155
Paradox of the Actor, The (Diderot) 115
Pardo, Enrique 17, 131
Paris Moderne movement 157
Paris Opera Ballet 90, 91
Passion Plays 37
Pavis, Patrice 20, 36, 202
Pearson, Mike 133
Pepys, Samuel 52
performance: definition of 68; instant of 150–1, *see also* performance writing
Performance Cosmology, A (2006) 13
Performance Studies 124–5
performance writing 74–5, 116; accuracy and truth 74; and expertise of writer 74
Performer's Energy, The (IWF project) 133
Performing Arts Journal 71
Perret, Jean 208
Peters, Julie Stone 202
Petit, Roland 90
phenomenology 25–6, 68
Physical State International 134
physical theatre: defining 81; emergence of term 14–17; hybrid pathways 53–72; roots of 34–52; and text 159–84
physicality, relationship with text 159–84
Pig Iron Theatre 16
Pip Simmons Group 94
Platel, Alain 81, 123, 207
play 5, 34, 38, 145, 146–7, 149, 150–1, 153, 154, 175–7, 207; popular playing 46–7; roots of 44–6; Trickster 49–52, 198
PLAY orchestra (South Bank project) 182
popular theatre 46–7, 113; and drama 47–9; and entertainment 49–52; mimesis and empathy 47
Possessed, The (1998) 162, 171
postdramatic theatre 13
Postdramatic Theatre 17
Potter, Dennis 205

Prague School 36
pre-expressive body 141, 199, 200
preparation and training 117–58, 199–200; as
cultural production 121–35; directors and
actors as trainers 121–3, 137; functions of
119–20; history and context 119–21;
pedagogy 117–19, 120; principles 135–57;
profiles of director-teachers 137–57; theatre
schools and universities 123–8; workshops
129–35
presence 21–2, 88, 122, 139, 141, 149, 150,
171, 200
Prometheus at the Winter Palace (Living
Theatre) 69–70, 182
Prometheus Bound (Aeschylus) 35, 37, 39
Pyramid Texts 37

Quad (Beckett) 179

Rainer, Yvonne 77, 81, 88
Rame, Franca 113
Read, Alan 11, 25–6, 118
realism, and the realistic 165–7
reception theory 31–2, 125
Reeves, John 37–8
Right Size 130
Ritchie, J.M. 67
ritual 35, 38–9, 49, 68, 70
Rorty, Richard 7
Rose, Martial 48
Rousseau, Henri 65
Rousseau, Jean-Jacques 65
Royal Academy of Dramatic Art (RADA)
123
Royal Hunt of the Sun, The (Schaffer)
159–60
Rubin, Rivka 134–5

Said, Edward 186, 187, 188, 189, 195, 205
San Francisco Mime Troupe 16
Saner, Bryan 109, 110–11, 112
Saratoga International Theatre Institute (SITI)
16, 142, 143
Saussure, Ferdinand de 21, 88
Savarese, Nicola 119, 140
Schechner, Richard 5, 30, 49, 119, 124, 186
Schleef, Einar 26
Schulz, Bruno 97, 105, 106, 107
Sea and the Poison, The (Goat Island) 107,
109–12
Sebald, W.G. 207

Second Shepherd's Play (Wakefield cycle) 48
Secret Art of the Performer, The (Barba and
Savarese) 119
See How they Run (King) 176–7
Seelig, Joseph 19
semiotics 23–5
Servos, Norbert 80
Séverin 58
Shakespeare, W. 3, 174, *see also Hamlet*;
Midsummer Night's Dream, A
Shared Experience 116
Shattuck, Roger 64, 65
Shevtsova, Maria 138, 139
Show Must Go On, The (Bel) 89
Siegmund, Gerald 89–90
sign systems 7, 36, 180, 184, 187; hierarchy
of 161–2, 165, 188
silence 171, 172–3, 207
silent scream 173
Skidmore, Jeffrey 192
Smith, Anna Deaveare 116, 185–6, 188
somatics (body sensation) 25, 35, 39, 51, 60,
119
Sontag, Susan 195, 202–3
Sophron of Syracuse 18
Soviet theatre 193, 194
space, as silent character 167–70
Spackman, Helen 71–2
Spencer, Charles 160
Spinoza, Baruch 135
Split Britches 31
Spoor, Will 14
Sprinkle, Annie 31
Sprung Theatre Company 124
stage directions 37–8, 162–3, 172–3
Staging of Wagnerian Opera, The (Bablet and
Bablet) 66
Stanislavsky, Konstantin 17, 56, 120, 121,
122, 124, 129, 138, 141, 142, 143, 154,
193
Steiner, George 173
stillness, articulate 170–2
Stramm, August 67
Strand Magazine, The 190
Strange Fish (Newson) 81
Street of Crocodiles, The (Complicité) 41, 97,
104–7
Striptease (La Ribot) 70
structures of feeling 28, 31, 76, 77, 93, 188
Studler, Gaylyn 62
Summit, The (2006) 97

Surrealists 18
suspension 141, 150, 151
Suzuki, Tadashi, training system 16, 124, 142, 143
syncretism 5, 37, 188

tanztheater 75, 76, 85
Tara Arts 8
Taylor, Paul 160
Tea Without Mother (2005) 128
text-based theatre, and physicality 159–84
Thatcher, Margaret 85
Theatre of Action 37
Théâtre de Complicité 15, 116, 130, *see also* Complicité (theatre)
Théâtre de l'Atelier 156
Théâtre des Funambules 57
Théâtre du Mouvement, Le 19
Théâtre du Soleil 93–6
Theatre Workshop 152–4
Thomas, Sian 133
Three Sisters (Chekhov) 170–1, 172, 180
Time Flying (1997) 103
TooBa 124
Total Theatre 15, 123, 130–1, 132, 134
total theatre 6, 57, 160, 178
Total Theatre Network 15, 130
Tricks of the Trade, The (Fo and Hood) 115
Trickster 132
Tripney, Natasha 160
Tulane Drama Review 77
Tynan, Kenneth 207

Ubu plays (Jarry) 65–7
Ubu Roi (Jarry) 41, 65
utopias, performing 201

Valeri, Walter 113
Varley, Julia 200
Veltrusky, Jiri 36
Verma, Jatinder 8, 188, 196
Véronique Doisneau (Bel) 90–2

via negativa 151
Vietnam War protest movement 142
Vieux-Colombier, Théâtre du 19, 25, 56, 122
Viewpoints 124, 142, 143, 144
visceral theatre 68–71
Visitation, The (Fischer and Spackman) 70–1
voice 10, 164, 208
von Kleist, Heinrich 66

Wagner, Richard 65
Wague, George 58
Waiting for Godot (Beckett) 42, 202–3
Wakefield mystery plays 48–9
Weaver, Lois 31
Wedderburn, Eve 59
Welfare State theatre company 48
Who can sing a song to unfrighten me (Forced Entertainment) 182–3
Wigman, Mary 76, 147
Williams, David 63, 95, 96, 107, 114, 185–6, 188, 202
Williams, Jay 187, 188
Williams, Raymond 27–8, 31
Wilson, Robert 16
Wilson, Tom 184
Winnicott, David 62–3, 65, 67
Winter's Tale (Shakespeare) 47
With the Whole Voice (IWF project) 133
Wittgenstein, Ludwig 7
Wollstonecraft, Mary 30
Women's Theatre Group 31
Wooster Group 16, 21, 89, 93, 107
world trade fairs 189
Worthen, W.B. 198
Wright, John 149
Wuppertal Dance Theatre 76, 77–80

Yarrow, Ralph 179–80

zachin 139
Zarrilli, P.B. 6, 68
Zidane, Zinedine 1, 181
Zimbardo, Philip 69